BEING ON
MISSION

BEING ON MISSION

A POWERFUL STORY OF PERSONAL
DEVELOPMENT AND CHANGE BASED ON THE
'10 PRINCIPLES OF LEADERSHIP AND LIFE'

Mark McGregor

ISBN: 1518655955
ISBN 13: 9781518655951

IN PRAISE OF 'BEING ON MISSION'

"My husband and I read this fantastic book together. We were thrilled by the story and strong key messages of 'being on mission'. These principles became essential for our professional careers as well as our private lives. (Ute and Norbert)." **Dr. Med. Ute Buschmann Truffer**, Fachärztin Neurochirurgie, Exec. MBA HSG Luzerner Kantonsspital

"Mark's high-energy approach to Leadership and Life comes shining through from inside an interesting and very 'readable' story. Each chapter delivers increased motivation to dig deeper in our personal quest for self-fulfillment through a balanced, happy and purposeful life." **Anthony Ameo** President and CEO of ECKART America Corp.

" 'Being on Mission' is an eye opener for those that are ready to see. See the life challenge, see how to bring back balance, and see how to bring a good dose of life intensity back in. 'Being on Mission' is about living, laughing, learning, loving and about taking a step back and recognizing this is about you, the way you live your life and how you will be able to unlock so many beautiful things that are waiting for you to be experienced.......If only, you are ready to see." **Bert Konings,** Director Marketing - Rosemount Europe, Rosemount Measurement, Emerson Process Management

"I've read quite a few business books but none that leave readers with enough knowledge to confidently execute the lessons being taught. Mark's book teaches a memorable and important message, helping to identify reader's real values and start their mission to find happiness and success." **Matthias** Becker, Executive Quality Head, T-Systems

"The idea of educating people on management and leadership by implementing theoretical knowledge into a novel is an exceptional and refreshing approach! It is much easier to comprehend the content when it is illustrated in examples. As are your seminars and the coaching with you, this book is a great guide for a holistic understanding of (self)management and leadership and a real page-turner at the same time. Congratulations!" **Bjoern Roeling** Senior Executive Vice President – Chemicals, Helm U.S. Corp.

"This book is a must read for all developing leaders in the 21st century. It is equally eye-opening, insightful and deeply touching. A true page turner!" **Dr. Katja Kruckeberg** International Leadership & Management Consultant, Germany www.kruckeberg.de

"In 'Being On Mission', Mark distills the essential elements of his trainings and workshops into a very readable and thought provoking story that highlights the ups and downs that every business leader encounters over the course of their career. It provides a roadmap to achieve true success by finding the right balance between one's professional and personal lives. I highly recommend this book to anyone looking for a fresh approach to leadership training." **Phillip M. Chalabi,** General Manager, Umicore Precious Metals Chemistry USA, LLC

"Feel the energy and enthusiasm of Mark McGregor in this life changing story about love, making the right choices, living them and enjoy life to the fullest. This page-turner almost reads like a thriller, with brilliant lessons for work, life and love. Learn about the importance of doing the right things, 'being on mission'and start doing what is most essential in your life. And remember there is always a reset button, so you can 'get up' when you 'fall' and always start again." **Annemarie Konijnenberg,** Management Consultant, Erasmus MC, Erasmus University Medical Center in Rotterdam

"This book is a real pioneer of edutainment in leadership- combining a well written,exciting novel with important lessons on leadership. A must for every manager who wants to make first steps towards becoming a true and genuine leader."
Dr. Axel Steiger-Bagel, Senior Bayer Representative Benelux

"Mark's vision of leadership, wrapped in a story everybody can identify with, is brilliant. My wife Mirjam was the first who read it in our family and she loves it, too. We think the book is really great and different to all the others out there. The content gives the ability to reflect and has the power to change life.... Thank you, Mark!" **Udo Hornfeck,** MBA and Eng., Dipl.-Ing., Vice President Global R&D, LEONI Wiring Systems Division

"'Being on Mission' encapsulates in a very readable story, how the simple messages and tools Mark has developed can really help anybody willing enough to develop, that leadership is a choice and that getting the right work / life balance builds from a set of strong values and a clear vision, both professionally and privately." **Julian Whitehead** EVP Finance, Airbus Defense and Space

"This book embodies the power of leadership and the ability to lead, combined with the important interdependencies between self-reflection, change and doing."
Axel Viering, HELM AG, Hamburg, BU Derivatives

DEDICATED TO

My wife, Faye, my own lighthouse.
Thank you for all your
love, light and support. I feel it everyday!
Together our foundation keeps getting stronger.

ACKNOWLEDGMENTS AND THANKS

Where to start, after the ten years dedicated to seeing this project finally come to life!

First, to my family… Faye, Ryan and Kaitlyn. Thank you for your patience and support, and the ongoing feedback and suggestions, and allowing the time necessary to complete this project. You are my purpose and my passion, and are what keeps me 'on mission'.

To my parents, Vivian and the late Pete McGregor, who always taught me to live, love, laugh and learn. I won the parent lottery and I know that.

To my sister Pam and her husband, Brent. Your continued feedback and support has always been valued and appreciated.

Elsie and Alex, for providing your love, home and support for my 'Canadian' office.

I need to thank my writing team. Together, we formed the high-perfomance team required to get a project like this completed. Thank you all for your part of the journey:

- Larry Danielson, for getting the ball rolling with me, and for the deep research and details that you helped fill in.
- Barbara Leslie, for your hours and hours of editing to bring my 400-page manuscript into a more reasonable 200 plus pages.
- Bob Leslie for sharing your wisdom and knowledge as a valued leadership consultant.
- Gillian Walter, my valued story consultant. You did such a great job of bringing in fresh energy and for being my sparring partner during my time in Bali and the final stages of the book.
- Steve Simpkin, for taking the time to read the final manuscript and assist with the final edits.
- Ayu Ikonen, thanks for falling into our lives when you did! You became my fingers on the keyboard, helping to make changes and add details during our sabbatical in Bali.
- Alex Borton and Dylanne Crugnale, I so appreciated your support in typing out and recording my thoughts and ideas.
- Lynda Dobbin-Turner, thank you for your commitment to this process over the many rewrites and various versions. Your word-smithing and editing have helped to bring this book into being.
- Cecil Turner, thanks for being Lynda's sounding board on two road-trips, reaching both coasts as she read the manuscripts aloud to you not once, but three times! You are a man 'on Mission'!
- To my administration supports Karin Schloms and Anita Walchhofer. You know none of this could happen without you! Together, we formed the high-perfomance team required to get a project like this completed. Thank you all for your part of the journey.
- Marcel Simon came in late in the project but had the important role of reworking the German translation and proof reading it to make sure it read well in German.

To my many ghost readers, and particularly those who provided such valuable feedback and suggestions: Andrea Gade, Iris Zeigler, Annett Lulow, Ute Buschmann, Pierre leinhrd, Philipp Mangold, Gayle Manculich, Olaf Ransom, Sven Gade, Franziska Ward, Tjalle Hijlkema, Sue Graham, Tine Kock, Annemarie Konijnenberg, Peter Kaltenegger,

Per Ulrich, Paul Rindler, Jackie Purkess, Nicole Loeffen, Dietmar Rohlf, Betty Lowe, Jim Graham, Andreas Mueller, Matthias Becker, Christian Rippl, Tore Birol, Stefan Buenemann, Darren and Barb Borton, Kathy Fischer, David Hartmann, Andrea Heckelmann, Marsh and Donna Kennedy, Claus Muhlfiet, Michael Neuhoff, Al Pirie, Carlo Reato, Anja Schleth, Axel Steiger, Achim Toper, Axel Viering, Peter William Ward, Anthony Ameo, Andre Bremm, Sandi Gilbert, Michael Gogoel, Frederic Klumpp, Tim Diepenbruck, Beat Emch, Ken McInnes, Annett Luelow, Margarete Loecker, Anke Linnartz, Sonja Lehnen, Jens Kuerten, Bert Konings, Rudd Knorr, Anne Gradl, Felix Grish, Phillip Chalabi, Gillian Walter, Timo Fritz and Rosina Gasteiger.

To those who have offered ongoing encouragement, have offered their help with content details and to those who were vulnerable enough to share the challenges that leaders in today's fast paced world have to contend with, thank you for your insight.

Thank you also to **Dr. D.H. (Dee) Groberg**, for his permission to use his poem "The Race" in the book. Also to **Robert Fulghum,** for his permission to use his poem "All I really need to know I learned in Kindergarten." Your talents have created some valuable teaching tools for others to reflect upon and are appreciated.

PREFACE

Throughout my ten-year writing process which began during my 2004 sabbatical in Australia, I have been asked the same question over and over; why did I write a story instead of a standard leadership book with clear and concisely presented content on 'How to Be a Better Leader'?

Quite simply, I believe in the power of a story. It's the stories and not the textbooks that you remember. I doubt you remember the material from that Psychology 101 textbook, although I'm sure some of the anecdotes your professor passionately presented are still as fresh now, as they were way back then. This book is a collage of real stories that clients have shared with me over the past two decades, including key moments and turning points of my own journey, and the result is an authentic picture of the main character, Michael Weber's, life. This authenticity helps readers to identify with the mistakes, experiences and lessons learned within the story on a more personal level. Identifying elements of one's self within a story can trigger powerful emotional experiences that deepen an interaction with a book and the strong messages within. Let the realistic anecdotes and personal reflections resonate with you and you will gain much more from this book than simple, bullet-pointed 'how to' lists.

Most importantly, it's because I teach leadership based on a whole person model. That is quite unique as it makes you reflect upon all facets of your own life. I truly believe that following Michael Weber's growth and development will motivate you to start your own process of personal and professional transformation.

Although this book is set out in a story-format, you don't necessarily have to read it as such. For the fast-paced, no-patience readers, I suggest starting at page 87, experience the leadership training component and read through the coaching session to the end of the book. You could, of course, read it simply as a novel and enjoy the story in itself. However, to get maximum value out of this book, I strongly recommend reading through the entire story and writing down *your* thoughts and emotions along with Michael in your own journal and *reflect upon* all the exercises and tools included.

To deepen your reflection even further, go to http://www.markm-cgregor.ch/cms1/index.php/survey/ and access the self-assessment questionnaire to evaluate how you live the "10 Principles of Leadership and Life".

Although much of the content can be found in the leadership course and coaching session, much more is embedded as lessons that Michael learns along his journey, which only develop as the story progresses. This recommendation is based on feedback given to me by over twenty clients who gained maximum value by working through the book this way. One client recommends this book as a story that has to be reread at different stages along one's personal journey. She actually went back to it four more times to get the most of her personal learning process.

Whether participating in one of my trainings or reading this book, my goal is to make a difference … one person at a time.

PART I

"ACTIONS BRING CONSEQUENCES"

CHAPTER 1

"Help me! Please help me!"

The pain-filled voice pierced Michael's ears, as he searched the fog that surrounded him. "Petra? Is that you? Where are you? I can't see you!" Panic rose in his heart as he strained to find the source of the voice.

"Help me...please somebody, can't you help me, please?" the tortured voice cried out.

The haze around him was so thick. "I'm here! Where are you? I can't see you! WHERE ARE YOU?" As he tried to focus his eyes and locate the terrified cry, a stabbing white light almost blinded him. It felt like a spear being thrust through his head as he struggled against it.

"Over here! Help me!" Petra? Or was it? He'd been so certain, but now Michael wasn't sure. He could still hear the shouting but why couldn't he open his eyes and see her or whoever was yelling? What was going on? As he struggled to make sense of it all, his leg suddenly exploded in a volcano of burning and terrifying pain. What was happening? He had to get to her and help...and what the hell was that deafening grinding noise?

"No! Help me! Don't leave me now..." The loud and insistent voice no longer sounded like her voice at all.

Michael suddenly went cold as he recognized the scream as his own.

He felt a hand on his shoulder and jumped.

"It's all right, Mr. Weber. Everything's okay."

He forced his eyes open and was surprised to find himself in a hospital bed. He felt his body trembling uncontrollably.

The nurse's hand remained on his shoulder, in an effort to settle him. "You've had an accident, Mr. Weber. Do you remember anything?"

"No, not much. Bright lights…loud noises, shouting…"

"You're in Erlangen. In our Intensive Care Unit. You came in by ambulance on Friday evening."

"What day is it today?"

"It's Sunday afternoon. You've had a critical couple of days, Mr. Weber. Your wife is here. We contacted her as your next of kin."

"Petra! Where is she?" Michael asked, trying to shift his throbbing body and look around the room.

"I think she just popped out to make a call," the nurse smiled, "I'll go and let her know you're awake."

Michael closed his eyes for a moment as his head pounded and his mind spun with the confusion of this distorted reality thrust upon him.

"I'm glad to see you awake. You had us all worried." He opened his eyes and saw Petra standing in the doorway as beautiful as ever, but something wasn't right. "You are a lucky man. You have been given a second chance at life, Michael. Perhaps now, finally, you will find the time to take a long, hard look at your life and decide how you want to live this new one."

He knew now exactly what was wrong; that hard and pained look on Petra's face had never been there before and, as she turned to leave and the events of Friday evening rushed back, he wished himself back into unconsciousness.

CHAPTER 2

After an hour of manning his company's trade fair booth alone, Michael Weber glanced at his watch. In his prime, he'd been a handsome man, slightly taller than one hundred and eighty centimeters with broad and muscular shoulders. He would have had an impressive build had he kept trim around his waistline with his old sports regime, but the familiar soft belly of a man who no longer took the time to exercise was drooping over his belt. Years of playing soccer had given Michael a permanently tanned face which suited his still-thick dark hair and brown- green eyes, eyes that now showed the signs of stress from late nights, constant travel and saying yes to one too many beers. After a decade of working hard for Plastics Engineering and Manufacturing Inc., 38-year-old Michael had fallen into the same trap as many men in his position; bad eating habits, weight gain, too little sleep and not enough time devoted to other aspects of his life.

As charming a salesman as he was, Michael was impatient with incompetency and tardiness, especially with members of his sales team and the two who were supposed to have relieved him thirty minutes ago were nowhere to be seen. He should be on the road home already if he was to make it to Frankfurt for the end of Petra's concert. He had promised her that he'd be there this time, a promise he intended to keep for a change.

Michael disliked working alone when things got as busy at the booth as they had with this Munich show. Where were those two? Trying to look relaxed, he greeted the three men who gathered around the aluminum injection molds, studying the latest innovative samples from the company he worked for. The new video of P.E.M.'s production work in Guangdong, China, was an enticing advertising tool and the new prospects stood in front of the big screen watching it closely. Michael put on his salesman smile and prepared himself for his sales pitch just as his two employees hurried towards him.

"Sorry, Michael," one of them panted, "the traffic is crazy."

Michael snatched his jacket, laptop, briefcase and call-back sheets from the back table.

"And I've got to drive back to Frankfurt tonight in exactly that crazy traffic," he snapped. "It's a busy show and there's plenty of interest so I'm expecting a report full of contacts and leads first thing Monday morning." With that, he stormed towards the exit sign.

Sliding in behind the wheel, he scrolled to Petra's number as he pulled out of the car park. He needed to call and let her know he was running late. He still looked forward to hearing her voice after each business trip.

"Hi, honey, it's me. I'm just leaving Munich. I should make it to the concert around ten thirty." Petra had become a professional cello player after college and Michael loved to hear her perform and see the passion in her face that only appeared when she played. As frustrated as he was with leaving late, he was looking forward to seeing her perform. His job, the travel and long working hours that it entailed, made attending her concerts a rare pleasure.

Silence. Had they been disconnected?

"Are you there, Petra?"

"Michael, it would be better if you didn't come," she said at last, her voice flat and cold, "I don't have much to say to you."

"Petra! What's wrong?"

"I've moved out, Michael. I can't do this any more."

"What? What are you talking about?"

"I heard about your night in Cologne. Why would you do that to me Michael...to us?"

For a moment, Michael was speechless. How the hell had she found out about Cologne?

"It's not like that. It was nothing… one stupid night. Petra, I can explain!"
Silence, again. Michael scrambled for words.

"I know I've been away too much. Not spent enough time with you. I don't know what you've heard, but it's not as bad as you think."

"I trusted you Michael. And it is that bad."

"Please. Wait. We'll talk when I get home."

"My key is in the mailbox. Good-bye Michael."

"Now you're just overreacting, just wait 'til I get…"

He stopped mid-sentence. She had hung up.

Numb with the shock of his stupidity and anger at being found out, Michael wove his way through the city streets, hardly conscious of where he was until he exited onto the A9. Traffic was picking up speed and Michael accelerated out into the fast lane. After all the years he and Petra had been together, could it really be over? They'd just been discussing a weekend away to celebrate their 10th wedding anniversary and now this! Michael's mind was swirling.

Petra was always so relaxed and calm about their marriage. Yes, he was away a lot on business, but she kept busy with her music and concerts. They were not a substitute for spending time together, but she never complained. She understood that in order for Michael to climb the P.E.M. career ladder, sacrifices would have to be made. She knew the plan. She understood, didn't she?

"Damn it!" He shouted punching the steering wheel. Who was he kidding? That was no excuse and he knew it. None of their plans had included another woman. He'd been stupid - end of story. But how could she have found out? Someone must have had told her, some one intent on hurting and undermining him. There were plenty who were jealous of his success, but would anyone really go so far?

Michael's phone jolted him out of his fury and he grabbed at it, certain that it would be Petra.

"Good evening Mr. Weber, it's George Schmidt."

The disappointment cut Michael like a knife.

"Yes?" he snapped.

"Well, sir, it's about next month's sales conference in Düsseldorf."

"What about it?"

"The conference runs Thursday and Friday, but your last email says we have to be there on Saturday morning for a sales planning session as well." Michael heard him take a nervous breath before he continued, "My little girl has her very first music performance on that Saturday afternoon and I was hoping to catch a flight out Friday night, so I could be there for her..."

Michael's fury overflowed as he snapped, "Come on, George, give me a break! You know how important it is to show commitment to the sales force, particularly from sales supervisors. What would it look like if everybody sacrificed their weekends except for you, because you can't be bothered to give one hundred percent? Don't you realize how your not being there would reflect on me? I think it is about time you reconsidered your priorities! I expect you to be there for that Saturday session, no excuses!"

Michael hung up without a goodbye. What the hell was the matter with everyone?

Furious, red in the face and out of breath after his rant, he flung his phone onto the passenger seat with more force than he realized and it bounced once before landing under the seat. Punching the steering wheel again he yanked and tugged at his seat belt, straining down to retrieve his phone. And, in that second, Michael's world changed forever.

CHAPTER 3

The emergency surgery to deal with his multiple fractures and traumatic pneumothorax had been complicated. The doctor informed Michael that he had been lucky. He would need more surgery, but he would live. Besides three fractured ribs, he'd broken the tibia and fibula of his right leg and both his ankle and kneecap were crushed. His ankle would need to be stabilized with a metal plate and screws and the kneecap fragments would have to be wired together.

Michael lay in his hospital bed after the doctor had left, staring at his useless foot and knee. What the hell? He wiggled his toes tentatively and wondered what lay ahead of him. He tried to clear his head but found trying to form any clear thoughts exhausting. He had often wished for more time to rest, but this wasn't exactly how he had planned it. He felt so hopeless and alone as the morphine took hold and dragged him into troubled dreams once again.

Michael was recovering from a second round of operations. He was still groggy from the anesthetic but brightened when he spotted the familiar figures of Klaus and Monika Mertens standing in the doorway.

Klaus and Monika had become Michael's family after taking him into their home and their hearts when Michael was seventeen. They took him in at the darkest time of his young life, having just lost his mother to lung cancer. She was only thirty-nine.

Michael blamed his absent father for that and so much more. His father was the one who had filled their home with tobacco smoke. For as long as Michael could recall, if his father bothered to come home at all, Michael and his mother had to tiptoe around his volatile mood swings while his father sat in front of the television with a pile of beer bottles growing on one side of him and a pile of ash on the other. Michael had watched, embarrassed and angry, as his mother made excuses for his father and struggled to keep some semblance of a home for them. She worked hard to keep up the pretense of a functioning family right up until the day his dad disappeared. One evening, his father stormed out of the house in a drunken rage and simply never came back. Michael had come to loathe the man but his mother continued to love him, to hope for the best and wait for his return. Michael never understood that. He would never forgive his father for what he'd put them through and when his mother died he had no intention of trying to find him.

Klaus had been his junior soccer coach at that time. Just as Michael was ready to give up hope on life altogether, Klaus offered Michael a home with him and his wife. Klaus was much more than a coach and not only for Michael. He was a mentor and a guide. He knew each of his players well; he knew when they needed space and when they needed him. Klaus knew Michael had started drinking heavily and was determined not to let him fall into the same pattern as his father. Thanks to Klaus and Monika, his future had taken a much more positive route. His career as a professional soccer player did not last long, but his decision, at the age of twenty-four, to move from a career in sports to studying engineering at university was one that they fully supported and no two parents could have been as proud at Michael's graduation as Klaus and Monika were. During his university years, Klaus encouraged Michael's continued involvement with the younger players as his part-time assistant coach. He had told Michael that it was a way for him to earn his keep but, in reality, they both knew how important Klaus' continued support and guidance was for him.

"How's my boy?" Klaus asked, striding across the hospital room with Monika at his side. "You scared the hell out of us, you know!"

With a twinge of guilt Michael looked into Klaus' concerned face. They had been like parents to him. No, less judgmental and more supportive than any parents he remembered. When was the last time he'd been to visit them, or even called them for that matter? Hell, how was he supposed to have time for them when he had precious little time for himself and yet, here they were.

"I won't dribble a ball, or be able to help out with your junior squad anytime soon," Michael tried to put on a brave face. "Sorry about the scare and thanks for coming."

"Petra called and told us about the accident. What happened?"

Michael confessed that his memories were all mixed up. He could barely remember the truck pulling out and his Audi flipping over. Michael blamed the truck driver who crossed into his lane and squeezed him into the railing but didn't add that he knew in his heart that he hadn't been focused enough on the road ahead to be able to avoid the extent of the terrible outcome.

"You're very fortunate," Monika said, as she stroked a petal of the yellow tulips on his nightstand. "Are these from Petra? It's just like her to try and get a little springtime in here."

"My company," Michael mumbled.

Monika was apologetic when he explained the change in circumstances.

"Oh, I'm so sorry...for both of you. She didn't mention..."

Her gaze was warm and reassuring and her tone was sympathetic and non-judgmental. She always managed to say the right thing and Michael thought, as always, what a great team she and Klaus made. He redirected his attention towards Klaus as he felt his throat constrict. Klaus Mertens still looked every inch the star halfback he had once been before becoming a great soccer coach, first, rising through the junior ranks and now, coaching a second division team in Munich. Noticing how fit and strong Klaus looked, Michael felt conscious of the bulk of his own body in the bed. Too many business lunches, snacks in never-ending meetings and junk food hastily grabbed on the road had taken their toll. Time for exercise was a distant memory. But how else was he supposed to keep up the pace that had got him to where he was today?

They talked for a while about Klaus' current, professional, second-division team and then drifted back into stories of players Michael had known during his playing years. If he missed a detail, Monika would lean forward in her chair and prompt him. Many of the players still kept in touch with them. A few had gone on to play professionally, but most, like Michael, had chosen other life paths.

"Your former teammates still ask about you too, Michael. You made quite an impression on my junior team players as assistant coach, you know. Coaching them wasn't always easy, was it?" Klaus chuckled.

"I'm glad none of them can see me now. Not much of an example to follow, am I?"

"Don't be too hard on yourself, son." Klaus rose from his chair and laid a package on the bedside table, "I've got something for you." Michael removed the paper from a burgundy, leather-bound book and looked quizzically back at Klaus as he flipped through the blank pages.

"I've spent some time in hospitals over the years myself with one injury or another and I know how frustrating it can be. But I also learned to appreciate the time, albeit forced upon me, and used it as an opportunity to rethink, or to reboot, if you like. I was given a book just like this years ago and told to write down my thoughts and goals and to clarify them. At first, I thought it was kind of strange and worried about writing the wrong thing or what other people might think, but it's actually one of the best things I've ever been given. I still do it, even now. Putting clear goals down on paper makes them real. It makes you face them square on. They look back at you, Michael, and ask, 'So, what are you going to do about me now?' Very few people bother to put their goals down in writing, but I've read that over seventy per cent of written goals actually get achieved. I thought being stuck in here would be a good time for you to try it out for yourself."

"Well, I'll certainly have the time, Klaus. I hope I can find the motivation."

"That's up to you to decide, Michael. Like I said, it's always worked for me. I constantly tell my team to go out and play like it's your last game. You know that, and it works for life too. You've been given the chance that not many of us get. The doctor tells me that Friday could, quite easily, have been your last day. You've been given a second chance to see another spring begin."

Klaus gripped his hand with a farewell smile. Monika leaned over, kissed him on the cheek and said softly, "All things work together for good, Michael. I truly believe that."

After Klaus and Monika left, Michael lay a long while, thinking of all the time he had spent at the Mertens' home after his mother had died. Never once had Klaus and Monika complained that he was in the way. And now, they never complained that he didn't have time for them. He opened the cover of the journal he had just received and saw, written in Klaus' bold handwriting:

"Goals: Write them; See them; Believe them; Achieve them."

Was it really that easy? With such a jumble of confused thoughts thrashing around in his head, when he was able to stay awake long enough to think at all, it seemed impossible for him to make enough sense of anything to set clear goals. What were his goals anyway? On the opposite page, Klaus had written a quote from Mahatma Gandhi that Michael remembered from somewhere:

Keep your thoughts positive because your thoughts become your words.
Keep your words positive because your words become your behavior.
Keep your behavior positive because your behavior becomes your habits.
Keep your habits positive because your habits become your destiny.
- **Mahatma Gandhi**

"Thoughts-words, words-behavior, behavior-habits, habits-destiny... Tricky when you can't make sense of your own thoughts in the first place," he mumbled to himself and threw the book back down. "Can my thoughts really affect my destiny? It can't be that simple!"

One goal he was sure about was getting in touch with the office but he just couldn't seem to stay awake long enough. When he finally felt up to it, he rang the P.E.M. office in Frankfurt worried about the state of his office without him. The receptionist told him how sorry they all were and put him through to his immediate superior, Karl Otto Fritsch.

Michael gave him a brief update and indicated that it might be weeks before he could return to the office. Mr. Fritsch assured him that there was absolutely nothing for him to worry about and he should just concentrate on getting well. Horst Nocker was managing the department very nicely in his absence.

Concentrate on getting well? There was nothing to do but wait, think his muddled thoughts, and dream his drug-induced dreams. Then wait and think and sleep some more. The rest of the world went on as usual, with or without him, as if nothing bad had happened. One day, giving it your best, busting a gut to win deals any way you can: giving up weekends and evenings to be with people you don't like, laughing at lame jokes and being a slave to the phone. Hell, even that woman in Cologne was a sales pitch that had gone way, way too far and he knew it. And for what? The very next moment, you're being assured that life is continuing 'very nicely' without you, thank you very much.

The possibility of that scenario had never once occurred to Michael. But what else could he do but wait? Writing goals in a stupid book? What was the point of that if his presence in the world didn't matter one way or the other and anything he had worked so hard to achieve could be ripped from him at any unsuspecting moment? What on earth did he have to be positive about? Who did he have to be positive about? His fury rose as he thought about Petra, Klaus and Monika. Didn't they know what he had to do, what he had to sacrifice to become the man he wanted to be for them? He was doing it all for Petra, after all. He so desperately wanted to give his wife everything, every luxury associated with being the wife of a successful General Manager at P.E.M. He was so close to getting that role, and she knew it. He wanted Klaus and Monika to be proud of him, and Klaus had always encouraged him to work hard. He couldn't get anything right!

Once again, his inner monologue became a negative spiral, pulling him ever downwards towards a bleak hole. A whirlwind of his own panicked thoughts and voices was dragging him towards it. He shut his eyes tight and felt unable to hold onto any clear and rational thought and soon he stopped even trying. Why bother to stop them? He was too exhausted to try. Was he losing his mind? The noise inside his head was deafening. His own tear made him jump as it dropped onto his sweaty cheek. His eyes sprang open, the noises stopped and the closed book that he'd thrown down lay there staring up at him with the words:

"Keep your thoughts positive"

CHAPTER 4

Michael did not sleep well. No matter how he positioned himself, he could not get comfortable even though the drugs made him so sleepy. He was determined not to increase his pain medication, knowing all too well that it meant swapping the physical pain for mental pain. But, shortly after lunch, he relented, called the nurse and soon fell back into another drug-induced flashback.

"Come on boys. You did well out there!"

"What? They killed us, or weren't you watching?" came a shout from the boys crowding around Michael in the team's locker room.

"I was watching and I saw great teamwork."

"What good is that if we lose the game?"

Klaus leant against the wall with his arms crossed and a smile played on his lips as he let Michael take the lead in the junior team's post-game session.

Michael raised his voice, "No match is solely about the final score. Wins will come with time, with training, with perseverance and hard work. I believe in this team and we will become successful! Can you say, 'YES, I did my best and gave all I had?' That's what's important. We may fall, but we get up and keep going, even when the odds are stacked against us! We choose to get better every day." Someone shouted, "No, I didn't", which brought with it a round of laughter and the tension dissappated.

Later, as Klaus and Michael were walking out of the dressing room Klaus said, "I'm proud of you Michael. How did you feel?"

"I was really nervous facing all the frustrated guys, but I knew that was the time to share my message. I think they're ready for a hard practice tomorrow. It felt good and I truly believe in them."

"And they believe in you, Michael."

Michael's mind couldn't focus anymore, as the vivid image of Klaus turned vague and the sound of his voice faded, Michael could still hear his praise: "I'm proud of you – you did really well. Now is the time to live that message." It was so real that Michael could even feel Klaus' hand on his shoulder.

He finally forced his eyes open to find Petra sitting in the chair beside him shaking his shoulder.

"Petra!" Michael stammered, uncomfortably wondering if she had been sitting there throughout his dream and realizing that he was covered in a layer of sweat. "What a wonderful surprise. I didn't know if you would come again."

"I wasn't sure I would. The nurse said it was okay to wait here." She still looked tired but the hardness was gone from her face. "You're still my husband Michael, I had to come and see how you were doing."

"Thank you," Michael struggled, adjusting his bed to an upright position. "I feel better for seeing you. How are you?"

"I'm working through things. I'm adjusting. I have a place of my own lined up for the first of May. Until then, I'm staying with my father."

Michael winced. "Oh. When you hadn't told Klaus and Monika that you'd moved out, I had hoped it was because you'd had a change of heart. Please don't leave me, Petra. I'm so sorry. I screwed up. I know that. But we can get through this, I know we can."

Petra shrugged, "There was a time when I thought we were perfect for each other. But everything has changed. I hardly even know who you are anymore and, what's worse, it's made me question myself. I thought we were working towards the same goals, but we've become strangers living under one roof. When I heard about Cologne I...." her voice trailed off, but not before he heard the pain in it.

Michael thought of a dozen excuses all at once but realized none of them were appropriate to say out loud. "Can you ever forgive me?" It was the best he could do, painfully aware of how pathetic he sounded.

"I honestly don't know. It's done, Michael, and it can't be undone. I need to take care of myself right now. I've been tolerating too much for too long, settling for the tiny, exhausted and distracted part of you that was left after work. It's not how I'd pictured my life, our life. I thought we'd be more somehow, but that's obviously not the case and I'm trying to come to terms with that." She stood up and put her hand gently on his shoulder, "Take care and get well. I'm sorry, I've got to go."

Petra gave him a long, sad look. "Goodbye, Michael." He saw a tear run down her cheek as she backed away. He wanted her to stay, to let him try and make this right, but she turned and headed through the door without looking back.

This was not how he had meant for their conversation to end. He loved her. One mistake and now she wanted to end their marriage? Was it really too late? If so, then what was the point of it all anyway? The extra hours, weekends spent working and stressful travel schedules. Why didn't Petra realize it was all for her?

His sense of panic returned and he had to have something, anything to focus on, to cling to in order to keep him from being sucked down into that hole he felt hovering below him. No! I'm not going down there! He reached out for the journal and read the first words Klaus had written from the Gandhi quote, 'Keep your thoughts positive'. He read it out loud over and over again until he actually heard what his mouth was saying. Now the hard part; write one positive goal. Come on, Michael, you fell down. Now, get up and write one. Just start with one.

Goal 1: Explain things again to Petra. Get her to understand.

He had no idea if he would even see her again, let alone get the chance to explain, to convince her, to show her that he could do better. The thought of having to keep that all bottled up was too much for him but he was desperate to concentrate his mind on something positive this time and stop the panic from rising. He began to write what he didn't think he would ever be able to say:

I'm sorry, Petra. I broke our trust and I take the blame. That woman didn't mean anything to me. She was just there at a moment when I was feeling full of myself, when I felt the thrill of the deal and thought I had the world by the tail. But I know all too well that something precious has slipped out of my grasp. What can I do now to bring you back? How can I make that happen?

CHAPTER 5

Exactly one week after the accident, a work colleague visited Michael in the hospital and their chat naturally turned to P.E.M. As Michael had already heard, Horst Nocker was the new 'Acting Sales Manager', filling Michael's position in his absence. Michael grimaced. It could take months to repair the damage Horst might do.

Michael hoped that Horst was doing his job well, but not too well. Michael had lots of irons in the fire that would bring him a nice bonus this year if he played them well. He was nervous that Horst would mess it all up or, even worse, make it look as if they were his successes. Michael knew it wouldn't be long before his boss retired and the General Manager's position became available. He had to be there to make sure he was the one impressing the right people with the right moves. Alone again, he dozed off with dreams of job advancement.

Michael felt the presence of someone in the room and opened his eyes to see Klaus Mertens. His surprise must have shown on his face.

"I had another meeting in Hamburg," Klaus explained.

"Must be something pretty important to bring you all this way again. What's going on, Klaus? Don't keep me in suspense."

His friend hesitated a moment, "The first division team has offered me a job as their head coach."

"Wow! Congratulations! You should have been called to the National League long ago."

"I'm still considering the offer."

"Considering?" Michael stared at him, dumbfounded. "What's to consider? Isn't it time you had some real money and appreciation for what you do?"

Money wasn't everything, Klaus asserted. He wanted to be certain it was the *right* thing to do. He felt a deep bond with the team in Munich and knew he could still contribute much there. And he had to think about Monika. She had a real passion for teaching and loved the work she was doing.

"She has a passion for *your* work too," Michael added.

"She shouldn't have to choose between the two."

Klaus was a persistent jogger and, if Michael knew Klaus, he would be running more than usual during the next couple of weeks using this time to think everything through before making his decision. It was the time when he reflected and thought most clearly and had the advantage of keeping him in great shape.

"And how are you doing?" Klaus asked. "I promised Monika a full report."

"Look at me, I'm a tangled mess." Michael gestured at his broken body.

"And emotionally?"

"Also a wreck. I would love to find out who ran me off the road and make him pay."

"It was a terrible accident, Michael. It must have been a terrible shock for the lorry driver, too. Let it go. Your past does not create your future. Make your future an open book that you write. The journal can help, you know." He pushed the book across the bedside table towards Michael.

"Michael, do you remember 'The Race'?" asked Klaus, watching Michael's face. Klaus had often read that old poem to his soccer teams, inspiring them to keep getting up each time they fell and keep moving forward. Michael felt as if he were back in his dream, "Well, it's time to pick yourself up again, my friend. The race is far from over for you. You need to keep moving yourself forward."

Michael nodded uncertainly as the two men shook hands. Klaus gave him an encouraging pat on the shoulder and walked out the door. Michael picked up the journal once more.

> So, my past does not create my future. Well, it's certainly affected my present. My past has ruined my future. That truck driver almost killed me. Horst is stealing my job. Petra has overreacted. And I'm just supposed to let it go? I'm the victim here and Klaus thinks remembering some old poem is going to make it better?

Michael looked at the empty doorway that Klaus had just left through and then at his journal.

> If my past does not create my future, then I guess blame, whys and what-ifs don't belong in my journal either. But that doesn't alter the fact that my life is falling apart and none of this is my fault.

CHAPTER 6

After four painful and difficult weeks and two operations later, Michael felt like singing when the doctor finally discharged him. The trip home exhausted him, but he was anxious to call the office. He called the colleague who had visited him in the hospital to find out what was happening there in his absence before officially calling his boss. He needed to know what Horst was up to, and then wished he hadn't. Horst was the new golden boy after landing the Lindeman account. Michael had worked hard for months to set up that deal and Horst had snatched all the credit while he was stuck lying in this damned bed.

Michael stared at the receiver after the conversation had ended. He had to get back to work. He had to put a stop to this. This news had completely knocked the wind out of him but he was way too restless to settle and wandered from room to room. His neighbor had his mail neatly stacked on the kitchen counter and the refrigerator was filled with microwave dinners but it was all so wrong. It felt completely empty with none of Petra's things there. He had been so eager to get home, to be back in his own place and get back to normality, yet now all he felt was the emptiness of his reality. There suddenly seemed little to celebrate.

For the first three weeks Michael religiously did his physio exercises and attended his outpatient appointments but then slowly started to slip. The rest of his life was unscheduled and unstructured. The apartment was starting to look like a mess. He went to bed when he felt like it and slept as late as he wanted. He had never taken much time for leisure since his college days and now that he had it in abundance, he hardly knew how to use it. He was not much of a reader, so he sat for hours in his recliner, surfing channels for anything to hold his interest. Munching on a bag of chips and sipping another bottle of beer, he decided he liked commercials best; they didn't pretend to be relevant or clever, they just wanted to sell. That, he could relate to.

Michael emailed Horst, offering to help with some of the office work. The only response was a copy of the March Sales Report, which he edited extensively. He was surprised how hard it was to concentrate on such a familiar task. He finished it at last and forwarded it to both Horst and Mr. Fritsch. There was no reply from either of them.

Michael kept his journal on the TV table for easy access, but his thoughts still seemed so muddled. At least writing was better than talking out loud to himself. All that achieved was to make the empty space feel even lonelier, not to mention making him feel as if he was going crazy.

I'm putting on a little weight, I think. But what else should I expect in the position I'm stuck in? Once I get back to work that will change. It should be easy enough once I'm up and active again...or is that just wishful thinking? Do I even care?

He dialed Petra's number for what seemed like the hundredth time, but once again, no answer. She didn't answer any of his emails or texts and he was slowly getting her message. But was it really over? He wondered if he should call someone else, but realized he wouldn't know what to talk about if he did. He had lost contact with most of the important people in his life. Michael had never felt so alone.

Klaus called a few days later, explaining that that he and Monika were in Frankfurt again. Michael eagerly agreed to meet them, jotted down the address and ordered a taxi.

The restaurant was a cozy, family-style place. Michael spotted Klaus and Monika at the far end of the room and made his way cautiously across to them on his crutches.

Monika leaned across the table and rested her hand on Michael's. "It's so good to see you up and moving again Michael. How are you doing?"

Michael knew that look. She was asking about more than his physical recovery. Monika read him well. She wanted to get to the heart of the matter, but Michael resisted. "I'm doing well. Keeping up with my physio, doing a bit of work for the office from home…"

"Michael, you know that's not what I mean. Have you heard from Petra?"

"Not since her visit at the hospital. I've tried repeatedly to make contact, but without any luck." Michael trailed off. He didn't really know what else to say.

Monika understood Michael's tone. "I know Petra is hurting too. This is such a difficult time for both of you. Klaus and I care for you both. Just keep reaching out and expressing your love to her." She knew he was at his emotional limit and let it go with a gentle smile and nod of her head.

Thankful to be able to change the subject, Michael turned to Klaus, "So?"

Klaus smiled slightly and answered Michael's question with one of his own.

"What would you have done in my place?"

Michael laughed, "The answer to that should have been clear from the first time you mentioned it. Better pay. More prestige. Working with the best players. When do you start?"

Klaus looked at him for a moment, "It's more a matter of… continuing."

Michael's confusion must have shown on his face and Monika quickly added, "Klaus turned down the Hamburg offer."

For a moment, Michael couldn't think of what to say. He wondered what strange reasoning had led his friend to turn down the head coaching position. He thought Klaus had more drive, more ambition. At his age, there wouldn't be another opportunity like this one.

"I'm sorry. I don't understand," Michael said at last. "You told me you had good news?"

"You seem disappointed by my decision," Klaus said.

"I'm certainly surprised! Isn't it time you got paid good money for the great work you do?"

"Financially, the offer was very attractive, but accepting it would be putting my personal interests ahead of my current team. A decision *not* to change can also be one that moves you forward. In life you also need know what you do not want. Don't forget that, Michael. I've taken the time to think about what matters most in my life. I always remind myself that the decisions you make and the steps you take determine your future. That made my decision much easier."

"Well, I'm sure you've thought it through carefully," Michael said.

"I have and it has not been easy." Klaus had considered not only his desire for advancement, but also the needs of his team and of Monika. He and Monica had made a decision earlier that they would never live apart and that they would always work in the same area. In the end, it came down to a matter of values, of being true to the ideals that had motivated him throughout his career and personal life. The Munich club had many good players and excellent potential, but was struggling financially. It would not be fair if he left them now. It would seem like a betrayal.

"Don't get me wrong, Klaus, I admire the courage of your convictions," Michael said.

"But you think I've thrown away my last chance at the big time."

"You're not getting any younger."

"No, but I hope I'm getting wiser. And sometimes saying no is the right thing to do."

Klaus changed the subject as the food arrived. "Tell us how things are going at your company."

"There's not much to tell, at least in terms of what I'm doing," he hesitated, "but I am worried about what's happening at P.E.M." Klaus listened intently as Michael told of the Lindeman account and how frustrating it was to see all the credit was going to Horst.

"It could be an opportunity to clarify what's important," Klaus suggested. "You no longer need to score all the goals you know, Michael. You're the captain. You're leading the team."

Michael shook his head. P.E.M. didn't go in much for team stuff. His sales staff, and in fact, the whole organization, were all individuals, out for themselves, with no real incentive to work together as a team.

Michael turned back to Klaus,. "So, what would *you* do in *my* place?" he asked.

"Transitions are difficult," Klaus began cautiously, "and I can't say what you should do. But for me, it starts with knowing what constitutes success."

"I've always had a clear idea of that," Michael said. "When I played for you, I wanted to be the top scorer, at university I strived for top marks in engineering. In my second year at P.E.M., I broke all their sales records and now, as Sales Manager, I've been working on a plan to boost profits and take market share from our competitor. Our General Manager won't be around forever. If I play my cards right, I could be in the right place at the right time to climb the next rung of the ladder. Seems to me that that's what it's all about."

"It's necessary to strive hard," Klaus said, "but you also have to think about your goals, both professional and private. Before you climb your ladder to the top, be certain you have it against the right wall."

"How can you be sure you've found the right wall?"

"You listen to your inner voice."

Michael laughed uncomfortably, "That sounds kind of mystical, coming from my old coach."

Klaus took little notice of the comment. "You know that I'm competitive and ambitious, even if I'm not going to Hamburg. But success, for me, is not only about winning or being in the highest league. It's about growing. It's about giving young men a good start and seeing where they go. Just like you, Michael. You're one of my successes. It's not all about soccer, it's about people and character development."

"I don't feel like anybody's success."

"I can understand that. You've been through a lot, but look how you're bouncing back. Soon you'll be back at work. No one in the world would wish for the kind of experience you've just had, but you'll be the stronger for it...as long as you don't play the victim!"

Monika cupped her hand over Klaus' and he read her message immediately.

He was silent for a few moments and then finished. "I don't mean to heckle you, Michael. But this is exactly what I've been thinking these past weeks. Success is more than just a bigger paycheck or some tactical move that advances our career. It's about what we're living for at home as well as at work. It's about having a sense of purpose, a reason for being. For me, love and successful relationships are part of success. When you think about success, do you see Petra as a part of your life?" There was a long pause. "I can tell by your body language that you do. So how are you going to reconnect?"

"I have tried many times, but nothing is coming back... nothing," Michael replied.

Monika, sensing the tension building and Michael's discomfort, changed the subject by announcing that they had some special news. She and Klaus had decided that next year, for their twentieth wedding anniversary, they were going on a sabbatical to Australia, a country they'd both longed to visit for years.

"Every year, for almost twenty years, we've talked about and dreamed about it and now, we're finally going!" Klaus exclaimed. "It has even been built in as one of the terms in my new contract."

The meal continued on a lighter note as the conversation shifted to their dreams and plans for the Australian tour. Michael returned home in a good mood but with pieces of the evening still resonating in his mind:

A decision not to change can also be one that moves you forward? Saying 'no' to what's not important allows you to say 'yes' to what is truly important? It's about what we're living for at home as well as at work. What should I be saying 'no' to? What is really important to me? Klaus said that success is a choice and 'if it's really going to be, then it's really up to me.' Can it really be that simple? It's not about winning, it's about growing and developing to be the best that I can be. Take the time to think about what matters most in your life, because the decisions you make and the steps you take, determine your future. And me? I'm alone in an empty flat...

Looking around the empty apartment, Michael put down his journal and thought about Klaus' definition of success, compared to his own. Should success feel this lonely?

He was impressed with their idea for the sabbatical and Klaus' words. "We want to get more living into our lives," had really resonated with Michael.

How can I put more living into my life?

He wrote the words down, knowing that he still had a long way to go before he even knew what that question really meant.

CHAPTER 7

Over the next several weeks, Michael felt a new vitality rising within him. The surgeon had x-rayed his ankle and knee again and declared they were healing well. It would be a long while before he could run, jump or even drive a car, but he was making progress at the clinic. Each tentative step brought him closer to his old self. Soon, he would be able to use a cane and return to work properly.

One Sunday evening, almost ten weeks after his accident, Michael excitedly laid out a suit, shirt and tie in readiness for his first day back.

"Oh, Mr. Weber," the receptionist exclaimed as he limped through the sliding doors on Monday morning, "it's good to have you back. We've missed you!"

She jumped up and followed him down the long corridor.

"It's okay," Michael said, fumbling in his left pocket, "I still have my key."

She looked apologetic. "Mr. Weber, sir, your things have been moved. They're in the Call Room."

She brushed past Michael, leading the way to a storage room on the right. Before Michael had an office of his own, he'd often worked in this space, placing his early morning cold calls. The room had no window and was a hot and stuffy place to work. Michael spotted three boxes stacked by the cubicle, a large cardboard one and two smaller file cases, all marked with his name.

"I'll let you know as soon as Mr. Fritsch arrives," she smiled awkward-ly. "Let me know if you need any help with those," she added, pointing at the boxes.

"So, you really are back!" Michael had been summoned to Mr. Fritsch's office. He waved Michael towards the chair and peered at him over his reading glasses, "It's good to see you all in one piece Michael. Have you seen how much our sales are up?"

Michael nodded, "Yes, that's good news. The team must be working hard."

Mr. Fritsch's face beamed, "They're doing splendidly. Horst has been doing the work of two men with his own sales and much of your manage-ment job."

"I'm sure he'll be glad to concentrate on his own sales again."

Mr. Fritsch cleared his throat and leant back in his chair. "I think it might be best if we ease you slowly back into things. You'll be helping Horst on the administrative side. He's not been able to keep up with the reports and that's something you're good at."

"I really am ready to manage things again," Michael insisted and felt his temper rising.

"We'll try things this way for a while," Mr. Fritsch replied, "Never change a winning team, Michael," he said as he picked up his phone indicating that the meeting was over.

Michael made his way back down the corridor, trying not to let his discouragement show. The door of his old office was open and Horst sat behind the desk, chair tilted back, feet perched on a corner of the desktop. The two men's eyes met and, phone in hand, Horst gestured for Michael to come in and take a seat. Ending his call, Horst swung his feet to the floor and reached out his hand across the desk. "Welcome back," he said, pumping Michael's arm, "it's good to have you on board to assist. With this surge in sales, I've been run off my feet and I can't keep up with all the paperwork. Did you hear about the problems with the goods shipped from China? The sales reps keep getting complaints and I have to deal with those, too."

Michael gathered his crutches and rose to his feet.

"Horst, I'll do what I can to help you catch up," Michael said, "but it sounds like you need to delegate more of the field work."

"Just the opposite, Weber. This is a *sales* department. Our job is to sell, not please the company's paper pushers. If you'd spent more time out in the field instead of letting Marketing waste your time with paperwork and useless meetings, we might not have so many disgruntled customers right now."

Shove it! Michael thought, as he headed back to the storage room.

He slammed the door shut, collapsed into the only chair and sat for several minutes trying to clear his thoughts. It was one thing to use this stuffy hole for a short list of calls and quite another to be stuck here for days with poor ventilation and no natural light. Michael could see no good reason why he could not handle the office side of the work. What was going on in old Fritsch's mind? Michael's journal had become his sounding board when there was no one else to listen.

Why am I the victim here? Why does it always happen to me? Why? Why? Why? I wonder what's really been going on here... How is it that they've found it so easy to replace me in such a short time, and with Horst Nocker? Am I that easy to replace? Something doesn't make sense. Were they planning on making this move even before the accident? Surely this is a bad dream. I won't let this spiral out of control this time. Make a plan. Set some goals!

His first step was to check the Sales Manager's account and see how much damage Horst had done, but every time he tried to log in, his access was denied. He called Mr. Fritsch's assistant to have his access reinstated.

"I have to clear that with Mr. Nocker," she said. "I'll put your request through right away."

Michael could hardly believe his ears. A Sales Manager cut off from his own account? What kind of control did Horst have over office operations? He swung his chair around and groped into the largest box, pulling out a handful of folders and flipped through them, dumping out all his sales books and binders onto the floor. What he desperately hoped to find was a market analysis he had been working on just before the accident. Unfortunately, that was the one file he could not find.

When his account was restored, Michael soon lost himself surveying the administrative disarray. The April report was poorly written and Horst had barely started the sales report for May, due at the start of next week. Much of the correspondence had gone unanswered, some of it dating back to late March. No wonder Horst was getting complaints from customers. When he clicked on Contacts, Quotes and Pricing Proposals, Michael got the old message—*Access Denied.* He reported the glitch in his account setup again only to discover that there was *no* mistake. Mr. Nocker was apparently handling these aspects personally.

Furious, but trying hard to focus, Michael settled into work on the May sales summary. If all the data were on hand, he might be able to complete it by next Monday's deadline, but the jump in sales was so puzzling. Figures were up across the board; by region, by product and by sales rep and they seemed to be driven more by customer demand than increased sales initiative. Had market conditions really shifted this much in just two months?

It felt good to lose himself in activity and feel the hours and then days flying by. He had progressed from using crutches to a cane, but still had to keep his right leg elevated much of the time. He enjoyed the return to a more normal rhythm even if it meant living on too many painkillers. At least he felt needed and useful again. His only reservation was that all his efforts compensated for a man who was doing a lousy job and becoming a sales hero. His only option, Michael thought, was to work hard and keep busy in his sweat-box of an office with summer approaching.

I helped develop Horst and the sales team and what thanks do I get? Nothing. There's no recognition in this company for hard work, loyalty and dedication. No pat on the back, "job well done", nothing. Why the hell do I bother? To make others look good? That used to be my old motto, but now I am not sure.

All weekend, Michael dwelled on the fact that Mr. Fritsch seemed genuinely impressed with Horst Nocker. His frustration and determination had built up by the time Michael sat waiting for him on Monday morning, "I know you're busy, Mr. Fritsch, so I'll get to the point. The paperwork is all caught up and I've made my readjustment. I'm ready to take over again as Sales Manager."

After an uncomfortable pause, Mr. Fritsch finally asked, "Before you...*went away*...were you expecting this increase in sales?"

"No," Michael admitted, "given everything I know about the market, it comes as a surprise to me."

"Have you discovered anything you may have missed before?"

Michael shook his head. "No. Quite frankly, I'm still puzzled by the increased sales, but I'll make it my top priority to find out what's driving it."

"I'm sorry, Michael, but something has caused sales to skyrocket while you've been away. We can't take a chance on changing our current arrangement. I am also really impressed by this market study Horst has written." Mr. Fritsch passed the report to Michael with a satisfied smile.

Strengths. Weaknesses. Opportunities. Threats. Michael flipped through the pages with growing disbelief...it was the market analysis that had disappeared from his files.

"I wrote that from start to finish. The only thing Horst Nocker contributed to that report was his name on the front cover when he gave it to you." Michael was furious and his pent up emotions became impossible to swallow down. Before he even knew what he was doing, he slammed his cane across the corner of Mr. Fritsch's desk, his exasperation uncontrollable. The cane snapped in two, the handle barely missing Mr. Fritsch.

"Mr.Weber! I am going to pretend that didn't just happen! You've been through a very difficult time, but the decision has been made, do you understand?"

Michael nodded, hardly able to believe what he had just done. His face flushed.

Mr. Fritsch continued, "You will have ample opportunity to demonstrate the range of your capabilities. We're assigning you to a special project, a customer satisfaction survey. Given your experience with sales and management, you're uniquely qualified."

Michael felt the knot in his stomach wrench tighter.

Special project, my ass! A nice way of saying we don't want you, but we can't fire you, so we'll drive you out one way or the other. I've got to figure out what Horst is doing that I wasn't. As the sales manager, was I over dominant? Did I micro manage? Was it too much command and control? But that was how I was taught! I was directive, telling them what to do and how to do it. Why are his sales up? What am I missing?

I am really stuck in this nightmare. My body's a mess, I'm weak, exhausted, overweight and alone. This isn't fair, it's not my fault but I'm trapped by it all. They have me where they want me and they know it! Right now I see no way out.

CHAPTER 8

Michael finally moved to a better workspace. He was still doing most of Horst's paperwork and now he had new demands from the marketing staff. He was expected to contact many of the company's major customers, assess their satisfaction with P.E.M.'s products and services, discern future buying intentions and identify prospects for expanded sales. If and when he returned to his Sales Manager position, the information from these calls could prove useful and he held on to that positive point. But, as long as Horst remained in charge, everything hung in limbo and everyone seemed genuinely dazzled by this unexpected rise in sales.

The survey he'd been assigned was proving much easier to conduct than the usual cold calls. His hunch that most customer concerns related to service quality was being confirmed. The strangest part of it all was that his sense of rejection now came not from customers but from his own company. He had never minded cold call rebuffs. They weren't personal, he told himself, just part of the process. 'No' was another step on the road to 'Yes.' Yet here he sat, in a remote office, cut off from his position, out of sight and out of mind. Michael's thoughts wandered to Petra. Where was she now? Was she seeing someone new? Did she ever think of him? He really wanted to know, but she was still not responding to any of his attempts at contact. Should he call her right now? But what would be different about today, when all his last attempts to call and text were ignored. He wasn't ready to give up, but he was slowly losing his confidence.

Even through the pain of my therapy this afternoon, I couldn't put Petra out of my mind. I miss her so much. I need to talk to her, to know how she's doing, to see where we stand and what I have to do to make this right...make her understand that everything was for her! The long days and the hours of travel were for the life I was building for us! But first I need to get my act together. If I'm ever going to have a chance of working things out with Petra, I have to prove I am still the man she married. We need to rebuild the trust that has been lost. How am I supposed to do that when the whole world is working against me right now? My job, my body and my relationships are all falling apart...I don't even know where to start and I am always so excruciatingly tired.

As Michael threw another pizza into the oven, grabbed a beer from the fridge and settled in front of the television, he wondered what Petra would think if she walked through that door right now? What would she make of the mess and the broken man he had become? Michael froze, the beer bottle mid way to his lips. The sudden realization that what she would see was the mirror image of his father plopped in front of the TV, letting the white noise and a cold beer numb him from the reality of his life. "What's happening to me?" Michael whispered as he lowered the beer slowly and felt himself sink deeper into despair.

The next morning at work, Horst barged into Michael's small second floor office, "I'm heading out on sales calls," he said. "You need to finish up my monthly report."

Michael eyed him coldly, "You want to put your name on something? Then write the report yourself."

Horst turned to leave with a provoking smile and Michael sat for several minutes trying to calm himself down. That guy really had a way of getting under his skin. Could he be trying to force Michael to leave? Michael grabbed his phone and called Mr. Fritsch to confirm he would submit his full report by Friday and would be ready to resume his Sales Manager position at the beginning of the next week.

Mr. Fritsch's end of the line fell silent and Michael knew this was not a good sign. "I said from the start, you're uniquely qualified to do this work, Weber. Marketing has decided to expand the survey to recent accounts and a new set of files is on its way over."

"Can't someone else take this over?"

"No, we want *you*."

Michael now knew exactly where he stood. His previous suspicions had been confirmed. He was stuck in the dreaded 'Project Position.' Sideline the employee, give him monotonous work and wait for him to quit. No messy severance package.

How did I not see this coming? I've manipulated others into intolerable situations for exactly the same reason! I'm beginning to know how it feels and I don't like where this is headed. How the hell can Horst get away with this? All these years of busting a gut for this place and where has it got me? This is like being stuck in someone else's nightmare!

For the next week, Michael threw himself into the expanded survey project. It wasn't as bad as he'd expected and it kept him busy. One of the most interesting conversations was with Ralf Escher, President and C.E.O. of Escher Electric, a small manufacturer in Düsseldorf. Mr. Escher confirmed that Escher Electric had recently placed an order with P.E.M. for mold work and the subsequent production of battery casings at P.E.M.'s affiliate plant in Guangdong, China. The P.E.M. order was for a new line of casings for solar storage batteries.

Michael launched into his list of questions relating to Escher's satisfaction with P.E.M.'s quality of service, but the C.E.O. explained he had no direct contact with the salesman and regretted he could not comment on his performance. Sensing the call drawing to a close, Michael asked about challenges facing Mr. Escher's company. He laughed, "How much time do you have?"

"Enough," Michael quipped, then listened closely to the major concerns, including an expansion project. Escher Electric had just acquired a small company that produced solar batteries with good products but weak management and a very different work culture. Had P.E.M. dealt with any mergers or acquisitions in recent years?

When the conversation was over, Ralf Escher had asked plenty of questions and Michael had confided more about himself and the work process of his own company than he had intended. *What new opportunities was he seeking in his career?* Michael talked of his desire to be more involved in strategic planning. *What vision did he have for his company's future?* Michael was caught off guard by that one. No one at P.E.M. had ever asked him his opinion before and Michael spoke of the need for better communication, externally and internally, for improved workflow for faster product delivery and the need to become more customer-centric and not product-centric.

Mr. Escher said he liked Michael's way of thinking and asked him more about his background, his work in sales and his training in engineering. Where was this leading? Mr. Escher seemed to understand there was more to growing a business than Horst's bullish mantra, "Sell like hell!" There was a lack of long term planning, a lack of leadership leading to a reactive culture. Most times they were flying by the seat of their caffeine fuelled pants. He was pleased when Mr. Escher suggested that they "talk again sometime."

"Your company is fortunate to have so perceptive an employee," he said as they concluded their conversation. "Engineers with sales skills, people skills and leadership skills are highly sought after. You seem like a low ego person with high ambition, which is exactly the kind of person I want around me."

I wish I'd asked for Escher's comments in writing. At P.E.M. I certainly don't feel "highly sought after". In fact, nobody even seems to recognize what I do. I feel "used and abused". How many people have I left feeling the way Fritsch and P.E.M. are making me feel right now? Too many, I know. How is it that a complete stranger has validated what I have to offer and shown more interest in my vision and goals than the senior leaders in the company that I work for?! I've sacrificed my health, my marriage

and my friends.... for what?? How many of my sales team have I left feeling this same way? Unrecognized, under appreciated and valued only for their contribution to the month end bottom line. Is everyone starving for that same recognition? Is that why it was so easy for Nocker to stab me in the back?

The next morning, Michael knocked on Mr. Fritsch's office door, intent on pleading his case for change and making him understand that he was ready to resume his Sales Manager position. He had even considered broaching the subject of his vision for P.E.M. after the conversation with Mr. Escher.

Entering the office, he saw Mr. Fritsch immersed in the pages of the project that Nocker had submitted. His project! Michael immediately knew that he couldn't risk another display of his frustration and weakness, so he ignored the file in Mr. Fritsch's hand.

"What can I do for you this morning, Michael?"

"Well, I have caught up on the project and the reports that I've been helping Mr. Nocker with. Frankly, sir, I am really quite impressed with our recent P.E.M sales success and you are right, I did not see that increase coming." Michael looked squarely at Mr. Fritsch and assessed that his boss seemed pleased with his change of heart. He continued. "You may be right that I underestimated Horst, but I'm only working with half the data. If you authorize my full access to the Sales Manager account, I should be able to identify the reasons for our sales success. It would help me to see what it was that I missed and it would help P.E.M to have a better understanding of what is needed to continue this positive change."

Mr. Fritsch looked relieved and pleased with Michael's suggestion. "Yes, yes, of course. I'll let my assistant know. All this technology stuff. Waste of time if you ask me. It's no match for the human spirit and good old-fashioned selling. Good to see that you are back as part of the team, Michael. I was beginning to have my doubts!". With a flick of his hand, Mr. Fritsch dismissed Michael, but as he exited the office, he heard Mr. Fritsch giving his assistant instructions to reinstate Michael's full account access.

"Good old-fashioned selling," Fritsch calls it. "Glad to see you're back on the team!!" What team? The team that stabs you in the back and kicks you when you're already down? No, thank you. I'm going to find out what Horst has been up to, besides taking credit for my work. The increase in sales just doesn't make sense in today's market. Companies are much too cautious to spend the way his figures suggest. I'm going to find out what's been going on behind my back if it's the last thing I do. I guess that's another clear goal and it feels good.

CHAPTER 9

Michael used his new password to look into Horst's cluttered mess. He dug into the back files of contacts, pricing proposals and unanswered complaints. It was time to solve the mysterious increase in sales. It took almost two days for Michael to discover Horst's secret. The surge in P.E.M. sales derived solely from unauthorized discounts. It was not evident at first and Michael had to work hard to piece together the whole story. Some of his staff members likely knew about it as well, but what surprised Michael most was that the controllers did not blow the whistle. The discounts had been small and intermittent at first, then more frequent and ever steeper as Horst sought to meet overly optimistic sales projections. During the last six weeks, not only was there no profit but the department had been operating at a loss. Michael smiled with satisfaction when he thought of what the bosses were going to think of their Golden Boy now. So this was his strategy to steal my job. Horst was playing a fool's hand and must have thought he could get away with it. Michael was eager to share his findings with Mr. Fritsch in a detailed report.

Michael's report got immediate, if not unwelcome, attention. Horst's disgrace seemed total. He was discharged immediately.

As Michael's new week started, he was kept busy fielding complaint calls. News of the unauthorized discounts had spread like wildfire and P.E.M. was besieged with angry calls from companies who had been informed of a 'terrible pricing error'. There would be no holiday time for anyone on the P.E.M. sales/customer support staff until this mess was sorted out. Employees were bitter over lost bonuses and forced overtime and Michael sensed they blamed him, the bearer of bad news.

> **I knew there would be some fallout, but I didn't expect this. I did what I needed to do. I hope I was right. I responded in a way that felt right to me. It got things moving around here, but there's obviously something new in the wind. Whatever it is, I just want my Sales Manager position back.**

In the days following Horst's dismissal, Michael's role changed again. Even though he still hadn't got his sales management job back just yet, it felt good to finally be out of the office, selling and driving one of the company cars again. His leg ached like crazy at the end of the day and the extra weight he was carrying added to his discomfort but at least he felt he was back in the saddle selling again. Fritsch had promised him his Sales Manager job back again by Christmas, if he proved himself capable of his old role in the coming months. Michael was determined to do just that and more.

His suit jacket and pants now tugged at the buttons and, if Petra were around, she would at least get him out for a walk in the evening. But she wasn't. Saddened, Michael realized with each and every day how much he missed her and he knew he looked terrible. What was it Klaus has said when they last met? 'A bad experience makes you stronger, if you don't play the victim.' Well, Michael thought, he was down, but not out. He'd always thrived on challenges and now he hoped that he was ready for yet another.

Things at P.E.M. seemed to be finally getting back to normal. By day, Michael was all business, focusing on his clients and adapting to the sales role when he started at P.E.M., but his nights were a different story. At home, he had no discipline, no structure and no energy. Michael spent most of his time watching television. Alone in his apartment, he wondered whether it was all worth the hassle, or in Klaus' words, 'if his ladder was against the right wall?' The career path that was once so alluring: Sales Manager, General Manager, Executive Board member of P.E.M. all seemed so empty now without Petra around to share it with. So many things just didn't make sense any more.

The next day, Klaus Mertens left a message to say he would be in Frankfurt again the next weekend and to ask when they could meet up. Michael knew he should call back immediately, but he put it off. He didn't feel up to another interrogation by his old friend, however kindly it was meant. What was the point in discussing his health, social activities, work and his whole sorry excuse of an existence? He just needed time to himself to think things through.

By Friday, he had forgotten Klaus' message altogether. His right leg throbbed more than it had for days. He took more pain killers, grabbed two beers from the refrigerator, limped to his living room chair and settled back just as the doorbell rang. Klaus stood there grinning at him.

"I hope you haven't eaten," he said, holding out a large wicker basket. He pulled back the cloth covering and Michael saw it was filled with fresh fruit, bread and two large jars of Monika's homemade soup.

Michael thanked him for the basket and carried it out to the kitchen, "Would you like a beer?" he called over his shoulder.

"No, thanks. We have time for a walk in the park. The leaves are beginning to turn and the sun is shining. It's quite beautiful out there."

Michael rejoined Klaus in the living room. "I get plenty of exercise at therapy and my leg's killing me."

"Fine. Let's clean things up a bit in here and then we'll eat."

Klaus opened both windows facing onto the street and a sharp breeze blew in. "Some beautiful autumn air might do you good. This place smells like a brewery," he said, looking at the pile of beer bottles lying next to Michael's TV chair. Michael winced. He knew his old coach was right, but he didn't like to hear it said out loud. Michael carried a handful of bottles to the kitchen and Klaus followed with another load, including the bottle Michael had just opened. As Klaus poured its contents down the sink, Michael struggled to hold his tongue. Klaus rinsed the sink, filled it with hot water and started washing dirty plates.

Klaus whistled when he opened the freezer to store the extra container of soup and saw the small compartment jammed full with frozen pizzas. "With a diet like that, it's no wonder you're gaining weight!"

"Could be, Klaus. So, how are the boys back in Munich doing?" Michael asked, desperate to change the topic.

"We're doing well, all things considered." There were still some financial problems, but he expected those would get sorted out.

While Klaus warmed a jar of Monika's homemade soup, Michael set the dining room table. It had been months since he had entertained anyone in his apartment and he was not certain he was looking forward to the dinner conversation without Monika to interject this time if it got too intense. Klaus was always the coach and, true to form, their talk soon turned to Michael's circumstances.

"Bring me up to date on what's happened since we last talked," Klaus finally said, looking Michael squarely in the eye. "I hear bits and pieces, but I want the whole story from you."

Michael sighed, and then started with his return to P.E.M. and the dead-end customer survey. He told the Horst Nocker dismissal story and explained how he'd returned to a sales position but was stuck with a smaller company car.

"Michael, you've had bad luck. Sooner or later, everybody does. But the future is in your hands and, as such, you need to take responsibility and move forward. Remember, 'If it's really going to be, then it's really up to me... .' I sincerely believe it but you have to tell yourself just that, rather than concentrating your energy on all that's going wrong."

"You think I deserve what's happened to me?"

"That's not what I mean. What's happened to you, Michael, is not what counts. It's what you do about it. We're not just victims in some predetermined chain of events. The question is, 'What are you going to change and how are you going to change it?'"

"Let's face it, Klaus, I'll never be the star, neither scoring goals in every game, nor in the sales world, so just let me live my life in peace."

"This isn't living and this isn't you!" Klaus stared at Michael. "What are you thinking? Have you given up?"

Michael stared at the floor for a moment and then, almost in a whisper said, "No, but it's just so hard. I can't even sleep at night."

"Ah, that certainly doesn't help, but my question's still the same, 'What are you going to do about it?'"

Michael continued to stare at a spot on the floor, so Klaus continu "You were given a second chance at life after your accident, Mic' Start to live again. Get help. Get more exercise. Get moving. Yr goals haven't worked out, so what? Set new ones. Don't just warm the bench thinking about how well you used to play and search for excuses, get back in the game! You have the journal I gave you. Use it. Write it all down so you can see the real issues more clearly. Be bold."

"Ha! It's not as simple as that."

"It's never simple, but that's how it starts. There are always ways you can improve your life at home and at work. You've got to start asking yourself four questions, 'What do I really want out of life? Am I doing the right things? What do I need to change? And where do I start?'"

"Are you saying I should change jobs?" Michael retorted. "You didn't do that when you had the chance. I seem to remember you being handed the chance and you staying in your comfort zone."

"What I'm suggesting is that you need a clearer purpose in life, a sense of direction and a destination that motivates you. You seem lost and very frustrated and, yes, maybe that means a career change. For me, it didn't. I chose to be where I can create the most benefit for the most people. That fits my values. Happiness doesn't only come from always getting what you want. It comes from knowing and being grateful for what you have. You're the only one who can change your situation, Michael Weber and I think you know that. So, where can you start?"

For the next hour the two men engaged in the most open and emotional conversation that they had ever had. It felt liberating and clarifying for Michael to open up and share his hopes and fears with another human being.

I'm clearly frustrating the only man who's always been there for me, no matter what. It is still amazing that he never gives up and always finds time for me. I'm so confused. I agree that I need a clear purpose in life, a sense of direction and a destination that motivates me. Right now, I feel like I'm going nowhere. Am I doing the right things? That was a good question. I'm pretty sure his key words were, "You're the only one who can change your situation, Michael Weber and I think you know that." Klaus has always had high expectations of me. But where do I start?

One Monday morning in early December, Michael received an e-mail from Mr. Escher, of Escher Electric. He was coming to Frankfurt on a business trip in the New Year. Would there be a chance of continuing their earlier conversation? Could they meet for dinner? His company anticipated an opportunity that required sales skills, technical knowledge and leadership and he hoped Michael might be interested. Michael's heart flipped and made a mental note to answer him as soon as he returned from the conference room where Mr. Fritsch had called all sales staff for an important announcement.

An attractive woman with long blonde hair and a perfectly tailored gray suit was standing in the corner of the room as Michael arrived. Mr. Fritsch walked to the head of the table and gestured for all to be seated. "I am proud to introduce Ms. Anne Hauser to you all today," he said, motioning for her to join him at the front. "I am pleased to announce that she has signed on as the new Sales Manager. Anne is an expert with key account management, has excellent leadership skills and specializes in running interactive customer events, something we most certainly need. Please join me in warmly welcoming her to P.E.M." Michael couldn't believe what he was hearing as everyone in the room around him clapped with their approval. This was the position he'd been promised from the beginning when Horst was fired. He had worked like crazy and got good results, but it seemed that meant nothing. For him this meant yet another broken promise from his senior managers. He decided then and there that his career at P.E.M. was over.

Mr. Fritsch looked pleased with himself as he introduced Anne to each member of staff, finally approaching Michael, whom he asked to introduce her to the operations of P.E.M. Michael tried to reply but it was like someone's fist was rammed down his throat. Composing himself as best as he could, he shook Anne's hand, welcomed her to the company and suggested they meet at reception in five minutes. He'd be happy to give her a tour.

He strode quickly to his small office, slammed the door behind him and braced his back against it. Angry, he thumped his head back against the door. With his eyes still closed, he took a long, deep breath and knew that this was the final straw. He moved over to his computer and typed a letter to Mr. Fritsch containing four key words: "I resign effective immediately." And, with that, Michael gathered his things.

After handing his letter to Mr. Fritsch, he made his way back to the main entrance, coat and briefcase on his arm. He approached Anne and explained, "I'm sorry but I need to inform you that I just handed in my resignation. It's a decision I should have made a long time ago. I've arranged for a colleague to give you the tour. Congratulations and good luck in your new position. You're going to need it."

And, with that, he turned and walked out of the P.E.M. premises for the last time.

> **Blindsided yet again. Horst Nocker is gone and instead of rewarding me for a job well done, they leave me in a sales position and hire a new Sales Manager. What the hell?!? Was this planned all along, or am I the victim of my own demise? How did I not see this coming? What did I do to deserve this?**

Panic, fury and confusion rose up inside him again until he actually heard Klaus' voice yelling through the din in his head - DON'T BE A VICTIM...

CHAPTER 10

J obless! Now what? As Michael dumped the contents of his briefcase onto his dining room table, he noticed his agenda and remembered the email from Mr. Escher. With all that had happened so suddenly he'd almost forgotten. Was he interested in meeting him? He most certainly was.

Michael felt a burst of positive energy after confirming a meeting with Mr. Escher and decided to do a little Christmas shopping. He wanted to find a little something special for Klaus and Monika. Frankfurt's Christmas Market was already in full swing and as he wandered in and out of the stalls, the lights, the music and the laughter of the children on the merry-go-round lifted his mood further. The smell of roasted chestnuts reminded him that he'd missed dinner and he walked over to stand in the queue.

"Hello Michael."

He looked around startled to see Petra standing behind him, smiling, "Hi! It's good to see you Petra. Wow... You look great," he stammered, self-consciously.

She smiled, "Thank you, I feel great."

"That's good," Michael knew he should be happy for her.

"I have a great coach who recommended a yoga retreat. I was skeptical at first but it really did me good and helped me to reconnect with myself and re-evaluate my life. I didn't realize how much I need it. Daily yoga. I was worried the time away might get in the way of my work, but quite the opposite as it turns out," her words came easily and he could hear how excited she was, "It's like everything comes even easier now and I have a passion for the music like never before. I was offered the cello solo in Brahms' Piano Concerto No. 2, which you know I love," Michael wondered if he did, "and it went so well that we're making an album and going on tour!"

Michael saw the happiness in her eyes. "I saw you play," he whispered, "twice, in fact. Didn't you get the roses I sent to the concert hall?" Michael slowly started to raise the volume of his voice and asked, "Why didn't you answer any of my messages? I've been going out of my mind. Why are you doing this to me?"

Petra looked up at him and the sparkle he'd seen a second before was gone so suddenly that it made him want to rip his words back. "Yes. They were beautiful. Thank you. I've been away. Yes, I got your messages, but…" She trailed off.

"But, what?"

"Michael, I only saw and heard your excuses, fingers of blame and circumstance. I saw and heard all that you want me to do to make things better. Not once was there a message where you accepted any responsibility for where we are. I've sorted through a lot and I'm feeling more positive, but that doesn't mean I'm willing to run back into an unhappy, one-sided relationship."

"Was it all really so awful?"

"Not always, no. I love you and I miss you, Michael. I miss what we once were, but I want and deserve better than what we became. I'm sorry. We took our relationship for granted." As she turned to walk away, she added, "When you take a relationship for granted, it falls apart. If you only take and never put anything in, at some point there's nothing left."

With that, she was gone, leaving Michael feeling more alone than ever.

Michael spent Christmas Day alone. He did try calling the Mertens' number, but when there was no answer, he chose not to leave a message. It gave him time to think. Rather, it forced him to think. So much had happened during the year: The accident, his breakup with Petra, losing his Sales Manager position, his return to sales and his resignation. After such a year of shocks and surprises, who would dare to predict what lay

CHAPTER 11

Michael immediately identified Mr. Escher when he entered the restaurant. He was a fit looking man, perhaps in his early sixties, wearing a corduroy suit and checked shirt, open at the collar, was seated alone and looked up expectantly as Michael approached

"We meet at last," Mr. Escher smiled, standing to shake Michael's hand and motioning him to sit at the other side of the table. "Would you like a drink?"

The waiter took their order and they settled into a conversation that was all about the batteries, solar in particular, manufactured by Sunstream, Escher's newly acquired company. The product was good, Mr. Escher said, but the company was asset rich and cash flow poor. With better management and marketing, he was confident it could become quite profitable. He peered through his rimless glasses at Michael with an intense gaze.

"When we talked in the summer, I liked your ideas," Mr. Escher continued, "particularly about using improved service to gain strategic advantage. I was really impressed when you mentioned getting closer to our clients and the concept of 'outside-in' listening. With the acquisition of Sunstream last June, our workforce nearly doubled to over 500 people. The expansion came either at the wrong time or the ideal time. Only the future will tell."

"Just what is it you have in mind?"

"We talked before about opportunities and you said you'd like to get more involved in strategic planning. I'm here to see if you're interested in a special project. It's a term position, six to eight months, but could develop into something more."

The position entailed overseeing the merger of Mr. Escher's two companies without alienating the best talents of either. Finding synergies and the retention of talent would be the two keys to success. As a third generation CEO, Ralf Escher represented tradition and stability. For a change of this nature, he wanted leadership from the outside with new perspectives and fresh energy.

"I presume you're talking with a number of candidates?" Michael asked as their main course arrived.

"Of course, but you're my first choice," Mr. Escher said as he refilled their wine glasses. "We understand battery making, but solar technology is different and the market is more volatile. We need someone who is smart and ambitious, someone with a good technical background, strong sales experience and a sense of how service builds a competitive edge. It's a tall order, but you seem to be more than qualified. I have only a few questions for you. First, as a leader, what do you see as your main strengths?"

Michael thought for a moment before responding. He was competitive and he thrived on challenges. He also had a long-standing interest in business trends. Most importantly, he encouraged employees to be more innovative, which required support from upper management levels.

Ralf Escher said little as Michael talked. He listened intently, occasionally nodding his head in what appeared to be satisfaction with Michael's responses. "You can probably predict my second question," he smiled as Michael finished.

"My weaknesses?"

Mr. Escher laughed, "Exactly. But I'm not asking you to hang yourself with your own rope. All of us have weaknesses. The better we know them, the more effectively we can overcome them. We can also hire to fill in for our weaknesses."

Michael braced himself, "I've learned there is a big difference between selling well and getting others to do the same."

Mr. Escher looked so pleased at this minor confession that Michael let down his guard and continued, "I've not had much luck motivating my colleagues. I seem to expect too much of them. I've always worked hard and pushed myself. I get frustrated when others won't do the same. I'm not a very patient person. "

"Those are things I can help you with. Being aware of them is the first step."

"I didn't just disqualify myself?"

Escher laughed again and shook his head, "You've been more honest than most and I like that. I believe in strengthening people's strengths and finding the ideal role for them that is customized so they can play to them. This allows people to become world class at what they do. By doing that we create added value for our organization so it can also become world class. I want to help you grow. You're a smart man with lots of potential. I would like to hire you for this term position."

"It's an interesting proposition, Mr. Escher. I'm certainly ready for a challenging change and I'm sure I'd enjoy working for you."

"And on the financial side," Mr. Escher leaned forward, wrote a figure on a piece of paper and handed it to Michael, who tried desperately to disguise his pleasure.

"I think that would be satisfactory, Mr. Escher," Michael responded as calmly as he could.

"I'm delighted to hear that, Michael. And you can start calling me Ralf."

That night, Michael opened his journal. Klaus had been right. It was a good way to help him see things more clearly. He sat at his dining room table, staring at the blank page then finally took a pen and began to write:

> **Interesting... a new boss who accepts both strengths and weaknesses as a natural part of one's character. I've always been afraid to even acknowledge my weaknesses, let alone admit them to someone else. It didn't phase Escher one bit. He said just be aware of them and hire good people with strengths in those areas. I liked what he said about strengthening my strengths and creating more value. I'd like to become 'world class' at what I do. Ralf seems to have more confidence in me than I have in**

myself. I hope he's right. It's good to feel wanted, respected and appreciated.

I cannot change the past, but I can choose my future. The events of today have presented me with a new challenge. I've closed one door and opened another. I do not know where it leads. But I know I must do my best to strengthen my strengths and fulfill my potential.

On a new page in his journal, Michael began to write a letter to Petra.

Hi Petra,

I know I couldn't find the right words the last two times we met so I'm going to try to put my thoughts on paper.

As you know, I've always struggled to express myself emotionally. Somehow it seems to be easier on paper. Maybe some day you'll get a chance to read my thoughts. As you said, our intimacy has been lost and I hope, in time, you will give me a chance to regain your trust. I feel like I'm starting to write a new chapter of my life and I wish you were here as it unfolds. At the moment, it's full of suspense, but I'm encouraged to keep 'writing'…I feel like I'm following the path of growth but struggling to see where I should begin…My first goal is to keep my words and thoughts positive and be grateful for this job opportunity. That seems like a good place to start for now.

PART II

"THE CHALLENGE OF CHANGE AND INTEGRATION"

CHAPTER 12

Ralf Escher was waiting with a hearty handshake for Michael when he stepped off the train in Düsseldorf.

Michael smiled, "So, here I am, Ralf, ready for a new challenge!"

"Yes, here you are, indeed! Now, let's create a new future for Escher-Sunstream."

Ralf dropped Michael off at his hotel after dinner. Michael was completely exhausted, mentally and physically, after two days of packing up his life in Frankfurt and preparing for the move. Nevertheless, he took the time to write a few short sentences in his journal. It was becoming a valuable exercise, a habit, to help him to see things more clearly. He smiled at how he'd felt when Klaus first presented him with this journal and remembered Klaus' words, words that he had not wanted to hear at the time. "If it's really going to be, then it's really up to me." That sentence had a whole new meaning for Michael now.

The next morning, Michael's taxi pulled up in front of Escher Electric, an old two-story brick building set back from the tree-lined street. The receptionist took him to the main office to meet with Mr. Escher.

"Good morning Michael, we're glad to have you join us."

"Good morning, Mr. Escher," Michael replied. "I'm very glad to be here."

"Please call me Ralf, remember? If we're going to work closely together, we'll need to be on a first name basis. Welcome to Escher Electric."

The room was not at all what Michael expected. It was more stylish and simple than any executive office he had seen. Japanese straw mats on the floor, a lattice pattern of wood and paper on two walls and a single silk scroll adorning another. A low table in the corner held a vase with three budding willow branches and a folding screen masked a filing cabinet in another corner. A glass bowl filled simply with rocks and sand was the only other decoration in the room. The cool simplicity gave a sense of quiet order and balance.

"Your office has a very distinctive décor."

"That's my wife, Marina's, touch," Ralf smiled. "She keeps me grounded and my mind uncluttered. We attended a stress management course together years ago and the benefits of a calming work space resonated with her."

"I like the look," Michael said with a smile. "It's relaxing, a feeling I've never associated with work!"

For the next forty-five minutes, Ralf Escher was all business. When he'd made the decision nine months before to acquire Sunstream, it seemed like it would be a 'good fit'. Escher Electric had decades of battery production experience. Sunstream offered similar products in a new market with the potential to grow. Sunstream, however, could not continue as it was and survive for very long. If it was to grow, it needed better discipline, better management and, in particular, better leadership. The integration process was off to a rough start. Viktor Fuchs, the founder and former owner, was to have stayed with the company for at least a year overseeing Research and Development. Unfortunately, he'd been diagnosed, almost straight afterwards, with lung cancer. The prognosis was not good. To make matters worse, there had been a downturn in the market. Orders had dropped, the sales team was struggling and cash flow was a problem.

"Do you see these changes as 'challenging' or 'crippling'?" Michael asked.

"Good question. Over the years, I've spotted opportunities where others see only problems. If we manage this well, we can be in an advantageous position when the economy picks up and that brings us to you."

Escher opened the file folder on his lap and retrieved a document entitled 'Integration Manager: Escher-Sunstream'. "This is the job description we have in mind," he said, handing Michael a bullet pointed list. "We've customized a role that will play to your strengths. I already know you thrive on a challenge, have sales experience, a good technical background and, from what I see, a fire in the belly. You're coming in with a fresh perspective and I'm expecting you to develop these skills to a world-class level. We'll do our best to make your next six months an interesting learning experience Michael, but we are counting on you being a leader." Ralf added with a smile.

Michael hesitated, "It will be an exciting challenge, but I do have some questions. Has any of this been started?"

The two companies had agreed to wait six months before making major changes, but many back office functions had already been integrated. The budget was finalized and its implementation would require discipline. Their Due Diligence Consultant, Nadine Peters, had adapted much of the policy.

"You'll meet Nadine this afternoon," Ralf added. "Next question."

"Besides you, who are the key leaders?"

"My 'right-hand man' is Lennard Stark, Operations Manager. What he doesn't know about battery technology isn't worth knowing. Nadine Peters, I've already mentioned. She conducted her study before Marina and I decided to buy Sunstream and she's stayed on a few months to help us get started on this transition period. You'll have a few days with her before she goes. And the founder Viktor Fuchs, now he's not with us, but you'll find his fingerprints everywhere you turn. A wizard with batteries, a great innovator and a visionary, but a poor manager."

"Anyone else?" Michael asked.

"Well now, of course, there's *you!*"

It's nice to be respected for my strengths, beliefs and abilities. I haven't felt this appreciated in a long, long while. I hope I can live up to Ralf's expectations. He's set the bar high, but Klaus always says the power of expectations is what makes you grow. Especially when those expectations come from people you respect and care about.

CHAPTER 13

The exterior of the Escher Electric plant was not particularly impressive. Michael was surprised, however, by its modern look inside and the fact that Ralf was able to greet each of the workers by name. Donning safety helmets and lab coats, Ralf took Michael on a tour of the facility. They started in a room where large gray blocks of pure, virgin lead stood in rows on wooden pallets, ready to be melted into battery grids.

"I hope this will help you to understand what we do," he shouted to Michael over the rumble of machines. "If you have any questions or suggestions, just ask."

The plant was highly automated. Even a minuscule variance in thickness could cause major problems when fitting cells into the battery casing.

"It's been a huge investment," Ralf said, "but necessary in order to ensure the high quality and volume of production."

"Have you had any problems with the automation?" Michael asked.

"The biggest challenge was retraining our workers. Some were so used to doing things manually, they couldn't make the transition."

Michael could well understand that. The whole automation process seemed so logical and efficient seen running like this, but he could understand how manual workers could feel overwhelmed.

Ralf looked at him, as if reading his thoughts. "We all have to keep learning," he added, "even you and I."

"There's no shortage for me to learn," Michael said before continuing through the rest of the plant.

"So that's the operation," Ralf finally said. "How are you feeling?"

Michael forced a grin. "Pretty rusty. Batteries were a part of my studies at the Technical University in Munich, but I've got a lot of review ahead."

"Don't worry. You don't have to be the expert. If you have any technical questions, just ask Lennard Stark." Ralf added, "I've planned for us to meet him over lunch."

Lennard was already in the restaurant when they arrived. He was a thin, almost gaunt man, who was hunched over the table top, writing in a small black notebook.

"Lennard, this is the engineer I've been telling you about, Michael Weber."

Stark rose and held out his hand to shake. He had an almost blank expression and a grip like iron.

With no time for pleasantries, Stark ran through the stats on current production. These made little sense to Michael but it appeared that Ralf understood all too well. "At best, that's just enough to break even. How long until you get the second station operational?" asked Ralf.

"If all goes according to plan, about three months, minimum."

Ralf asked what he could do to help speed things up and the conversation turned to delayed parts and back-ordered cell assembly equipment.

"Let me make a few calls and get back to you," answered Ralf, shaking Lennard's hand warmly at the end of the meal and making his apologies before leaving the two men.

Lennard sat silently on the drive to Sunstream, a brick building topped with a dozen solar panels. The building and carefully landscaped grounds were smaller than Escher Electric but, at first glance, considerably more modern.

Lennard saw Michael admiring the panels. "It's a demonstration unit that Sales uses," he smiled for the first time. "Mostly it keeps the coffee hot."

Inside the front door, Michael crouched to examine the row of batteries laid out on display.

"Best deep cycle batteries on the market," Lennard boasted, "...and the most expensive."

"I guess the expense is something we'll have to change."

"That's your problem."

Turning to the executive assistant, he added, "Hannah, please show Mr. Weber around the building and let Nadine know we're here."

Hannah Krauss stood and offered Michael a firm handshake before leading him on a short tour of the visitor's lobby, the solar control unit, down a short corridor and past an unused office stacked with file boxes, to the board room. "This is Mr. Fuchs' office," she offered as they stopped at a small office with towers of papers and file folders stacked everywhere. A strong smell of stale pipe tobacco hung in the air. "He hasn't come in since last fall. But he's the heart and soul of this place, a real wizard. The lights in the research lab used to burn day and night."

"When do you expect Mr. Fuchs to return?" Michael asked.

"Not anytime soon," Hannah said quietly as she turned off the light and shut the door.

Michael stood in appalled silence as she flicked on the lights in the worker's lounge. It was hard to imagine anyone relaxing in this dull, badly furnished and claustrophobic space. The adjacent locker and shower facilities were an uninviting, dirty yellow and were dimly lit. He was relieved when they moved swiftly on to a large storage area without comment.

Pallets of white battery casings were stacked on floor to ceiling shelving and workers in blue overalls were working hard. A machine with flaming gas jets was spewing streams of hot lead into the molds before being cooled with water making the air hot and humid.

Michael's right leg ached and his breathing became labored as they moved quickly up a circular stairway. Once he got settled into his new job, he resolved to start an exercise program.

A loud buzzer went, signaling the top of the hour, and to Michael's amazement, all of the workers stopped and switched places. Hannah saw his inquiring look and explained that this was one of Viktor Fuchs' innovative ideas. It eliminated boredom, ensured quality work and helped to cover any absent operators. Michael made a mental note that despite its laggard equipment, perhaps Sunstream would have something to offer to the integrated production process.

After the noise of the previous work areas, the next room seemed eerily quiet. There were hundreds of batteries linked together with red and black tipped cables. Two workers were wiping the battery casings and sticking *"Fuchs-6 Volt"* labels on them.

A man with white hair and long sideburns came walking jauntily up the aisle, his overalls unzipped almost to the waist revealing an oil-stained t-shirt.

He was introduced to Michael as Martin Hess, Sunstream's shop foreman. Michael held out his hand, but Hess kept his fingers tucked in his pockets. He looked Michael up and down and said, "If you last more than a couple of weeks, I might try and remember your name."

Pretty impressive that Ralf knew each of his employees by name. Either he's got an amazing memory, or he really cares. It is a sign that shows his respect. I've had senior leaders who asked me what my name was after years of service!

Lennard Stark impressed me as a professional type of guy, but that Hess is something else. If I'm going to be going up and down those stairs every day, I'd better get back on my physio program. My leg hurts like hell after one day and the extra weight I'm carrying doesn't help. I was impressed by the hourly duty change. That's an innovative approach to cut boredom and create a flexible work force.

CHAPTER 14

As the tour concluded, Michael headed up the stairs to meet Nadine Peters, an impeccably dressed young woman with an efficient manner. She gave Michael some documents to read to bring him up to speed. The due diligence report seemed a good place to start. He skimmed through the financial statements, legal and environmental audits and marketing overview. It was a concise report, providing an excellent summary of economic data relating to the Sunstream acquisition.

Michael soon focused on three areas that seemed most critical: production, management, and marketing. From the onset, it was apparent that Sunstream had to become more productive. The management section made it clear why Viktor Fuchs was willing to sell. Much of his time during the last two years had been spent in creditors' offices, trying unsuccessfully to refinance the operation. Cash was very tight now. On the production side, Sunstream products had to become more affordable if their technical superiority were to be a marketable advantage.

He paid particular attention to details that Nadine had highlighted. Sunstream excelled at product development, but lagged behind its competitors in the production process. It had almost as many employees as all of Escher Electric, yet its output volume was significantly lower. Fuchs-designed batteries got good technical reviews, but customers were pushing for them to lower the overall price. Sunstream, unlike Escher Electric, lacked a standard set of policies and procedures, had wide discrepancies in salary scales, a poor employee evaluation system and an almost nonexistent employee training program.

"What have you learned so far?" she asked, as she brought Michael a coffee.

"I'm not sure I'd have bought the company."

"Your lack of nerve, or its lack of prospect?"

"Mostly the latter. I'm not sure the return will justify the effort, expense and risk."

"The Eschers made their decision to buy Sunstream because they're able to think long-term. It's a good thing, or a lot of people here would be without jobs, yourself included."

"After the Escher plant, this place is like stepping back in time."

Nadine nodded, "It was a good process fifteen years ago, but working by hand is no longer competitive. It doesn't generate a profitable volume. Fuchs was always more interested in battery performance and new technology than profitability. Soon, he didn't have enough money to stay afloat, let alone upgrade his plant. It's great that the sales guys have a big contract lined up, but it's going to take almost perfect execution for it to succeed. If we fail here, we could all be finished."

Michael also learned that Nadine had been commissioned to work on an Integration Plan for the two plants, though it was far from complete. Sunstream had an existing workers' council, but she had met with them only once, "If you get too close to employees you can't be objective about the difficult decisions. Besides, all these people do is complain and demand. Writing policy is one thing, but chairing 'moaners meetings' is not something I have the time for."

Ralf suggested that he 'get to know the floor' and show the men he could get his hands dirty. In the locker room at Sunstream the next morning, Michael found an old pair of blue overalls. Walking through the storage room, he took a closer look at the white battery casings he had seen on his tour and noticed the familiar P.E.M. logo and beside it, stamped into the plastic, 'Guangdong.' What a small world. Only months ago, he was promoting orders for these and now, here they were stacked high in his new employer's production facility.

Michael found Lennard and his assistant totally focused on aligning a track for the new conveyor belt. Michael joined in and they made good progress. His bad leg meant he worked at a slower pace, but he could tell the men took notice of his participation and it felt good doing something with an immediate result. When the hour shift ended, Michael approached Stark and shouted, "See you tomorrow!"

"Looks like you've got your hands dirty for a change!" Stark shouted in return.

Ralf has a great understanding of people. He knows each of his employees by name in both plants. People really respect and like him. I can see it in their eyes. I can picture Ralf rolling up his sleeves on the production floor. He seems like the kind of leader who would want to know what his workers are doing. They know he cares and being involved helps me care. I've got work to do! It's the first time I've felt energized in ages. I have my new apartment now and my quality of life has definitely improved!

CHAPTER 15

M ichael was prepared when he returned to Nadine's office. He wanted the names of the employees representing their departments on the workers' council. He also asked if the big contract she had previously mentioned had anything to do with the battery casings in the storage room.

"Yes, in my opinion, that shipment of casings was the final stage of a very poor strategic decision. Walter Fischer, our sales manager, lined up a big deal with Hartrand Battery in Ohio. Everybody was euphoric at first but, in reality, it's a make-or-break deal. It demands four fully automated stations running at full capacity for at least ten weeks. We had to make a big financial investment in the automation and it almost stretches us to the limit. There is an early August deadline for delivery and huge financial penalties if we do not come through on time. It could endanger the company's existence if we fail."

Michael calculated the timeline, "Wow, that means a mid-May start-up. Can Lennard do it?"

"He's as good as they come but it is way too much pressure. I'm concerned that he might burn out first. He's got two plants to run, besides overseeing this automation project. Much of the equipment is still back ordered. I don't know what Ralf was thinking. Remember Michael, your workers council team is not aligned and very close to dysfunctional and that really adds to the challenge here."

As the seriousness of the situation sank in, Michael decided to change the subject, "Anything else I should now about Viktor Fuchs?"

Quite a bit, as it turned out, "He has no management skills. Everyone regarded him as a fountain of knowledge, but he couldn't see beyond the next new battery. Sunstream workers were fanatically loyal to him and now that new owners have moved in there's a 'Viktor cult' at the plant. Even minor changes are deemed as acts of disloyalty. Speaking of being fanatically loyal, you'll need to be wary of Martin Hess, the shop foreman. He could make your life hell." She handed him a thick personnel file with Martin's name on it.

Michael returned to his apartment that night in a brooding mood after Nadine's answer to his last question: Is there anything else I should really know? In response, Nadine slid a thick, neatly bound report across the table, her final recommendations to Ralf Escher. Michael looked at her.

"I've recommended that Ralf sell Sunstream. Spending more money at this point prolongs the inevitable and risks the whole business."

"Sell Sunstream? Have I jumped aboard a sinking ship?" Michael thought to himself as he walked slowly back to his office.

It was a long weekend and he wished more than once that Petra had been around to be his sounding board as she used to be. She was always such a good listener and used challenging questions to make him think from alternative perspectives.

Michael was waiting for Ralf on Monday morning and got right to the point, "Is Sunstream going to be sold?"

"Michael, you said last week you had an appetite for a challenge. Have you changed your mind so quickly?"

"I wasn't expecting anything so extreme."

"Nadine said what she felt she had to and, maybe, she's right. I'm not convinced. What do you think?"

Michael began to breathe easier, "It's too soon for me to tell and I have a vested interest. I don't have another job waiting."

"Fair enough. Let's keep things honest between us."

"Is there a bottom line that I should be aware of?"

Ralf Escher sat quietly before speaking. "The welfare of my workers is important," he said, "but a company like ours doesn't exist purely for employees. To survive and thrive, we must serve the needs of customers and make a profit. Remember, we are in business to make a profit. When running a business 'cash is king' and, right now, we are short of it."

"On the people side," Ralf continued, "as Nadine warned, if we can't get the staff onboard, we all go overboard. I know some people are against change but we have to get them involved and win their hearts and minds to be successful. If we don't get this right, the whole organization could be in jeopardy. My decision, as to whether we sell Sunstream or not, will depend entirely on the success of the Hartrand project. It is a game-breaker."

With that, Escher turned his focus to the week ahead: How did Michael intend to begin the Integration Plan? What was his agenda for today's first workers' council meeting? What was the most productive thing he could do when he left Escher's office? He should organize an 'all hands' meeting on Thursday or Friday to introduce himself and the immediate changes. Ralf stood up to end the meeting and said, "Remember two things, Michael. One, work smarter not harder and two, in the meeting, be real, share your values and be yourself. A little vulnerability goes a long way. That is how you start to build trust."

Michael began planning by making a few notes in his journal.

> **I've got to do this right. As Klaus said, 'It's not only about doing something right…it's about doing the right thing.' Now, how do I connect to their hearts and minds? I found it very helpful preparing mentally for the workers' council meeting and the all hands meeting with Ralf. Through his questioning, I could visualize the step-by-step process much easier. I will remember that he suggested I share my values and let them see who I really am.**

Several hours later, Michael was laying copies of his agenda on the boardroom table at Sunstream as the men and woman started to arrive. When all twelve chairs around the walnut table were occupied, Michael called the meeting to order and began with introductions. He kept his introduction brief and the others followed suit. Michael used Ralf's strategy to learn the names of the men and women, identifying some detail to help him to remember each person. Though it took longer than

Michael anticipated, he now believed such preliminaries were vital to building good will and, in turn, a high performance team. The meeting then began formally with a review of the agenda and the main aims of the meeting.

He asked each rep to inform their staff of an all-hands meeting in the last half hour of Thursday's shift. The subject was no secret, Sunstream's output must dramatically increase and automation was a key step in that process. The task of this workers' council was to anticipate issues and solve problems that arose with such change.

"All big decisions have been made!" Martin Hess challenged. "We're just here to 'rubber stamp' them."

Here it comes, Michael thought, the first test to my authority.

"It is true," he said, looking at Hess, "that important decisions have been made. Mr. Escher made the decision to accept Viktor Fuchs' sale offer, to keep this company going and to take the production of a great battery to a new level. The key decisions on how best to proceed reside with this council. You're here as leaders of your departments. If you're only here to 'rubber stamp' the decisions of others, I suggest you leave now and we'll find someone who is willing to lead."

Michael's voice sounded strained and sharper than he had intended, but he meant every word. No one else said anything, so he continued. He distributed draft copies of an Employee Policy Manual, most of it based on one already in use at Escher Electric.

"You're messing with our pay rate?" Hess snapped.

"Some of you are getting the short end of the stick," Michael said as calmly as he could. "So, yes, the remuneration scales need to be aligned. The principle is 'equal pay for equal work.' This draft is a starting point. Read it through and discuss it with your staff. I'll ask for your recommendations at our next meeting."

Michael pressed on to his main point; completion of 'phase one' of the automated production process by mid-May.

"The way it's going now," someone commented, "it'll be months longer than that." Others chimed in with their agreement.

Michael thanked them for their comments, but voiced his confidence that Lennard Stark had gauged his timeline carefully. What was vital was that all staff offer their full cooperation to speed the transition along. "Before we go on to other issues, I just want to mention how important it will be that we come together as a team. We must communicate the same message consistently to our people and they all must feel a sense of urgency" Michael explained.

"There's no reason to be in such a bloody hurry," Hess declared. "We should sort all of this out when Viktor comes back."

"That may be a very long while," Michael said, as gently as he could.

"You don't know Viktor," another insisted. "It'll take more than a little bout of cancer to keep him down."

Another voice continued, "We lost both our sales guys and nobody's been working on a new battery since last fall. How do we know this Escher guy isn't just running us into the ground? How do we know we won't lose our jobs?"

"First," Michael replied, "our sales reps are still with the company. They're just working out of the Escher plant. As far as I can tell, we've gained a larger sales team as the Escher sales staff are now selling both product lines."

Michael looked around the table. All the members were listening intently, "I can't answer your question about the new battery development today but I know it will be a big part of our future. Innovation has always been and always will be an important value of this company. To address your second concern about losing jobs, you may not know it, but I am here on a six month contract to help with this transition phase. So, the only person here who may work himself out of a job is me. I feel the pressure everyday and I want this to be a successful integration process. In six months, I may no longer be needed but Ralf Escher will need all of you. He took a big risk when buying this company and it's not fair for us to run *him* into the ground. If Sunstream is going to survive, even with his support, we have a lot of work to do and some hard deadlines to meet."

No one spoke. Finally, someone broke the silence, "Can I ask a question?"

Michael waited for him to continue.

"How is it that your boss has all this money for fancy machines, but won't spend ten cents on the crummy dump where we have to eat?"

"What do you suggest?" Michael asked.

"Fix it up."

"And what about the showers?" Came next.

"What about them?"

"There aren't enough."

There would be enough showers if they all worked. For months, hot water had not been available in three stalls. Why Viktor Fuchs had not dealt with the problem seemed beside the point. Michael summarized what they had agreed upon as the meeting ended and once again shared how important teamwork would be in the future. At that point the meeting ended and Hannah handed Michael a long list of notes to consider in the days ahead. The workers' council had made all the progress he could expect for one afternoon.

CHAPTER 16

B ack in his office, Michael drafted a plant-wide communication announcing the all-hands meeting. The annual budget was set but
certainly there was enough margin to repair the Sunstream showers and to start basic renovations on the lounge. Michael delegated this
project to one of his team members.

What next? He had quickly learned that he had to proceed on a number of fronts at once. He grabbed a pen and started to list the tasks need-
ing immediate attention. He had resolved to complete the Integration
Plan by the end of the month, eleven more days. He must start work on
it today. "Plan your work and work your plan," Ralf had told him in one
of their Monday one to one sessions. It was time to put that advice into
action. Michael stared at the growing list with determination.

> **Think, Michael...what is the best use of your time right now?
> Ralf has given me some good advice: Plan your work. Work your
> plan. Decide which item is most important. Keep things in per-
> spective. Do the right things first.**

The next morning, Michael asked Hannah to straighten up Mr. Fuchs'
office and air it out.

"Are you sure?" She stammered. "Mr. Fuchs gets angry if any one
touches his papers."

"I'll deal with Mr. Fuchs when he comes back. For now, I need somewhere to work."

At the end of the last shift, the buzzer sounded and the noise level dropped. Slowly, the workers began to gather at the back end of the storage area. Michael stepped up onto the temporary platform. He turned on the microphone and introduced himself, "I want you all to begin by thinking about the three 'gifts' that we've received in recent months. The first came from Viktor Fuchs, the battery genius, when he created the technology for our new battery. You have every right to feel proud of the Fuchs - Six Volt or as some of you call it, the Six Pack, and it is finally getting much wider distribution and better promotion. It is cutting edge technology."

The employees listened closely as Michael continued, "The second gift came from Ralf Escher. He saw your achievements, he believes in you, and is investing in your future. We're working in a competitive market and survival depends on being innovative. Our success depends not just on *what* we make but *how* we make it and on how our new equipment will help us become more productive and profitable."

One of the men raised his hand.

"Question?" Michael asked.

"Yeah. How would you feel going from craft work to servicing a robot?"

Michael cleared his throat, "Certainly no one wants to play second fiddle to a machine. But that's not what's happening here. These machines handle the dull, repetitive work leaving the employees free for more of the 'added value' work. Viktor Fuchs isn't here to lead us through this change, but it is one that he knows is necessary."

"Since when did *you* become an expert on Viktor Fuchs?" Shouted Hess from the back of the room. A bold and direct challenge hung in the air.

"You don't have to be a Viktor Fuchs expert, Martin, to know that he is the heart and soul of this company and that he had its best interests at heart, even when selling. It's up to us to make this work for him."

From the grins on the employees' faces, Michael could see that he had hit the mark, "We're all feeling the pressure of change and I know it's not easy. Our colleagues at the Escher plant felt the same way when they faced this change but, if you talk to them now, you'd find they wouldn't go back to the old way. Some of you may be worried you'll lose your job to a machine. The reality is, without these new machines, we will all lose our jobs. We will need some retraining, all of us have to keep learning, but in the end you'll find it provides jobs that are better, safer and more secure."

"What if we don't *want* to change?" The man standing next to Martin smirked.

"Good question," Michael said, pausing to make certain he was listened to, "It's important you have a job that suits your interests and abilities. For anyone who's not willing or able to face this change, Escher's personnel staff will help you to retrain or even relocate if needed."

There was an uneasy stir and Michael was quick to add, "I'm confident that all of us are up to this challenge. Viktor Fuchs and Ralf Escher believe in you and that brings me to the third gift. It's our turn now to give those men a gift in return by embracing the change they know is necessary and achieving the challenging goals they've set for us all."

The volume in the room rose further, but a few heads were nodding approval.

"I know you are eager to get home, but before you go I want to mention one more gift. It may not seem like a big deal, but now all the showers have hot water and you'll be pleased to know that Mr. Escher has approved funds to renovate a new lounge in the old Sales and Marketing office. Our budget is limited, but with your help, we can make it go much further."

Everyone looked pleased except Martin Hess, who scowled and quickly left the room.

Survived my first all-hands meeting! The air was tense for a while, but I believe I conveyed where my values lie. Listen to me. I've never taken the time to think about my values before, let alone share them. I've always been too busy getting the job done, or doing the real work. But I truly believe that good results come from committed people who take responsibility for their own actions. Relocate? I thought I'd have a mutiny on my hands! But I think my message was delivered loud and clear. Now, how do I deal with Hess?

CHAPTER 17

Michael accepted an offer from Walter Fischer, the recently appointed head of sales for Escher-Sunstream, to meet at a bar on Friday evening for a well-earned drink and the conversation quickly drifted into sales talk. Walter was pleased to be working for the larger company. The new Escher-Sunstream broader portfolio made it easier for him to earn a good commission. The huge Hartrand sale had been great for his personal bonus, but it now put tremendous pressure on the whole organization. He had been surprised, but happy, that Ralf Escher had agreed to the deal.

For much of the next hour, they sipped their drinks and swapped stories, recounted sales triumphs and mishaps. Michael had not laughed so hard in months. He felt like he had made a new friend and it felt really good.

> What is it they say? "Laughter is the best medicine?" Have I lived my life until now, too busy to laugh with Petra?
>
> As I look back, I realize that I didn't take enough time for our relationship. I hope it's not too late to get her back in my life. Just the other day, I made a list of all the reasons why we fell in love and what makes Petra so special. It makes me miss her even more. How could I forget these things?

And he smiled sadly as he read the list again.

Ralf Escher looked surprised to find Michael seated behind Viktor Fuchs' desk on Monday morning.

"Not too noisy?"

"Too smoky is the real problem."

"It's a wonder you found any room to work here."

"I've tidied up a bit."

Ralf said nothing as he surveyed the mess of files heaped on the counter behind Michael. "What will you do when Viktor comes back?" Ralf teased, "I spoke with him last week and he says he's feeling better."

"I guess I'll move to the janitor's closet. It'll probably smell better."

Ralf laughed and they got down to business, starting with the ever-present automation timeline topic. Michael suggested that some outside help to meet their production deadline would help and outlined key Hartrand contract pressures. He reported on concerns arising from the first workers' council and the positive feedback after the all-hands meeting, including appreciation for the shower repairs and new lounge project.

Escher asked his usual question. What were the most productive things he could do now? Michael used that mantra to throw himself into his work in the days that followed. He was enjoying himself more than he ever had at P.E.M. The learning curve was steep but fulfilling. His days took on a predictable rhythm: Assisting Stark, hours of paper work, reporting and research in Fuchs' tiny office, conferring with the council reps, driving home for a hurried supper and then brushing up on his technical knowledge with books borrowed from Viktor's shelves until late into the night. Viktor's almost illegible, scribbled notes in the margins helped him get to know the great battery wizard.

Most of all, Michael enjoyed his Monday morning one-to-one sessions with Ralf. He had accepted Michael's Integration Plan with only minor tweaks, but what Michael really liked was the way Ralf challenged him through his use of questions and intense listening. It brought clarity to Michael's thinking and helped him to nail down his priorities. It certainly made a difference from the P.E.M. meetings where Michael either tried not to fall asleep, used his Smart phone to check his emails or even play games just to get through the monotony of people droning through bullet points that they all had a copy of anyway.

By mid-April, the members of the workers' council had clarified plant tasks. It was important, Ralf insisted, that each employee knew who was responsible for each task. "Clear values and vision lead to clear roles and goals, Michael. This applies to organizations, teams and individuals." Michael was still not sure if he completely understood this and how it all tied together. How does this apply to an individual? It all seemed so obvious and aligned to Ralf, but sometimes Michael felt lost and was worried that other people may also feel lost. Ralf said he needed to simplify complexity because complexity blocks execution, but what did that actually mean for him? Michael turned more and more to his journal to clarify and find solutions to his own questions.

Ideas were starting to come up from the employees on the plant floor and that was very positive. The best idea to improve the training process was given to Michael by one of the reps at the workers' council meeting, workers were to go to the Escher plant and work with operators there. The Sunstream practice of trading work positions every hour now proved to be a godsend in freeing up one or more workers each day. Michael smiled to himself that such a good idea came from the 'bottom up'. He joined the workers commuting to the Escher plant on occasion and spent his time speaking with the operators about the automated equipment they used and their thoughts on the change that would soon come to Sunstream.

> Ralf's words really stuck today: Clear vision and clear values will lead to clear roles and goals. Complexity blocks execution. Therefore, we need to simplify complexity. How do I get five hundred people clear on our vision and values? I do feel more involvement from my team members and our meetings are becoming more lively and interactive. Ralf sees them as positive first signs that we are creating more trust and that is the first step in creating a great team.

On April 20th, the first stage of automation at Sunstream went flawlessly. Michael was beginning to visualize what the fully automated plant might look like. Walter offered a suggestion for the Fuchs' Six Volt promotion and when the next stage of automation was ready, they could invite reporters and a few key customers to see what Sunstream was doing to improve affordability. Michael liked Walter's vision. Lennard Stark was skeptical, a reflection of his perfectionist temperament perhaps, but Michael recommended it to Ralf anyway. He was open to the idea, "I'll talk with Lennard. He's a bit set in his ways."

In most of their one-to-one sessions, Ralf listened carefully and said little. At the close of one session, he had a question for Michael, "You've been a good salesman and you're doing well as a manager. How are you evolving as a leader?"

Now it was Michael who sat silently, pondering a response. There were only so many hours in a day. What else was he supposed to do?

"I can't squeeze much more into my schedule," Michael said at last. "I'd welcome any tips you can offer on managing my time."

"You're working hard enough, that's not the issue. It's time we consider a different approach, time to figure out how you can work smarter. You have to constantly find the high leverage activities that get the most return on your investment. That means to do the right things first. Be ruthless with time."

"Work smarter...not harder" That has a message in it for me! I work hard and I thought I was reasonably smart. I explained to the workers how it applied to them...but how does it apply to me? Can I be more ruthless with my time? I need to find the high leverage activities.

The next Monday, when Michael entered Ralf's office, he saw that the decorative bowl of sand, pebbles and rocks had been emptied and moved to the center of the room. Ralf wanted to share a lesson he had learned years ago. The task had been to place all the sand, pebbles and rocks into the glass jar. Michael had tried what seemed like the logical solution of pouring the sand into the jar first, smoothing the layer by shaking the jar, adding the pebbles and then the rocks. But regardless of how he arranged them, he always had a few left over. The task seemed impossible.

"Interesting mind puzzle," Michael laughed, "But what's the point?"

"The point is, Michael, you're finding you can't squeeze one more thing into your work schedule. As I said last week, it's time to consider a different approach."

The solution was to start with the big rocks first. Once they were all in the jar, the pebbles could be placed in the spaces between them and the fine sand could be sifted into the crevices. Michael did not need Ralf to explain the connection to his weekly schedule planning. If he started with the big rocks, he would find space for the pebbles and sand in life.

"I try to never forget this, Michael. I first saw it demonstrated at a workshop with Gregory Marks years ago. He took it one step further and poured a bottle of beer over the sand and gravel and added with a smile, "There's always room for a beer." We laughed but his message was a serious one: The importance of finding time for a social life. I think I told you a little about it the first time you came to my office. The main theme was the **Ten Principles of Leadership and Life**. Perhaps you've heard of him?"

Michael shook his head.

"He's a leadership coach, a Canadian. He played and coached professional hockey before becoming a business coach. His work with building effective teams and prioritizing what's really important in the moment has affected my career significantly. I still remember his message to 'Be on Mission', to always deal with the big rocks first. It's a lesson I've never forgotten. If you're interested in a session, the company could cover your costs, it would be of benefit to both of us."

"Will I learn about time management?"

"That and a lot more."

Back home that night, Michael poured a cold beer and thought about the 'big rocks first' advice again. For the first time ever, he drafted a detailed weekly schedule and tried to prioritize his many tasks. At the top of the list were the big rocks: Monitoring the automation timeline, assessing the Hartrand contract progress, preparing for workers' council meetings and, last but certainly not least, his workouts at the gym. He'd called Greg's office that afternoon and registered for the High Performance Leadership session to be held in Davos, Switzerland at the end of May. Once more, Michael felt he was on the threshold of a new beginning.

> **I've learned more during the past three months working for Ralf Escher than I learned in nearly ten years at P.E.M. Ralf certainly has a different way of looking at the world, always calm and clearly focused, not giving way to the frantic demands that nip at his heels. Perhaps a workshop with Gregory Marks is just what I need.**

Michael's journal entries were structuring his thoughts and goals and making them more tangible and clear. One of Ralf's questions still puzzled him though, *how was he going to evolve as a leader?* The answer, it seemed, lay not so much in what he did as how he did it. Michael sat for a long while, but the answer refused to come. And then he almost leapt to his feet. Of course! It was all so simple, so obvious. It had been there all the time, but he'd missed it.

> **I cannot manage others and I cannot lead others until I learn to lead myself. Is that the foundation? That means finding the priorities for my own life. That's what the rocks in Ralf's bowl were all about! It's an Ah-ha moment! Ralf said leadership starts by looking inside... not outside. So, when I do look inside, what do I see and where do I start?**

Michael grabbed his phone and tried to call Petra.

"Hi, you've reached Petra. Please leave your number and a short message after the tone and I'll get back to you as soon as I can."

"Hi Petra, it's me, Michael. I just confirmed a place in a seminar in Davos. Remember how you said you wanted to try skiing there someday? Well, it's a Gregory Marks leadership workshop. I think the time is right and Ralf Escher believes it will be good for me. I don't know what to expect, I'm nervous, but I'm looking forward to looking inwards. Listen, the reason I called, I'm dropping in on the Martens the weekend after my course on my way back so, er, I was wondering how you felt about meeting up? Dinner, perhaps? All four of us again, just like old times? No strings."

Michael's cell phone rang the next morning while he was shaving. He rarely got calls outside of work hours and felt a moment of panic wondering if there was an emergency, or if it was Petra returning his call.

Michael laughed when he heard Klaus' voice, asking him what he's been up to lately, "I've been busier than you'd believe," he said and began to tell Klaus all about his new job at Escher Electric and Sunstream. "It's a term position, but it might lead to something more. Even if it doesn't, it's been a great change. I'm learning so much."

He thanked Klaus again for the journal and assured him that he was using it and adding to his goals, "And you'll be glad to hear I'm managing better," he said. "I'm managing *myself* better."

"That's good. You need to look after yourself. Just changing your position doesn't change the situation."

"Speaking of positions," Michael asked, "How is your club doing?"

"Financially, the club has had some hard sailing, there is a back pay issue but we see the light at the end of the tunnel and that's what we're focusing on. I have no doubt that we made the right decision and that brings us peace of mind."

Michael glanced at his watch and noticed the time. He told Klaus that he would be attending a workshop in Davos, Switzerland at the end of the month and planned to stop in Munich on his way back. Could he come by to see them?

"We'll look forward to your visit."

"Good. See you in a few weeks."

PART III

"LEADERSHIP: AN INSIDE-OUT PROCESS"

CHAPTER 18

T he mountain air felt crisp and refreshing as Michael arrived in Davos, home to the famous World Economic Forum. Ahead on the right, perched on the mountainside, was the stately Steigenberger Hotel Belvedere. He stood in awe for a moment at the front entrance thinking of all the leaders of state and captains of industry that had stood here before him.

Michael's fourth floor room was luxurious and faced south, overlooking the mountain village. He wondered if someone famous had occupied this room before him and was glad he only had the problems of Escher-Sunstream to concern him and not the problems of the world as they perhaps had to deal with.

In the breakfast room on Monday morning, Michael found a sunny table near the window. The workshop was scheduled to start at ten o'clock and he was looking forward to settling down to enjoy his food and read the morning paper. The ping of a text message sounded on his phone and he was surprised to see a short 'Call me ASAP' from Ralf's assistant.

"AB Robotics called," she said. "They're running behind on another job and can't start work on our job until June 12th."

"That won't work for us! That's too late as it is only one day before all the press comes for the launch!" Michael felt panic rise up within him.

"That's why I thought you should know as soon as possible."

Michael asked her to find the names of three alternate fabricators and promised to call again in the early afternoon. Leaving his breakfast and paper untouched, he popped an antacid pill and headed for the door and some desperately needed fresh air.

Short of breath, Michael arrived back at the conference room at 9:55. Gregory Marks was standing by the double doors with a friendly smile and a strong handshake. He introduced himself as 'Greg' as he greeted Michael and welcomed him to the Leadership Workshop and Michael looked carefully at this man that Ralf Escher respected so much. A tall trim guy in his early fifties perhaps. He looked ordinary enough for someone who carried so much weight with Ralf. Greg ushered Michael into the room and pointed to the last name card on a small table. The tables were arranged in a horseshoe pattern with two flipcharts at the front of the room. Michael found it surprising that there was no projector in the room. He picked up his card and joined the other nineteen participants.

Greg welcomed everyone to the three day **"The Ten Principles of Leadership and Life"** workshop and briefly introduced himself. He was born and raised in Canada, received a teaching degree, began his career as a professional hockey player, went on to coach teams in international competitions and eventually became a leadership coach. He admitted to failures along the way. He had seen his teams lose vital playoffs and had also been fired from positions of leadership. The lessons he taught he had learned firsthand.

Leadership Development is an Inside-Out Process

"What I teach is not new," he said. "Much of what we're going to talk about is common sense, but common sense is not always lived. Just you being here tells me that you are ready to 'lead' and I believe your key competitive advantage is trying to develop yourself as a leader. That means stepping outside of your normal, busy life to reflect on what you're doing, finding time to think about it, to talk about it and to ask yourself, 'How can I become more effective?' That's the key question that I want you all to keep in mind from now on. That's why you're here." Greg continued, "The development of leaders and leadership, if your company gets it right, will give you a tremendous advantage against the competition for years to come. What I teach is based on a whole person model. You are more than just a manager. To become an effective leader, you have to look at who you are as a person, think about your vision, clarify your values, know what's important to you, then begin 'the inside out process'. This is what you're going to start here over the next few days."

"Leadership is difficult to teach, but I believe that leadership can be learned," he continued, "You choose to lead and the word 'lead' is a verb, an action word. Leadership is a decision you make and the actions you take. Hopefully you will continue to work on this beyond today. Some people tell me that there are natural born leaders and that it is somehow in their DNA or genetics. I disagree. I have never seen or heard of a doctor picking up a newborn baby and yelling out, 'Oh that's a natural born leader!' I believe leaders are formed and developed, not born."

They began the morning with a game, 'Indiana Jones, a lateral thinking leadership problem.' The participants paired off and Michael joined a man named Sam. The premise was that four characters needed to cross a rickety wooden bridge in the darkness of night. The hero, Indiana Jones, needed to get himself, a beautiful young woman, a Swiss banker and a Bavarian executive across the bridge to safety. The bridge had many holes and could only support the weight of two people at a time. Pursued by a villain who would kill them, they had only one hour to complete their task before a bomb detonated and destroyed their means of escape.

Greg scribbled the details on a flipchart page. The hero, Indiana Jones, could cross in five minutes, the woman in ten, the banker in twenty and the executive in twenty-five. They had only one flashlight, so one person must always return to enable another to cross.

"When two people cross together, you use the slowest person's time. You have three minutes to create a strategy and then I want your solution-Go!"

Immediately the volume in the room shot up. Michael huddled close to Sam, so he could hear as they plotted their approach.

"Two minutes to find the solution!" Greg shouted.

As, "Time's up" was shouted, only one team had found the solution. Greg beckoned the successful pair to the front. They would be the directors of the Indiana Jones movie to demonstrate the correct answer. Their five actors would play each role, four being the characters trying to cross the bridge and one playing the role of the bad guy. Seeing the players move back and forth over the imaginary bridge, the solution seemed obvious. It didn't all depend on Indiana Jones. Sam thumped Michael on the shoulder, "Why didn't a smart young fella like *you* see that?" he joked.

Greg picked up the cue, "Because we get caught by old paradigms, not just in games like this, but in our work and life. We stick with our assumptions and rules and can no longer be flexible. But this game isn't just about a different way of thinking and shifting paradigms. What else does it show us?"

"It's about teamwork," said Daniel, "not just working with your partner to find the solution, but the teamwork needed for everyone to get safely across the bridge."

"Exactly!"cheered Greg. "What else, Sam? I saw the shift for you, what else is this exercise about?"

"It reinforced that you have to have a good strategy and the right person in the right role. As leaders, we need to simplify complexity, because complexity blocks execution." Michael's ears pricked up at hearing the simple answer to Ralf's criptic statement.

"Yes!" Greg continued, "And it's about leadership, because as a leader you need to think about these things. How do you create that high performance team where the right person is in the right role to be the most effective? We need to get synergy out of the members of the team. It's also about having a vision, in this case getting across the bridge, and it's about values; making sure everyone gets across alive. Clear vision and clear values give us clear roles and goals. Strategy follows clear vision and values. Systems and structures follow strategy. It is a process. Effective leaders also create a sense of urgency for change. So let's get started."

On the second flipchart he listed the main topics he intended to cover: *Paradigm Shift, the M.C.C.L.S. Model, Ten Principles of Leadership and Life, Your Leadership Brand, Three Intelligences, Production Game, Hot Seat, My Executive Team,* and *One Year to Live.* A few more options were offered and the majority of the group voted for *The 100 Day Challenge,* which would focus on energy management and health.

A page marked 'Appointment Clock' was distributed. The instructions were to find four partners in the next two minutes, one for each quarter of the clock face. Everyone stood up and Michael made appointments with Saskia for twelve o'clock, Tim for six, Stefan for nine and Daniel for three.

"Okay, let's do some quick introductions, sit with your twelve o'clock partner with your notepad in front of you. Flip it over to the cardboard side and create a 'passport' for your partner. Our real passports provide a glimpse of who we are. These are going to do the same. Ask your partner the following questions: What's their name? Where are they from? Who do they work for and why are they paid? I want that answer in a sentence with a maximum of nine words. The words 'I am paid to....' do not count. For my example, I am paid to **help people see their potential** and **get sustainable results**. Then ask, what are two of their strengths? What is their hobby? Their drug of choice: Tea, coffee, alcohol, tobacco? How do they reenergize? Finally, on a scale from 1-10, ask them to rate their level of vitality and the level of charge in their battery. Write all that down and, later, you'll have a minute to introduce your partner to all of us."

Michael turned to Saskia, sitting on his left. "You first," she said.

Michael explained that he now worked in Düsseldorf helping Sunstream, a solar battery company, to integrate with its new owner, Escher Electric. He was paid to make a profit. He prized his ability to work hard and, when he had the time, he enjoyed gourmet cooking. He hadn't smoked since university, but never said "No" to a glass of Scotch, drank seven or eight cups of coffee per day and perhaps drank too much beer. The reenergising question was harder, so he mumbled something about watching TV to relax.

His partner was Saskia Brussé, a quantitative risk analyst employed in Amsterdam. *Her strengths?* Explaining quantitative ideas to people with little financial background. Her drug was mild, a cup of Pickwick green tea. Her hobby was coming to the mountains.

After the introductions, Greg moved swiftly on, "I'm going to be referring to paradigm shifts frequently in the next few days. The Indiana Jones game is a classic example of a paradigm shift. Indiana Jones had to go back and forth each time and most of you assumed that he was the most important character, but he wasn't. That was your paradigm, not reality. He didn't have to cross the bridge each time and do all the work."

Greg continued, "Your paradigm is basically how you see the world and your own, ingrained, set of rules. I believe that, if you cannot change your paradigm, you cannot change. Your behavior is always aligned to your paradigms. We have to challenge our old assumptions in order to change our behavior. We need to change glasses or the filter that we look through to see the world, otherwise we will always fall back to our old behaviors and habits. Our individual paradigms are created by our experiences and our assumptions. Things happen in our lives that condition our thinking and these experiences shape how we see the world and what we do. They may contribute to our success, or they may become self limiting beliefs unless we can learn to shift them."

"That is exactly what happens in our lives all the time," Greg continued. "We get locked in on our preconceived notions and create our own map of the world to guide us. But what if that map is wrong? That's exactly why you couldn't solve the Indiana Jones problem. The question is, 'can we challenge these old assumptions and our conditioning? Can we break some of the old rules and find a new way to see? Can we become aware of self-limiting beliefs? Can we change our behavior? If we can, then that new behavior leads to new habits and sustainable results. 'A person can only change by the people they meet, the courses they take, the books they read or by the CD's they listen to.' That's what I believe facilitates change."

Encouraging the participants to keep that thought in mind, he began to guide them through a paradigm shifting leadership model he called "**M.C.C.L.S.**" He called on Kevin, an analyst from Hamburg.

"Kevin, why are you paid? I want your answer in nine words or less."

"Because I wouldn't work without being paid," Kevin finally blurted out to chuckles around the room.

Greg shook his head, "That's your *motive* for working, but not why your boss pays you."

Michael raised his hand, "I'm paid to make my boss look good!"

Everyone laughed now, including Gregory Marks.

"That's not an answer, Michael. That's an evasion. Just what do you *do* that makes Ralf look good? And remember, I want a nine-word answer."

Michael had not expected his old motto to be so quickly discounted, nor that Greg was so good at remembering names and individuals.

"Well, I organize...I'm paid to... I manage... " He stammered to a halt.

"Why are you really paid? It seems like a simple question," Greg said, "but it stumps most of us because we get caught up in the details of daily business and operational issues. In reality, you're paid to live four or five roles: *Managing, coaching, clienting* and *leading*. This is called the **M.C.C.L.S.** Model. If your company is like most, it is over managed and under led. Let me repeat that: Your company is over managed and under led. Some of you are even paid to live a fifth role of selling. The people with the selling role are sales leaders in their organization as they need to live that role as well." In just a few minutes, Michael had two and a half pages of notes. He grabbed his journal and scribbled:

We are over managed and under led.
From management to leadership.

CHAPTER 19

"You all have three basic intelligences which influence your behavior and over time, will create your leadership brand. Your leadership brand is how others view your actions.

The first is **IQ**: Intelligence Quotient or our intellect, how smart we are based on a particular scale that measures analytical and logical thinking. Some people would say it measures our processing power.

The second is **EQ**: Our Emotional Quotient or intelligence. This is our ability to connect and empathize with people at a level that assures them they're being understood. It is about understanding and using our own emotions in order to better understand others. Some people call this 'women's intelligence' or 'soft skills'. Men, this stuff can be learned!

Finally, we each have **PQ**, which is our Physical Quotient. How we manage our energy, nutrition, stress and fitness to maintain sustainable performance. This mix of intelligences and skills come together as our leadership brand. It is formed by what you say, what you do and even how you look. These three intelligences have a big impact on all these things and therefore, on your leadership brand and your future. We'll go into all of this a little deeper over the next couple of days, but it's important for you to have a fundamental understanding of these intelligences as we discuss the **M.C.C.L.S.** Model further.

"That's a scary idea," thought Michael, "if I can't change my paradigm... I cannot change. And I want to change. My behavior is always aligned with my paradigm. Key question to ask: Why am I paid? My three intelligences: IQ, EQ, PQ. I know nothing about my body, zero physical intelligence. If my PQ remains as it is, will I have the energy to maintain long-term results? EQ is not something I have naturally and the lack of it has destroyed my private life.

Greg talked about the feedback given to one of his clients from his team during a leadership workshop when they focused on the topic 'My Leadership Brand', IQ, EQ, and PQ. The feedback from his team shocked him into the realization that he was a giant on IQ, very short on EQ and his limited PQ had his team seriously concerned that he was slowly, but surely dying. "That is not a good leadership brand and not how I want to be seen, but it's not far off where I'm at right now." Michael thought to himself.

OVER MANAGED-UNDER LED.
IQ: My intelligence and knowledge.
EQ: My people skills and ability to connect.
PQ: My energy and resilience.
THE FIVE ROLES OR PARADIGMS: Managing, Coaching, Clienting, Leading, Selling.

"So, let's start with **Managing**. Managing draws most strongly upon your IQ. It's comprised of operational management, daily business, short-term execution and dealing with systems, fostering order and creating structure. It's about reporting, administration and problem solving. It's mostly carried out behind a laptop and no one can lead from behind a laptop. It's dealing with details and being involved in execution. It is also firefighting or being 'Mr. Fix-it'. It is reactive rather than proactive. It's short-term and internally focused. Management is more top-down, with lots of telling and controlling. It is the boss often saying, 'I think and you turn the screws' or 'when I want your opinion, I'll ask you for it.'

As I said, most management work is done from behind your laptop, but remember, we manage things, not people. In most companies good managers get promoted but the question is, can they evolve to become good leaders? How many of you have a boss who is strong in management?" Everyone in the room laughed as 90% of the participants put their hand up.

> **Managing: maintaining order, reporting, creating structure, controlling, internal focus, short-term excecution. Top-down, micro-management, telling people what to do, giving orders. Being the administrative clerk. High IQ helps with management activities.**

"This was all we learned and did at P.E.M.. It was what defined our culture – no wonder we were losing good employees. The leaders at P.E.M thought this was real leadership. No one wants to be managed like that." Michael thought as he saw the logic of this, "This is what I did every day as Sales Manager at P.E.M." Then the realization hit him, "and now I'm doing it all again, unconsciously, as Integration Manager at Sunstream. I didn't even realize! Maybe this is why Ralf wanted me to come here. If I create an over-managed culture, we won't be developing future leaders and people won't feel empowered." Managing had always been Michael's strength and was definitely Horst's weakness. Michael was finding it tough to keep up with Greg's input while it was giving him so many insights and food for thought.

"**Coaching** is the next role or paradigm that we are going to focus on." continued Greg. "Coaching relies strongly on your **EQ** and involves the one to one interactions you have with your people. It involves supporting them to reach both their individual and company goals. It requires understanding, feedback, listening skills and the ability to propose challenging questions. Effective coaches help their people to develop clarity, understand their roles and set goals. It gets them focused. It means helping them recognize and utilize the potential within them. Strong coaches help their people to constantly grow and develop."

Greg continued by asking some thought-provoking questions, "How many of you have ever had a boss who was strong in coaching?" This time, only four hands came up. "How many of you ever had an empathetic boss? How many of you have a boss who finds time for one-to-ones? How many of you have a boss who uses quality questions to help you get clear on your priorities? How many of you have a boss you think is skilled enough to be able to coach their own children? This time, no hands came up at all. Michael couldn't believe it, as only one, two, or even no hands came up each time. "Many of my clients share with me that after the course they had trouble finding additional coaching time, but they felt the quality of their coaching and the quality of their questions improved so dramatically that it still helped them get huge results. They finally realized that they could be a coach."

"Our biggest weakness at P.E.M was the lack of coaching, and that defined our culture," Michael reflected upon his lack of ability to empathize, not only at work, but also in his private life.

Michael made a few hurried notes in his journal:

Good managers get promoted, but can they evolve? For the old-fashioned manager, is it evolution or revolution that is needed? You don't lead from behind the laptop. If there is no coaching there is no personnel development and therefore no future for the organization. Coaching needs a certain level of IQ in order to create high-quality questions and the ability to challenge to gain clarity. Emotional intelligence, EQ, is needed in order to connect with people and make them feel understood.

Telling is not coaching. 'I told you' is not coaching. Finding time for one-to-one interactions... encouraging and challenging employees. Klaus did it with soccer players, just as Greg did with his hockey teams. Ralf is doing it with me. I see it now. It's about helping people to find their own solutions. I knew it was not one of my strengths. I told Ralf that the first time we met...but it's something I can work on...

A person can only change by the people they meet, the courses they take, the books they read or by the CD's they listen to. Change also happens when we take time to process our experiences - good or bad. That's what facilitates change.

"The second C stands for **Clienting**. This skill also calls upon your EQ to build and deepen relationships. It's about getting closer to your internal and external customers. Clienting is purposeful networking, making time to engage in both social and professional activities that are going to create improved relationships. It can mean going for dinner, playing a round of golf, or enjoying a beer with a colleague, or customer. It's something that most of us don't spend enough time doing. At one of the banks in Holland where I work, they have this poster on the wall," He turned over the flipchart page:

Client Rule #1
Don't Be Interesting....
Be Interested!

"It's all about relationship management."

Michael smiled when he saw the poster revealed. "Yes!" he said to himself and quickly jotted it down in his journal.

> **Don't be interesting, be interested. Easy to write, hard to live. Sales people are naturally good at clienting. You build a relationship by investing in one-to-one time with that person. Get closer to your internal and external customers. It is networking with a purpose.**

As Michael was writing, Greg asked, "How many of you have a boss who is good at clienting?" This time about forty percent of the hands shot up.

> **Clienting: Getting closer to people. Building positive relationships with customers.**
>
> **For example, a good 'clienter' could go golfing, go to Oktober Fest or just go to dinner with their clients. You've really got to like people.**

"Easy", Michael thought to himself. He could write a book on client-ing, that's exactly what he had used to clean up the mess that Horst had created with his unauthorized discounts. Initially, he focused on the relationship and built the trust needed in order to win back their business.

"Over managed and under led!" startled Michael to the present and he looked up at the flipchart and again saw:

Over-Managed
Under-Led

He was eager to learn more about leadership, but didn't under-stand why Greg seemed so critical of management. As if reading his mind, Greg elaborated, "Don't misunderstand me on this. We need managers and management; the business world couldn't function without those who have the ability to manage well. But, we need to understand the difference between managing and leading. I believe a poorly managed company is out of business in two to three years and a poorly led company is out of business in five or ten. I call much of the daily problem solving 'Monkey Business.' Let's say you're busy working in your office and one of your staff comes in to share a prob-lem (their 'monkey'). Your typical reflex is to give a couple sugges-tions and send them on their way, but before you know it, they've left their 'monkey' on your shoulder and once again you're 'Mr. Fix-it'. Then, while you're sorting out how to fix their problem, someone else calls with their problem, then an email arrives to announce a piece of equipment has malfunctioned and, hey - presto, you're car-rying everyone else's 'monkeys'. Suddenly, the day is over and the priorities you set haven't been dealt with because it's turned into a zoo and you are covered in 'monkeys' and 'monkey poop'! Does that sound familiar to anyone?" Greg' animated description of a manager carrying around a load of monkeys had people laughing and nodding their heads.

"This is not leadership. **Leadership** is about developing a vision and creating a strategy to make that vision a reality. Remember, you don't lead from behind the laptop. We manage things and we lead and coach people. Leadership is about creating and having clear 'vision and values' and being able to communicate and sell those effectively to your people. You need to get into the hearts and minds of your people. It's also about you living those values with integrity and walking the talk. It's about innovation, change, paradigm shifts and team development. A leader also needs to sell the 'why' to the organization so they understand the reason we are doing certain things and what it means for them. The employees need to know where we're going and why we're going there."

"**Management** is about keeping the status quo, while **leadership** challenges the status quo. Leaders empower and enable their people to function as a high performance team. The ability to facilitate and run an effective workshop is a valuable **leadership** skill. We need to get people on board and create synergy. People want to be involved. Effective leaders provide a platform to enable their people to come together, to identify problems and obstacles and create their own ideas, solutions and action plans. Celebrating success with your people is also an important leadership behavior. Positive feedback, appreciation, constructive criticism, listening and making people feel valued are the things that will get your team working happier and smarter."

"Team building and team development are important areas of **leadership** that are often neglected. Remember, great teams are not born, they are created. The same applies to great leaders. Effective leaders are good at selling their vision so it gets into the hearts and minds of their employees, forming an emotional connection. They are constantly trying to expand the influence they have in the organization."

"To close this **leadership** topic, I have a few questions about your bosses' strengths. You can be honest as they are not here! How many of you have a boss who is strong at creating a vision? How many have a boss who is good at communicating and selling the vision? How many have a boss who is strong at getting people involved in the strategic process? What about driving and leading change? Explaining and selling the 'why' behind our strategy and what we are doing? Whose boss is strong at facilitating change and can find synergy in their team? How many of you have a boss who is strong at developing teams? Who has a boss who can be open, even vulnerable, when speaking to their team?"

Michael was shocked to see how few hands came up after each question was asked. He felt very lucky to have a role model like Ralf Escher to learn from. He remembered clearly how Ralf had suggested that Michael be himself and vunerable during his meetings. Michael also realized that Ralf was very strong at explaining the 'why' to people and he was good at passionately selling his vision.

"You can't criticize a boss for not living the leadership role because if they haven't learned it they can't live it. If the only tools they have are a hammer and a laptop, all they can do is hammer out e-mails and tell people what to do. That's the culture we're stuck in. That's why we need role models like you to develop the next generation of leaders. People can so easily become numbers, but think of it more personally; if your son joins your organization he will need to see someone leading to learn leadership. How else will he learn? Going to a business school and doing twenty case studies a week will only help him to become a case study expert, not a leader. He needs to see and experience leadership in order to learn it."

"If the culture in your company stays as it is today, would you want your son or daughter to spend five years in your company? If the answer is no, change the culture."

Greg then shared an example of a strategic workshop and team-building session he had recently run for a large HR organization. At one point in the workshop, it became obvious to all that this team was not at all clear on their values, mission and vision. Their operational and strategic discussions were useless without that clarity and they knew it. Suddenly, it was as if everyone pointed a finger at the head of HR and wanted an answer from him. They wanted to know the mission, vision and values of the HR organization and what it meant for them. When put on the spot, he really struggled to articulate it well enough to satisfy the team members and the frustration in the room increased even more. He felt overly challenged and began to point his finger back at them."

"The real problem was that he had never learned the tools or methods necessary to create a powerful vision, mission and values process with his team. He also did not know how to break down the corporate vision statement and explain what it meant and how it applied to his team. This process is teachable and can be learned. Posters and stickers hung on the wall at the corporate headquaters, but they had absolutely no relevant meaning for that team beause they weren't involved in the process of creating them, they were not, therefore, committed to any of it. Trying to tell them top down what the vision and mission was useless."

At this point, the meeting turned 180 degrees and the boss asked Greg to turn the session into a vision, mission and values workshop that would align them with the corporate vision and values. Greg knew that the team members had to take ownership and get emotionally involved. The mission and vision had to get into their minds and hearts in order to get results. Everyone got really excited when they started working on the creation of vision and mission after they had created their own core values. "The boss had finally realized that leadership is a choice and that he had to get his people fully involved in this process in order to get their full commitment."

"In the end, it turned out to be a successful two days that brought them clarity and alignment, was a great team builder and ended up being a lot of fun. That is leadership in action." A year later, the HR director shared with Greg that his department now had one of the highest ratings in the whole company on the engagement survey.

Greg went to the flipchart and wrote down a key message:

"If you don't get them involved... you don't get them committed!

Flipping up the chart papter, on the next page Gregory Marks wrote:

The process of creating mission, vision and values, is just as powerful as the outcome.

Michael scribbled more notes:

No involvement... no commitment.
To lead is a verb. A decision you make. Actions you take.

Creating and selling the vision is part of leadership. Empower more, control less.
Trust is the key, be vulnerable, it starts with me.
Change management = leadership.
People get excited when given ownership and are empowered to create a vision

"The last role, that only some of you have, is **Selling.** What I mean here is selling real products and services to real customers. Selling ideas within your organization, or to your boss or team is all **Leadership.** The real **selling** process starts with understanding your customers' needs and their business. If I do a good job of clienting and form the relationship, my customers give me permission to sell. As the customer shares their needs, you can eventually sell your solution in order to help and deliver benefits. Remember, sell the benefits not just the features of your product. People buy benefits. If the benefits outweigh the cost, the customer will say yes the majority of times. This is called solution-based **selling**. Some good salespeople even find the 'pain-point' or what keeps the customer up at night. They then sell their solution for that pain or the big 'need' of that company. The final phase is closing and getting a win-win agreement."

Michael reflected back on Ralf's questions. He thought he'd been talking about doing more, about taking on more responsibility when he used the word 'leader'. He needed to become more of a leader and not just a manager. It was clearer now. He had to find the right balance between the two.

Over managed, under led. You don't lead from behind the laptop. You manage things, not people, no involvement, no commitment, sell the benefits, not just the features. Leadership is a decision you make...

Being vulnerable builds trust in the team. I need to learn how to do that. No trust, no team ... just a working group. If you only give a man a hammer and a laptop ... he can only hammer out emails from his laptop.

Live the change you want to see in your organization. Start by leading your team. Cultural change happens one team at a time. Leadership starts with me.

To lead is a verb. We need leaders who are role models.

I will need to get out of my comfort zone if I am truly going to lead.

Michael's hand was flying across the page, trying to keep up with all these 'gems' that suddenly made so much more sense to him. But the more he reflected upon the M.C.C.L.S. Model, the more he started to understand about these five roles or paradigms, it became very clear he was not living them. He was trapped like most in the M paradigm. He remembered the key question: Why am I really paid?

CHAPTER 20

G reg was back at the flip chart explaining the next exercise. It would be an 'Executive / Coaching Session' focusing on the M.C.C.L.S. coaching model, "Keep the same partner you had in the passport exercise. You are going to work in pairs. One of you will be the coach and the other one of you will be coached, or, the 'Executive' as we are going to call it here. Whoever went first will be the 'Executive'. The other will stay here with me for training as the 'Coach'. I'm going to walk through this step-by-step with all of you once and then the executives will leave the room to finish their preparation. The preparation consists of four phases I also need to get the coach mentally ready and give them a few tools that they will need for this session. He wrote as he spoke,

"We are going to learn how to coach our partner and I want the 'Executives' to get their thoughts on paper in the next 20 minutes:"

M.C.C.L.S.
1 to 1 Coaching Proccess

Phase 1

o   Where do you spend time now? M.C.C.L.S. %

o   How was your time spent two years ago? M.C.C.L.S. %

o   What are your strengths and weaknesses in each role?

o   What are your values in each role? What is important in each role?

o   Who are your role models in each role? What do they do well?

Phase 2

o   Where do you want to be 18 months from now? M.C.C.L.S. %

Phase 3

o   What is your motive for changing your M.C.C.L.S. %?
    What is your reason for changing?

o   What are your benefits privately and professionally?

o   WIIFM → What is in it for me?

Phase 4

o   What is your action plan?

o   The next 100 days?

o   What do you need to:

- Start doing?
- Stop doing?
- Do more of?
- Do less of?

As Michael finished writing the questions down, Greg said, " 'Executives' please answer all of the questions and fill out this matrix during the preparation session. Make sure to copy down the example matrix of the **M.C.C.L.S.** model on the flipchart to my right. This example shows a sales leader who had no time to coach, client or lead. He was very busy but not really effective."

MCCLS
Coaching Proccess

	Past	Today	Future	Strengths	Weaknesses	Role Models	Values
Managing	85	75	20				
Coaching	0	2	15				
Clienting	0	3	15				
Leading	5	5	20				
Selling	10	15	30				
	100%	100%	100%				

"Executives", Greg instructed, "please go out and do your homework for the next twenty minutes, coaches, stay with me for your preparation."

Michael grabbed his notepad and told Saskia he'd do his preparation in the lobby.

So, where was his time spent at the moment? Planning the integration process, problem solving, working on automation schedules, reviewing weekly progress, doing weekly reports and administrative work. Being 'Mr. Fix It', dealing with 'monkeys' and putting out fires took up a lot of time as well. He estimated these tasks consumed at least eighty percent of his time. This is my strength, but also my comfort zone.

Michael wrote down, five percent for **Coaching** and another five for **Clienting**. That left only ten percent for **Leading,** not enough to impress

Ralf Escher. Michael remembered that selling ideas was part of leadership and, as he currently was not in a sales role, he put down 0% for selling.

Where did he want to be in 18 months? Michael grimaced. He had no assurance he would be working with Escher-Sunstream beyond another few months. He could not even be certain that the company would still exist. For whatever time he had available, he must manage more effectively, but that should not consume all of his attention. If his work was to avoid Nadine's prediction of, "prolonging the inevitable," he must develop as a leader.

He reflected for a minute on the question 'Why am I really paid?' It had become a real mind-worm. He would meet more often with the council, delegate more important tasks and help the members to develop necessary skills. He would think beyond the immediate survival of Sunstream and more about 'thriving'. He wanted to create a vision, increase involvement, get more buy-in and empower his employees. Living the coaching role and doing more internal clienting would also be vital parts of the process.

Michael put his thoughts onto paper:

M.C.C.L.S.

Today
80
5
5
10

In 18 months
25
20
25
30

Saskia slipped into the chair beside him and then asked after a moment, "So, in your company in Düsseldorf, how do you spend your time?"

Michael recounted the percentages he had jotted down: *80, 5, 5 and 10.*

"Are you happy with this distribution and how has the realization made you feel?"

"I'm sure they're not ideal," Michael said, "but I haven't had much choice. My company's struggling to survive. So it's mostly reactive, not proactive. It doesn't feel good, but it is reality."

"Is this how you spent your time two years ago?"

Michael explained the P.E.M. situation where it was mostly a top down, telling people what to do culture. He then articulated that he had been doing less managing and more selling. Back then he had been paid to lead, but had never really understood leadership, even so, he felt his new position with Sunstream was a good step forward. Saskia listened without commenting.

Michael continued, "I am making a little progress and Klaus always reminds me that a 'little progress is still progress'. My strengths are execution of daily business and solving problems as well as my analyticial skills and getting things done. My weakness is coaching." They spent the next few minutes focusing on how he could strengthen his strengths. It felt good to see them on paper as Saskia jotted it down in front of him.

"Looking ahead to the future, how do you want to invest your time on the **M.C.C.L.S.**?"

Michael's thoughts raced forward. What would change if he thought more like a leader than a manager? If he could make the paradigm shift, he would definitely take steps to align Escher Electric's sales and marketing with Sunstream's growing production capacity. He would organize an offsite workshop to help the employees to focus on vision, values and team development and establish plans of action for the future. He would provide his team with a platform to identify problems and obstacles while developing good ideas and solutions. He would need to become more the facilitator and less 'Mister Fix-it'. Michael felt exhilarated and excited at the vision for the future but scared by the realization that it would lead him way out of his comfort zone.

"In eighteen months, I would like to see my **M.C.C.L.S.** rating as 25, 20, 25, 30."

"Who are your role models for each role?" Saskia asked.

Michael smiled, "I'd like to manage like Britta, the former executive assistant at P.E.M., coach like Klaus Mertens, client like I did in my prime, lead like Ralf Escher and sell the benefits like Peter Lang, my first sales leader at P.E.M. He could sell anything to anybody!"

Saskia smiled as Michael went on to explain his role model choices and what they did so well. She then asked Michael to explain the benefits he would get both privately and professionally if he could make these changes over the next eighteen months. Michael wasn't expecting the deeper level of thinking or the emotion that came with it and he tried to laugh off the question but Saskia was persistent in making him articulate the benefits and the motives for a change.

They had just begun to discuss what steps he would take during the next weeks and months when Greg arrived to announce lunch. Michael leapt up promising to join them soon after a couple of urgent calls.

"Not so fast, Michael, we need to finish," insisted Saskia. "First, tell me what your next step is going to be. I want to know what you're going to start doing and stop doing before we go to lunch and we still need to create a 100 day plan."

Michael was caught off guard by actually having to make a real commitment.

"Well," he stammered, "let me think...my plan is obviously to improve my coaching ability and increase the time I spend doing it. I could start by designating time to meet one to one with some of my staff. Maybe start with the workers' council. The council members have already shown some initiative by offering good ideas and suggestions. Maybe they should be the first to focus on and help develop further. I also want to read all the coaching tips that Greg has included in this hand-out and put some of them into action."

"Good! So when will you start this action?" Michael confirmed that he would start next week. "Now, two more questions before we go to lunch, one word answers only. I'd like you to take a minute to think about your life and how you live. First, what do you want 'more of' in your life? Second, what do you want 'less of' in your life?"

Again, Michael had to think hard before finally replying, "Less management. More relationship." As the words slipped out, Michael realized that this was the first time he had acknowledged to anyone that the relationship part of his life was suffering because of his professional commitment. Now what?

In the closing phase of the coaching Saskia asked him to write down four words to describe how he felt. After this she asked him what was clearer for him now and finally she asked him to rate his commitment to these changes on a scale from one to ten.

1. **Exhausted**
2. **Exhilerated**
3. **Focused**
4. **Motivated**

When Saskia ended the session, Michael bounded up the stairs to his room as fast as his bad leg would allow and called Escher-Sunstream. The sudden action set his heartburn off and he searched for his antacid pills as the phone rang. He got the details of three companies but none were able to help. On a whim, he tried one last company who confirmed they could start on the second of June with a ten-day turnaround. That would only leave one day to spare before the media launch, but it was better than the alternative.

Michael needed a few moments to calm down and get his thoughts into some sort of order before returning to the workshop:

Is this an example of manage by panic?
I always get pulled back into details
I need to delegate more
My journey from management to leadership has now begun.
I will not get dragged back into this monkey business!

"Why does everything have to come down to the wire?" he asked himself as he entered the dining room and sat down across from Saskia, who looked at him quizzically.

"Dealing with monkey business, Michael?" She asked.

"Sometimes, Saskia, I feel like I'm a zoo keeper!"

CHAPTER 21

G regory Marks welcomed the coaches and executives after lunch, asking if their time together had been worthwhile. Michael nodded in agreement with the majority, making a mental note that finding an effective solution for monkey business might be a solid first step.

"You all have the potential to solve your own problems. **Coaching** helps you find solutions to overcome these challenges. There is no 'right' formula for the **M.C.C.L.S.** model. The percentages are as individual as the people in this room. Your percentages will be affected by your boss' expectations, your strengths and weaknesses as well as the strength of your team. It's a good idea to get feedback from your team on how you are investing your time.

"If your team is weak, you will be doing a lot of '**M**' yourself. My personal secret is to have a really strong executive assistant and that makes all the difference in my life. Sometimes I do leadership training with a team just to help them create a common language for better and clearer communication. Many of my clients create a weekly plan to live the **M.C.C.L.S.** model. These five roles need to be lived each week. This model offers a clear view of how you are actually working. It enables you to think about how you could work more effectively and helps to clarify what steps you need to take to get there. It simplifies the complexity of the professional world. Remember, complexity blocks execution. Professional sports coaches are exceptional at breaking down the complexity and that helps their players perform at such a high level.

With that, Greg flipped over another flipchart page to reveal the following list:

Coaching Tips

- Clarify the goal
- 20/80
- Leading pen
- No home movies
- Pacing/leading
- Positioning
- 8/38 second rule
- More of, less of
- No tips
- SMART goals
- Follow up plan

"These are the coaching tips that I gave the coaches before the morning session. I believe that teaching is the best way to learn. Coaches, please pick a different executive and teach them the coaching tips."

"Okay, I hope I can remember," Michael's partner, Gitta, smiled sheepishly,

- "In the initial phase of coaching, the coach and the executive should agree on the goal of the session. What do they really want to take away or focus on?
- Next comes the 20/80 rule, which means that when you are coaching, you should only speak 20% of the time. 80% of the time you should be listening to what your executive has to say.

- The 'leading pen' means using your pen to bring your executive's attention back to something important or to highlight something on the page. It helps to focus their attention and lead the conversation. It refocuses them on that key word or phrase.
- 'No home movies' means don't share your personal experiences too often. This is about the executive, not about you. Keep yourself out of it.
- In coaching there are two phases; 'pacing and leading.' In the 'pacing' phase you make a connection by matching the tempo, tone and body language of the person you are coaching, in the leading phase you begin to lead the conversation by asking the right questions and keeping the coaching 'result-focused.' Keep the goal in mind. Always remember, it is the quality of your questions that determine the quality of the coaching. Challenge them to think."

"This is making a lot of sense, Gitta."
"Thanks, Michael. I'll keep going while I still remember."

- 'Positioning' is making sure you sit in a position with your writing hand between you and the executive. This makes it easy and natural to make notes and they can see what you're writing. Ideally, sit at the corner of a table.
- The 8/38 Second Rule means always wait at least eight seconds for an answer when you're coaching and, if coaching a really analytical person, sometimes even longer, perhaps up to 38 seconds. People need time to formulate ideas and responses.
- 'More of/less of" makes people think deeply about what they want more or less of in their lives. Stating it out loud verbalizes an intention that may support them to make changes towards those ends.
- 'No Tips' means we shouldn't make suggestions or give advice about what we think they should do. It's a natural reflex to want give a tip every time we hear a problem but we need to control that reflex. Don't be 'Mr. Fix-it'.
- 'S.M.A.R.T' goals is an acronym to help you set clear goals: Specific, Measureable, Agreed upon action, Realistic and Timeable goals.

- 'Follow up plan' means make a plan to connect with each other at some point in the future and provide an update on how things are going. It makes people accountable."

"Good grief, I did it! I never thought I'd remember all that!"

"Time!" Greg called above the steady hum of voices. "Was everything clear? Do you need help explaining anything?"

"You did great," Michael exclaimed grinning at Gitta, "I doubt I would have done half as well remembering all that."

"Let me elaborate slightly on **SMART Goals**," Greg continued when the room had quieted, "If the goals are unrealistic, people set themselves up for failure. Make sure they think about that before they write those goals down. The act of writing sets the intention and internalizes the goals. Good job, everyone! I mentioned earlier that the best way to learn is to be the teacher and I think my teachers have learned a lot."

"Now," Greg wrote **'Leadership Roadmap'** on the nearest flip chart and turned to the assembled group, "This morning's coaches become executives this afternoon so listen closely. Part of living the leadership role in the **M.C.C.L.S.** model is developing teams. As a leader, what are you going to do to create a stronger, higher performing team? How do you build commitment, increase trust and accountability? Building teams is not about a monthly operational meeting with cookies and coffee. There are management meetings that focus on operational issues and leadership meetings that focus on vision, values, strategy, team development and trust building. Most meetings are purely management meetings. They consist of PowerPoints, lots of talking and not much listening. Most people work on their laptops and smartphones while someone else is presenting."

"Executives, in your preparation session I want you to think of the following questions: What could you do to increase involvement and encourage your team members to get to know each other better? What is your plan? What tools and methods might you use? Executives, you have thirty minutes to create your 'Leadership Roadmap' for the next 18 months on flipchart paper and reflect on your **M.C.C.L.S**. matrix.

Take your passports and your own **M.C.C.L.S.** notes with you. Your coaches will come and find you later." Michael noticed that most executives looked a little uncertain, as they had never thought of the concept of creating a 'Leadership Roadmap.' He was glad he was a coach this time.

Greg told the coaches to start by deepening the passport and getting a snapshot of the M.C.C.L.S. matrix as part of the pacing phase of this coaching, "When working on the passport, really challenge them about why they are paid. Make them articulate this clearly. That is the pacing phase of the coaching and a good warm-up. The focus of this session is to get these executives clear on what they are going to do this year to develop their people and their team. This session will help them create their leadership roadmap. This is the outline I want you to follow for this coaching:

Leadership Roadmap Coaching process

Phase 1:
Review and deepen their passport

Phase 2:
Look at M.C.C.L.S. percentages:
today vs. future and find two actions

Phase 3:
Focus on strengthening strengths
and create developmental plan

Phase 4:
Identify key leadership challenges
and create action plan

Phase 5:
Identify how to increase spheres of influence

Phase 6:
Create leadership roadmap on flipchart.

"After looking at their passport, get them to share their M.C.C.L.S. percentages with you and once again get them to focus on their strengths. Then ask them what their key leadership challenges for the next twelve months are. Ask them to decide how to expand their sphere of influence in their organization. At this point, move into the leadership roadmap part of the coaching."

He then challenged the coaches who remained to use questions such as: "What kind of workshops or training sessions might be planned? Where could the team go for its offsite learning?" He reminded them that strong, high-performance teams spend three to five days a year at offsite workshops.

"What would you do at those offsite workshops? What techniques could be used to break up bureaucratic and interpersonal barriers? How could you increase trust and get people to open up and become vulnerable? How could you create more of a feedback culture in those workshops and also help people get to know each other? How can you create a feedback culture and encourage healthy conflict? Coaches, you need to use these kinds of questions to help your executives to create their plan. Ask them to think about an effective leader they have worked with in the past, a good leadership role model, and consider what best practices he or she used to develop high performance teams? What did they do to create great teams? Coaches, get your executive to lay out their plan on a flipchart sheet so it looks like this."

My Leadership Roadmap

Today   9 Months   18 Months

My Plan to Develop my Team /Extended Team

Greg then turned back to his flip chart and started a new page:

Coaching Tips #2

- **Atmosphere**
- **Communication Rule**
- **20%W, 30%T, 50%BL**
- **Hilti/Black 'n Decker technique**
- **Open ended questions**
- **3rd person example with storytelling method**
- **Next week's goals**
- **Strengthen your strengths**

"After lunch, the morning coaches took the time to teach you some of the tips that I had previously shared with them. This is your next set of coaching tips, so listen closely, because later you will become the teachers!" he smiled, "And right now, I have high expectations that you will use some of these tips in this session."

"The right coaching 'atmosphere' is essential, find a quiet and comfortable place where you won't be distracted. '20%, 30%, 50%' represents how we communicate, though most people don't realise it. 20% of our communication is through words, 30% of what we communicate is through our tone and a full 50% is conveyed through our body language. Keep that in mind. In this session, I want you to focus on using more tone and body language. This will be especially important for you engineers, don't just be a 'talking head.' It's not just about IQ. Use the 'Hilti Drill' like a master craftsman to keep probing, keep asking 'why'. Press them to go deeper, to be honest with themselves. Ask open-ended questions and use paraphrasing to be an active listener. Ask questions like, 'Why is that important for you?' 'How did that make you feel?' 'What will it look like in two to three years?' Draw the information out of them."

"This morning we talked about 'No tips', not being Mr. Fix-it and not sharing 'Home Movies', but there is power in using a third person storytelling technique. For example, if your executive is struggling with poor communication on his or her team, you may tell them a story about a friend of yours who had the same struggle, but found great tools and ideas in a book by Patrick Lencioni called 'The Five Dysfunctions of a Team.'"

"The final coaching tip is the idea of strengthening strengths to become world class. It is something I truly believe in. The key is to affirm and help them see their strengths and create a developmental plan to strengthen those strengths. Finally, challenge them to tell you what they are going to do next week to get started. Make them commit to an action. Understand? Good! Now go find your executives and make me proud! You have 45 minutes!" Michael gulped and already felt some pressure, as this time they were getting feedback from the executives.

Michael survived the coaching session, broke quite a few of the rules without thinking, but did manage to live the 20/80 rule and only gave two tips near the end of the session. Saskia's feedback helped him become aware of his coaching skills. Michael realized that he had also learned a lot when she shared her 'Leadership Roadmap' and some of her best practices. She was an effective leader who really had a plan to develop her team. She really knew why she was paid and Michael was impressed.

I need to work on the pacing and leading process.
Body language and tone can make such a difference.
I have to quit sharing so many home movies.
I must not be Mr. Fix it!
A leadership road map is needed to develop a team.
Without a plan nothing will change/nothing will develop.

CHAPTER 22

F ollowing the afternoon coffee break, the focus shifted towards the **The Ten Principles of Leadership and Life,** as the workshop title had promised. The majority of people around the table were showing signs of exhaustion from the pace of the training, but Greg showed no signs of fatigue as he drew a large triangle on the next flipchart page. Michael felt his coffee sitting uncomfortably and took another antacid so that he could concentrate better.

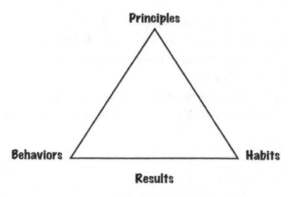

He wrote 'Principles' at the top, 'Behaviors' at one corner and 'Habits' at the other. He scanned the room making direct eye contact with each one of the participants, "With the person you're sitting beside, your 'Home Buddy' as I call it, define what each of these words mean to you. I would also like you to brainstorm ten or twelve words that you associate with 'Being on Mission'. Think about how this pyramid influences, or is connected to the results that you get in your private and professional life." Five minutes later, Greg asked for volunteers to share.

Daniel, who had solved the Indiana Jones problem, raised his hand.

"If principles are lived, habits get formed and this should lead to good results," adding with a smile, "I remember that from one of the off-site team building workshops you conducted for our company. Its focus was on the habits of high performance teams and it left a strong impression on me."

Gregory Marks beamed, "That was a very intense and exciting three day process. I'm glad you had some important 'takeaways'. Leadership development is not only an 'inside out process', it's ongoing and I'm always thrilled to have people in my seminars for a second or third time. It shows a commitment to lifelong learning. Thank you for that, Daniel."

"Principles are like an internal guiding system that give us direction," Greg continued. "They steer our actions and help us make decisions just like an internal GPS. Remember that principles can be lived or not lived, but the principle is always there. They are universal laws akin to gravity. These principles are timeless, universal and not new."

"In the pyramid, principles guide us and affect our behaviors and actions. Our actions create our habits and it's those habits that create our results. As leaders, we need to be constantly hitting the 'Reset Button' to ensure that our behaviors are aligned with our principles, thus creating habits that are principle-based. These keep us moving forward. Is that clear?"

Everyone nodded enthusiastically. Greg added, "In the workshop that Daniel mentioned, his boss got feedback from the whole team on how he lived **The Ten Principles**. That was important for him as it allowed him to adjust his behaviors. It showed his team that he listened, that their feedback was valued and that he could change. He was able to learn how to become more aligned, more congruent to the principles and get sustainable results. As the boss shared his strengths and weaknesses with his team, both privately and professionally, he became very vulnerable. That created tremendous trust in the team. That is **leadership**. This will become clearer in the next two days."

On another page of the flip chart was written

Ten Principles of Leadership and Life.

"For the last assignment of the day you'll be reading and discussing these principles that I believe are universal and can be lived by all of us. Today, we will work with them on an intellectual level and try to understand what the principles really mean. You'll be reading and discussing this with a partner and creating your own core definitions, which will be presented tomorrow. You will be finding role models for each principle and you will constantly be reflecting on how you live them yourself. At the end of the day you will carry out a self-evaluation that goes into more detail on how you live the principles."

"There is a questionnaire at the back of this handout for you to fill out. Tomorrow, you'll be working in groups to deepen this process and then I will be presenting my understanding of the principles. At some point, you will then get my feedback on how I think you live the principles and we will compare our two points of view. After my feedback, you will also get feedback from at least five other people in this room and, even though it is just first impression feedback, it should still be very interesting for you. At that point a coach will be selected to deepen your reflection and help you create an action plan to move forward.

Greg continued, "Now it's time to work with your six o'clock partner."

Michael went to Tim and they turned their attention to the **Ten Principles**. Tim proposed that he and Michael save time by defining the principles alternately.

"Faster, better, cheaper," he smiled. "That's why I'm paid."

"Okay," Michael agreed uncertainly, "Let's give it a try."

Michael took Principle 1: **Responsibility**. He read through the page long text, underlining key words and sentences as he went. "…Taking responsibility for our attitude, actions and future…exercising our freedom to choose…a 'Yes I can' proactive mindset, knowing that I can create my own future. It's in my hands…pulling my own strings…the opposite of being a victim…the ability to make a promise and be able to reset my life. I can choose to start again.

He fussed with his phrasing until he was fully satisfied. He recalled all too clearly Klaus telling him to stop being a victim. That had hurt so much, yet here it all sounded so matter-of-fact and sensible. He knew he was in the habit of blaming others. That had to change.

Tim copied the **Responsibility** definition from Michael quickly into his notes and then read out his own on **Clarifying Values**. He seemed preoccupied with finishing quickly. Michael resolved that he would find time to look at all the principles again for himself. They worked steadily through the pages summarizing their thoughts on each principle.

> **The words are different but the ideas are those I've heard many times from Klaus. As Greg said, what he teaches is not new. It's simply not consistently lived. I certainly don't live it when I'm caught up in the grind of daily business and pumped full of caffeine and adrenaline. That's when these principles get forgotten.**

Michael had just finished work on the ninth principle, **Relationship Deposits**, "Strengthening a relationship by doing small things that matter to the other person…giving compliments and praise…showing recognition and saying, "thanks", making someone feel special and important…

It is little acts of love. It's showing love by loving. An emotional connection coming from an emotional deposit." Michael was pleased with his final definition.

"I don't buy that," Tim sneered, "Too touchy feely. It's manipulation! No one gave me any compliments or praise and look how I've moved up in my company."

Greg was writing personal feedback on the back of peoples' name-cards at the table across from them, "Tim, I don't think it's manipulative to say 'Job well done' or 'I believe in you.' It only has to be real and you have to mean it. If you want to build the next generation of leaders, you have to find ways to affirm their potential so clearly and strongly they start to see it in themselves."

Tim sat with his arms crossed. "I still say it's fake."

"It may seem that way to you, but it can be done sincerely and effectively. I'm not here to tell you how to think, Tim, I'm here to share some principles of effectiveness that I believe really work. You will have to decide for yourself if you want to live these principles. That's your choice," Greg smiled as he made his way to the adjacent table.

"It's time you tell me about Principle 10: **Re-energizing**," Michael said to Tim.

Tim quickly explained, "It is the principle of self-renewal, which has to happen on a variety of levels; mentally, emotionally, spiritually, socially and physically. Vitality is a choice and you have to listen to your body."

Tim and Manny announced they were heading off to the Wellness Center to practice the renewal principle. Michael laughed but declined, saying he wanted to work on his self-evaluation assignment immediately.

Michael sat down at the desk in his room as he only had a couple of hours to himself before the group went out for dinner. He spread out his thick pile of hurriedly scribbled notes:

Paradigm shift. M.C.C.L.S. Model. Ten Principles. Coaching Tips. Definitions.

Greg had provided no major tips on managing time, but there were ideas to consider. Michael found that the stories that Gregory Marks had shared were very powerful. Somehow, the messages were made louder and clearer when put into context. They were real examples that made him look inward.

> **Leadership is not a job title, it is a decision you make, an action you take. A promotion does not make you a leader. Your boss does not make you a leader. Having a team does not make you a leader. You need to lead to be a leader. I am a manager in transformation to become a leader.**
>
> **These principles get forgotten, and what gets forgotten is not lived.**
>
> **Monika told me, "When I am ready to learn, the teacher will appear." Is this the case now? If I'm the student who is the teacher? Gregory Marks? Ralf Escher? Klaus? Petra? Am I ready? Leadership is difficult to teach but is able to be learned. I like this whole person model that Greg uses as a foundation.**
>
> **The change process starts with each of us. It comes from the inside out. It starts with me.**

After re-reading **The Ten Principles** handout, Michael clarified them further for himself by expanding upon Tim's brief sentences. He glanced one more time at the list of all ten principles.

Principle 1: **I am Responsibile**

Principle 2: **I Clarify My Values**

Principle 3: **I Have a Vision**

Principle 4: **I Am on Mission**

Principle 5: **I Strive for Life Balance**

Principle 6: **I Actively Give and Take**

Principle 7: **I Value Empathy**

Principle 8: **I work with Involvement and Diversity**

Principle 9: **I Make Relationship Deposits**

Principle 10: **I Re-Energize Weekly**

Satisfied with his understanding, he turned to the Self-Evaluation form. It had ten categories, each with six statements and each statement with a rating scale of 1 to 6. The categories were obviously meant to correspond to **The Ten Principles**, but many of the statements gave a different perspective than either he or Tim had recorded. Michael started filling in the self-evaluation questionnaire, stopping often to reflect.

- Values: 2.3 "I know what is important to me and regularly reflect upon this." Michael shook his head and jotted down, **2 out of 6**.

- Vision: 3.5 "I know who I am and the kind of person I want to become." **Probably 4 out of 6.**
- Vision: 3.6 "My definition of professional success is clear." **4? No, 3 at this point.**

Most of the statements required more thought than Michael had anticipated and he found himself debating his choices. His responses had only a few fives and no sixes. He remembered Greg's words about these principles being a 'whole person model' and tried to delve more deeply into the questions.

- Mission: 4.2 "I know the most important aspects of my life and I focus on them first and foremost." How should he answer that? At Sunstream, he tried to stay focused on the biggest concerns: The automation project and the timely completion of the Hartrand contract. Is that what was meant by 'the truly important activities in one's life'? In terms of work, perhaps this was, but definitely not anywhere else in my life. **4.**
- Mission: 4.3 "My actions have meaning and connect to my mission in life." Some people may not consider managing the integration of two battery facilities to be 'meaningful', but at this point it certainly was for Michael. It challenged his organizational, planning and management skills. With over 200 jobs on the line, it had real meaning for him. Real people and real jobs. **2 out of 6**

Much harder to know, was how such achievements might contribute to his 'overall goals in life.' What was his overall goal in life?

- Relationship deposits: 9.2 "I do what I promise and stick to my commitments." Michael re-read the questions and suddenly realized this was one of his biggest weaknesses, he just hadn't made Petra feel special, loved or needed. **2.**

    Forty minutes later, Michael finished rating himself on the final statement.
- Re-energizing: 10.6 "I am conscious of my nutrition and my sleep." **Not so good. Quite poor, actually. Only 2 out of 6.**

He computed his score for each category and charted it on a graph provided at the end of the booklet. The result looked like the silhouetted mountains outside his window, a series of steep peaks and deep valleys with scores lower than he'd expected. Had he been too hard on himself? That his numerical results rated him 'Poor' and 'Very Poor' for **Life Balance** and **Re-energizing** came as no surprise. He did not have to come to Davos to know that.

He had 'Good' for **Responsibility, Give-and-Take** and **Team Diversity** but only 'Fair' for **Values, Vision and Relationship Deposits**.

His rating for **Principle 4, Mission**, was one of the low points on his chart with *18 out of 36*. He was disciplined in carrying out his daily plans, but was poor at saying 'no' and not consistently living his values. That meant he was very busy instead of very effective – more of a manager than a leader.

What pulled him down were the statements connecting **Mission** to **Values** and **Vision**. Was he really doing the right things? Was he 'aligned and congruent' as Greg called it?

- Values: 2.5 "I often ask myself what is my purpose and my inner voice has the answer'"

  Michael had scored himself a **2, 'Poor'**. When Klaus had talked about listening to his 'inner voice,' it had sounded pretty mystical and Michael remembered laughing. The crisis at Sunstream gave him a strong sense of purpose at work but, beyond that, did he have a purpose in life? It was not something he thought about. Did he even avoid it on purpose?

- Values: 2.6 "The time I spend on personal reflection brings me clarity."Here, too, he had marked himself **2, 'Poor'**. What were his values, anyway? Work hard, do your best, get an education, use your head, don't give up, get a good job. He had set out determined to make something of himself but was that what was meant by values? Were these his values? Michael had never really thought about this question before.

His **Vision** was just as unclear. Do you really need to have a vision? A vision could also set him up for failure and it would mean that he would have to take risks. For most people their vision was to retire at 65. Was that also his vision? Where was he headed? Upward? Maybe. Unemployed? Probably. Does real happiness have to wait until retirement? What did he even want to do with his free time at 65? The thought of retirement scared Michael. He didn't know what he would do without the structure and purpose of his work. He thought back to how quickly his life had crumbled to unstructured meaninglessness after the accident. He felt no clarity and he certainly didn't have a vision that had him springing out of bed in the mornings. He might be working harder than ever before in his life, but what was his vision? He was doing his best to manage the challenges that came at him every day, but now he heard Gregory Marks talking about companies being over managed and under led. Was all of his hard work misplaced? Was he just another busy but visionless manager? Did he know what he did *not* want? He had some tough decisions ahead.

Michael thought back to the story of the manager who got feedback from his team and realized how powerful this would be. He realized he had to do this with his own team and he knew it would build trust. The most interesting feedback would come from Petra and with this thought he pulled out his phone to call her but, again, only got her answering machine.

CHAPTER 23

At breakfast, Tim bragged it had taken him only twelve minutes to complete his **Ten Principles'** Self-Evaluation, "And that's more time than it was worth! I already know who I am," he insisted at breakfast the next morning. The Wellness Center, on the other hand, garnered his full approval. Michael was not surprised that just twelve minutes on the evaluation form yielded little value if you work on the premise that you get out what you put into it. Even so, he was determined that he, too, would find time that evening to enjoy the Steigenberger pool and hot tub. Wasn't that part of **Life Balance**?

Just before the session began, one participant was excitedly sharing an experience from the night before and Greg asked him to share it with the entire group as his energy was visible. He then started to recount his night:

He had gone to his room with the intention of carrying out his self-evaluation and realized that getting feedback from his life partner could be one of the most useful things he could do. He explained he was German and his wife came from Hong Kong. He Skyped his wife for 3 hours, went through the questions and asked her for feedback. At first she was skeptical, but eventually started enjoying it. Her feedback really helped him see the reality of how he lived the principles. She even asked him for feedback on how she lived them. He said they had spent three hours skyping and had a great discussion. In the end he had said that his next step would be to have the same courage to ask his 14 year-old daughter for her feedback.

Gregory Marks was very excited by the story and exclaimed that getting feedback from your life partner is a huge step. The people you live with know you best, sometimes better than you know yourself. This feedback often initiates the change process and this will be even more powerful as your life partner can lovingly support you through this and hold you accountable.

The morning session started with Greg asking everyone to stand, "We're going to play a paradigm shifting game to start the day."

I will read out the text on the flipchart and if you think I made a mistake, please sit down. If you think I made no mistake, remain standing." With that he opened the flipchart and read out, "Germany in the spring, Australia in the fall,"

'Germany in the the spring, Australia in the the fall'

One person sat down with a big smile his face. Next, Greg asked Manny to read the words.

"Germany in the spring, Australia in the fall," He read as directed.

"Everyone who agrees that Manny read it correctly, remain standing. If you disagree and think he made a mistake, please sit down."

Three more people sat, the other sixteen remained standing. Greg spoke directly to the four people who were sitting and said, "If you see a mistake when someone is reading it out loud please put up a hand. If they make another mistake, put up the other hand so they will get instant feedback from you." Greg called on a man to Michael's left to read.

"Germany in the spring, Australia in the fall," he read. This time two more people sat down and the four people sitting had both hands in the air and big smiles on their faces.

"Thomas, will you read the sentences for me?" This time three people sat, Michael among them, totally annoyed for not seeing the obvious much sooner.

"Iris, I noticed you were one of the first to sit down. Can you please read the sentence for those still standing?"

"Germany in the THE spring, Australia in the THE fall," She clarified accentuating the extra 'the' in each sentence. With lots of laughter, the remaining people standing took their seats.

"It's okay, don't be embarrassed. Instead, notice how often we overlook the obvious. We get caught by our assumptions or paradigms and, therefore, don't see things as they really are. Keep this in mind as you go about your day. How many situations might you look at just a little differently?"

In groups of four, the participants then shared and compared their '**10 Principles**' definitions and each identified a role model for each principle, someone they knew who lived it strongly. Their mission was to identify the best behaviors and best practices that demonstrate how this person lives the principle. Michael put forward his boss, Ralf Escher, as a strong example of **Life Balance**. Even in the midst of a crisis, he remained calm and collected. He took time away from work for his wife, family and friends and he seemed to have a strong partnership with his wife both in their business and private life. Michael felt acutely aware that very few of Ralf's 'Best Behaviors' applied to him. He always seemed to be happy.

Michael was somewhat shocked by the fact that most people really had trouble finding role models for the principles from within their own company. How can you learn if you have no good role models? He was so thankful he had Ralf to look up to. Some people actually had parents who were role models for some of the principles. Greg said that those participants had won the parent lottery. Michael knew he had not.

In the hour before lunch, Greg explained the meaning of the **Ten Principles** and presented his definitions of them. He had a list of the ten principles on the flipchart at the front of the room.

Principle 1: **I am Responsibile**

Principle 2: **I Clarify My Values**

Principle 3: **I Have a Vision**

Principle 4: **I Am on Mission**

Principle 5: **I Strive for Life Balance**

Principle 6: **I Actively Give and Take**

Principle 7: **I Value Empathy**

Principle 8: **I work with Involvement and Diversity**

Principle 9: **I Make Relationship Deposits**

Principle 10: **I Re-Energize Weekly**

Greg then walked to the other side of the room and flipped over to the next page of the second flipchart to reveal a picture of a lighthouse that was divided into ten layers.

Ten Principles of Leadership and Life

Be a Lighthouse

"I use a visual symbol to connect the principles together. Visual memory is a very powerful thing and can help you to remember them. For me, the lighthouse means even more; a lighthouse has a solid foundation, it is a symbol of strength, it is aligned, it can withstand storms, and it has a continuous message and for me, is a symbol of leaders and leadership."

"The first four layers of the lighthouse," he explained, "are mostly about self, the 'inside' work. They form the foundation. **Principles 6 through 9** relate to 'outside work', or 'working with or through others'. These deal more with **communicating, coaching, leadership** and **relationships. Principles 5, Life Balance,** and **10, Re-energizing,** support the others and make them work. Without living these two principles, the others will be negatively affected and the results will not be sustainable."

At this point Greg went to the flipchart and wrote the word 'Responsibility' on the rocky foundation of the lighthouse,

"**The Principle of 'I am Responsible',** the foundation of our lighthouse. It is all about having a choice," Greg declared. "You all seemed pretty clear on that. You know you can 'push the reset button' and make the choice to change. You are not victims. You are creators." Michael felt himself nodding along. "You can make a promise to yourself to start again based on your vision and values. For some of you, my feedback on the back of your name card stated, 'believe in yourself and your skills more' and to 'have more of a 'yes, I can' proactive mindset. Keep pulling your own strings.' That is what this is all about. You are not a victim."

"The process of **Clarifying Values** is not easy," Greg continued, moving on to his next principle. "It often takes years of deep thinking and searching to understand what matters most in your life. Sometimes, people need an external force to help them gain clarity. For example, some people wait until their first heart attack until they realize how important health is or wait until their partner leaves them until they realize how important love is. This process of clarifying values is an important part of building a solid foundation for your vision."

He put a quotation from the poet, T.S. Eliot up on the flipchart:

"We shall not cease from exploration, and the end of all our exploring will be to arrive where we started and know the place for the first time."

T.S. Eliot

Michael wondered what it was supposed to mean. The statement seemed profound, but Greg had already moved on to his next point and there was no more time for Michael to reflect on it.

"When we talk about **Leadership**, we're talking first and foremost about a clear **Vision**. It's your vision that gets you out of bed in the morning and makes your day purposeful. Only a small number of people actually have a written vision. A lot of athletes do and it is very powerful. This **'vision and values'** process should start with yourself on an 'I' level. The next step should be with your life partner at home, getting clear on the 'we' level. You need to define success and be clear on what you want to be, do and experience in the next years of your life. Of course this can be done with a team and an entire organisation. The process of 'doing' it is the most powerful part of it."

Michael smiled. He should have an advantage then. He always took detailed notes and when he finally figured out what his vision was, he would definitely write it down.

Clear Vision and Values Give you Clear Roles and Goals

Greg became passionate about this topic and his words came faster than Michael could record, "These principles are life changing!" Greg declared, "We come back to them again and again. Our paradigms, self-limiting beliefs and conditioning can all limit our behavior. But, once we **clarify our values, create our vision and find our mission**, we'll not just be busy people; we'll be effective people, we'll be people on mission. The key to **Principle 4, I Am on Mission,** is to start saying 'no' to what does not matter and 'yes' to what really matters. This is where you create and live a weekly plan that makes sense for you. You find time to live your values and all the roles you have in life. This is the principle of discipline and execution. You start to consistently execute them based on your vision and values. These actions align Principles 1-4 as you start to create habits of effectiveness. That leads us to **Principle 5, I Strive for Life Balance.** As you start to move towards your vision and values you will find happiness. When I look at people, I look at their eyes as they smile because a true smile, with true happiness, has 22 muscles contracting and 14 muscles relaxing at the same time. If I see real happiness I know they have a good life balance. These first five elements must be aligned, must be congruent," Greg emphasized. "Otherwise they will not survive the storms and the crashing waves. Clarity is needed at each level." Greg then moved to the flipchart and added **Principle 5, I Strive for Life Balance**, which then completed the first five layers.

Ten Principles
of Leadership and Life

Michael grabbed his journal and summarized his thoughts.

'We shall not cease from exploration,
and the end of all our exploring will be to arrive where we started and
know the place for the first time.'
-T.S. Eliot

That statement will require some thinking... And I like what Greg said... Once we clarify our values, find our vision, and create our mission statement, we'll not just be busy people, we'll be people on mission... I understand so much more than I did a few days ago. Nothing has changed. Yet everything has changed.

I realize now that it is an inside-out process which needs to start with myself. Principles 1-5 are all about me as a person. They are interconnected and sequential.

It starts on the 'I' level and then goes to the 'We' level. I hope I get the chance to do this 'We' process with Petra. Maybe some day we might have the chance to do a course like this together!

Greg continued with **Principle 6, I Actively Give and Take**, "This is about finding solutions that are good for both sides, it takes time, energy and patience, but it leads to a long-term relationship. You show respect and fairness for the individual and you show you care. This principle is lived when we sell and negotiate. Perhaps showing the opposite of this principle will make it clearer. I've seen some bosses and some fathers continually creating win-lose agreements. 'Father wins, child loses'. Over time, what they end up with are weak employees and weak children. That's the last thing you want. We need to have patience and show respect for the other side."

"That brings us to **Principle 7, I Value Empathy,** which I also call the **Coaching Principle**. This is the principle the coaches lived so well in the first two coaching sessions. They made the executive feel totally understood. One of the biggest needs we have is to be understood. A coach who only waits for his turn to reply, to give their solutions or recommendations is an example of someone not living this principle."

"**Principle 8, Team Diversity**, can also be called the **Leadership Principle**. Try to picture a boss with the mindset of "I think, you do: I decide, you just turn the screwdriver. It's the old-fashioned, top-down, 'just do what I say' way of managing. This example is the opposite of principle 8. I've been in meetings where I see a team and they all look, think, talk and dress exactly like the boss. Where is the diversity? To live this principle, you need to get full commitment and buy-in from your team members. It focuses on valuing differences and using team diversity. Facilitating an effective workshop is a great example of this principle in action. This results in synergy and creative solutions."

Greg openly shared his own experiences as he reviewed **Principles 9 & 10: I Make Relationship Deposits** and I **Re-energize,** "The essence of the **relationship deposit principle, Number 9**, is doing small things to show appreciation, recognition and respect. It means making someone feel important, needed and special. The key to re-energizing with **Principle 10** is to understand that renewal needs to happen physically, emotionally, mentally, socially and spiritually."

"The principles are easy to understand, but as we come under pressure and filled with adrenaline, they are very difficult to live, especially before we accept the first principle of responsibility. Before you take that responsibility, you are blinded to many things in life."

"As a professional hockey coach, I really struggled to give praise, recognition and real understanding to my wife and children during the difficult phases of the season. I started to take their relationships and love for granted, I took my health for granted and before I realized it, my life was not functioning well – physically or emotionally. I was constantly stressed and tired, and when I did get home I wasn't doing the small things to make my wife and children feel loved, special and important. At the time I just couldn't see it or did not want to see it. It was like I had a pair of rose tinted glasses and thought that everything was perfect and just the way it had always been. I just couldn't see reality. It affected my children's confidence and had an impact on how my wife felt about herself. It really affected her emotionally.

After coming through some difficult years, I learned that awareness is the key and living these principles is an ongoing process where you have to continually challenge yourself to actively live the principles. I was fortunate that my wife and family stayed with me through these hard times. When my life hit the low point I realized something really had to change. It was the time to take off my rose tinted glasses and actually see my reality.

I took responsibility for my life and that helped me to be open enough to receive feedback from my wife and start the change process.

Luckily for me, it wasn't too late and I was able to make the major changes that were needed. Over time, I saw and felt the benefits on all levels of my life. Before this point, I was doing no exercise. I thought I had no time for sports and kept making all the usual excuses. When I finally had a blood test, I realized what a predicament my body was in.

In the good old days, before I was under so much stress, when I came home my son and daughter would jump in the air and give me big hugs BUT I was not making relationship deposits back. I took their love for granted – then during my 'dark days', when I walked in the door the best I could expect was, 'Oh hi Dad, you're home.' Taking responsibility for all areas of my life and making the necessary changes according to the 10 Principles had a huge positive impact on my family... forever. When the principles are lived, they are so powerful."

Greg's vulnerability and openness, as he shared his personal examples, clearly had some of the participants emotionally reflecting on their own lives. Michael got a terrible feeling in his stomach as he realized he'd lived so far from these principles and how exactly this had affected him and all his relationships, especially with Petra.

Greg walked to the flipchart and added the last two principles to the lighthouse, "As you can see, these ten principles together form the lighthouse which is a symbol of strong leadership. My expectation for you is to become a lighthouse."

Ten Principles
of Leadership and Life

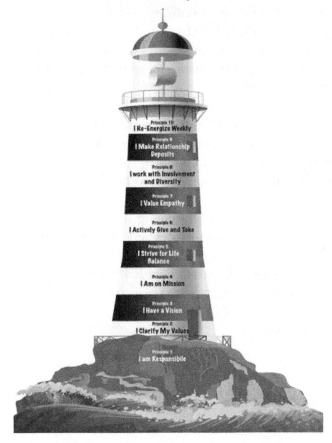

CHAPTER 24

At this point, Greg drew their attention to the **Ten Principles** feedback he'd written on the back of their name cards the previous day. Michael scanned the notes and symbols on the back of his card.

Under the heading 'Strengths' were the numbers 8, 1 and 2. Near the bottom of the card, under 'Weaknesses' Greg had written the number 10, with 'increase H2O' and 'work on energy management' beside it. In the opposite corner he'd written 3, 4 and 5. Beside 3, he'd written 'invest more time & define success'. Be clear on what you want out of life. Think beyond your comfort zone and build your vision based on your strengths and your real potential. By number 6 he'd written, don't be so dominant, be patient and find the win-win. Beside principle 7, empathy, use more tone and appropriate body language. Don't give so many tips. Next to number 8, Greg had written to increase involvement and hold back your own opinion until you get the others in the boat. Increase the amount of deposits and catch people doing the right things was beside principle 9, relationship deposits.

As Michael tried to make sense of the scribbled notes, Greg explained, "We've only had a day and a half together but I have been watching each of you closely. On the top half of your cards, I have circled the **Principles** where I see strengths. Most of you will see **Principle 1, I am Responsible** as one of your strengths. You've chosen to be here and that shows me you have taken your life in your own hands and that you believe in yourself. You made the decision to invest the time and the money in improving your leadership skills and continuing your personal and professional development."

"The circled numbers at the bottom are two or three 'mission critical' principles I suggest you need to work on first. The other notes I will explain more when I meet with you individually for a one to one feedback session. Now, take a look at your own self-assessment graph and see if my observations are in alignment with your own. If we totally disagree, I will want a phone number so I can call your life partner and get a third opinion," Greg joked.

After comparing his own chart to his name card assessment, Michael glanced around the room. Most of the expressions he saw confirmed that Greg was pretty accurate. Manny asked the question that he was sure many wanted to ask, "How do you know this? What do you look for?".

"I look at many things. I look at your eyes, smile, chin…or chins, the brightness in your face. I watch your concentration, your energy level, early and late in the day, what you eat, what you drink, how much sugar and caffeine you consume, how you coach…I take note of your belly, your hips, and your back. I pay attention to how fast you talk, how fast you walk. I look at your posture and I watch how often those 22 muscles around your eyes move. I look for real smiles and real happiness. I watch how you network during meals and how much interest you show in other people. They are all clues. Other than that, I'm just guessing," he grinned. "It's not just my opinion that counts, so, in order to prepare you for the next coaching session, I'm going to build some teams and have each person sit in the 'Hot Seat' and get first impression feedback from the team members on how they see your strengths and weaknesses based on **The Ten Principles**."

With that, Michael joined his assigned team and volunteered to sit in the Hot Seat first. He heard Greg say that feedback is a gift and some people say it's the breakfast of champions. **The Ten Principle** feedback he received was well-aligned with his own self-analysis. The other members agreed that Michael urgently needed to work on **re-energizing** and **life balance** and they questioned whether he lived the **give and take** and **empathy principles** consistently. Three people thought he was weak on **vision**. When the session ended, Michael felt awful, but thanked his team for their honest assessment. They had helped him clarify where he needed to focus if he was going to develop into a strong and more effective leader.

"Now, find your three o'clock partner for the **Ten Principles Coaching** session, decide which of you will be the executive for the next exercise then return to your seats. You've got one minute. Go!"

Michael and Stephan greeted each other in the middle of the room. "I would really like to work on my coaching skills this time," Michael said before Stephan had a chance to speak. "I can see how coaching really helps people and I certainly need to practice." Stephan happily agreed to be the executive this time round.

"As preparation, I'm going to do an exercise with the whole group before the coaching takes place." Greg slipped a disc into the CD player, "This is a great tool. It's a reflective vision and values exercise with some relaxation and mental preparation. There will be a relaxation phase, a 'brain writing phase' and finally a coaching phase. At the end of the relaxation phase I will ask you to look down at your paper, open your eyes and then write continuously whatever thoughts come to your mind. It is non-stop and your pen should constantly be in contact with the paper."

Calming music filled the conference room. The participants put everything down except a clean piece of paper and a pencil, relaxed, then sat with their feet firmly on the floor and closed their eyes as Greg continued speaking in a smooth, calming voice, "I want you all to take a deep breath in, ...out, in, ...out, ...feel yourself relaxing and this time as you breathe in, imagine breathing in clean, white air...picture it. As you exhale, picture the tension or frustration that's trapped inside you leaving your body as a black breath."

After several repetitions he continued, "Keep breathing deeply and slowly. I want you to concentrate on one finger. Think about the blood running through your body from your heart. Follow it as it flows through your arteries into that one finger. Can you feel it? Concentrate on finding your pulse or feeling that heartbeat in your finger."

"Now I will slowly move into the mental phase and start asking you a variety of questions regarding your values and vision. Think about what matters most in your life. What do you value? What is important for you? Think about the different roles you play. You are more than the job you do, more than the company you work for. Are you a father, a son, a mother, a sister? Are you part of a community, a church, a team? You are a whole person so, as you think about all these roles, what do you want to be remembered for twenty or thirty years from now? Is it your kindness, your understanding, your compassion? Is it your willingness to help? Is it your commitment to a cause? Think about each of your roles. If I asked the people in your life to give me words to describe you, what would they say? Think about those words for just a moment."

"Five years from now, what would you *want* them to say? If your life were a message, what would it be? How can you get more 'living' into your life today? What do you see yourself doing fifteen years from today? Where are you? Who is there with you? What does your life look like? If money were no object, what would you be doing? What would you try if you knew you could not fail? If you had a three-month sabbatical, where would you go? What would you experience? Who would you be with? What would be your priorities? How would you invest your time?"

The gentle music continued to play in the background, "Slowly, when you are ready, open your eyes, look down at your blank paper and start writing. As the questions are repeated, just get it all out. Write it all down. What do you want more of in your life? What do you want less of? What qualities do you want people to remember about you? What traits do you hope your children will inherit from you? Adventure? Creativity? Family commitment? Keep writing. What values should define you as a person? What do you *really* want out of life?"

Michael felt the questions fill his mind and his hand flying across the paper. He couldn't believe the power of the exercise, how deeply it had taken him into himself, looking for answers to questions he had never thought to ask. 'Where do I want to be in fifteen years? Who do I want to be? How do I want to be remembered? As a leader, how do I want to be seen ten years from today? What did I contribute? What did I bring to the table? What was my leadership brand?'

He felt his mind and pen beginning to slow and Greg's voice brought him back into the moment, "Executives, please find a new location outside of this room for the next phase of the exercise. Take this brain writing, your Principles graph and passports. I would like you to write down five words that describe how you felt during this exercise. Also write down what you saw, what became clearer and what your message from this process was. I'd also like you consider the purpose of this exercise. Then, review your self-assessment of the ten principles. Are there any adjustments you might make based on our earlier discussions? Examine what you wrote during this last exercise and choose two principles that you would like to improve upon. Create an action plan for the first steps. You have twenty minutes to prepare."

At this point Greg turned to the next page of the flipchart:

Feedback/ reflection

- **How did you feel? (5 words)**
- **What did you see?**
- **What is clearer?**
- **What was the message?**
- **What was the purpose?**
- **What is your next step?**

Michael and the other coaches remained behind and joined Greg at the front of the room. "That exercise was all about gaining clarity on **Principles 2** and **3**, **Values** and **Vision**," he began, "You can't move ahead on **Principle 4** and '**Be on Mission**', until your values and vision are clear to you."

Michael felt self-conscious at rating himself low on **Principle 4**. He knew he wasn't aligned on the first four principles. Further, he realized that his real mission was about so much more than his Sunstream job. He listened intently to the tips as Greg explained them, "In this coaching session, I want you to try the most popular techniques in sports psychology, 'visualization' and 'seeding'. I want you to help your clients to see their futures. Ask them:"

- **'What will it look like five years from today?'**

- **'What will be different from today?'**

- **'What is your ideal life ten years from now?'**

"The 'seeding' technique happens when you ask:"

- **'How will it feel when you've achieved that?'**

"If they can physically describe and share that emotional state and the feeling of success that they crave, the seed has been planted. This leads to increased motivation and commitment and in turn, nurtures that seed to grow into their vision. For an athlete, this means visualizing, and even feeling, a gold medal hanging around their neck before the competition starts. The seed is planted and that's the motivation."

Greg looked at each of his trainee coaches before continuing, "This way of coaching is less about goal setting and more about letting your executives open up about their brain writing. For some, this will be very difficult and will need gentle coaxing. Our goal is to help them gain clarity and articulate their values and their vision. I call it the vision finder exercise. I want you to put their values in the center of the paper and then put their visionary thinking and their definition of success on the outside around that. You are creating a mental map for them on paper. It will help them see their future."

"As a pacing technique, start by having them share how they felt during the relaxation phase of the mental session and the brain-writing. In this pacing phase of coaching, you need to share and be vulnerable as well. You can use some of the following questions:

- ## What became clearer for them?

- ## How did they feel?

- ## How did the exercise help them clarify their vision and values?

Get them to describe how it's going to feel when they have achieved that vision. Now, go and make me proud because this is where we can make a difference!" He then turned one more page on the flipchart.

Essence of Coaching

to affirm their Potential so Clearly ... they see it in Themselves

Michael went in search of Stephan, determined to do better this time. No home movies, no tips, talk 20/listen 80. He was determined to do the best he could and sat down strategically beside Stephan making sure that his writing hand was between the two of them.

Fifty-five minutes later he was exhausted, but had to admit it was the most interesting and intense one-on-one session he'd ever experienced. The coaching after the mental training was so powerful and emotional, Michael couldn't believe Greg's ability to get people to open up in such a way. In hindsight, he wished he could have had the opportunity to be the executive as he was eager to see the outcome out of the session for himself and his own life. He also wondered if he could have been so open and vulnerable and if he would have been capable of articulating his vision clearly.

Michael's biggest takeaway was the vision finder tool. It was sort of a mind-mapping process that created a visual picture of a person's inter-connected values and visions. Getting it all down on paper brought great energy and clarity for his partner. Michael could see the passion and excitement in his partner's eyes.

CHAPTER 25

A fter the intensity of the **Values and Vision coaching**, the Production Game that wrapped up the afternoon activities was a welcome bit of fun. The goal was to produce a product at the lowest price. Michael joined Sam and Kerstin and the men immediately started to dominate and shared their ideas on the best strategy. Twice, Kerstin tried to interject with her idea to produce the best outcome, but they quickly shot her down, "Sorry, Kerstin," Michael snapped, "but this is what I did day in, day out in my old job. I know what I'm talking about," and continued to plan with Sam.

Just as he and Sam had agreed on the optimum approach, Greg shouted, "Oh! Your company has been merged! Your new coworkers will be joining you now."

Saskia, Manny and Daniel joined them and Michael outlined their plan. Daniel shook his head, "Sorry guys, but we're way ahead of you. Here's how we'll do it."

"Daniel, that's not the best alternative," Saskia cut in, "I think we need fewer employees at the table!" Kerstin joined in agreement, but the men didn't seem to hear her. Daniel controlled the discussion, but neither Michael nor Sam was about to concede. Their group was still arguing as time ran out and the game began. Facing fierce competition, they lurched from one strategy to another with predictably miserable results. Michael reflected on Greg's comment that, "Complexity blocks execution" and they had not even begun to simplify the complexity of the challenge.

When the final scores were tallied, the winning team had chosen a strategy very similar to the one Saskia and Kerstin had suggested. "You're not bad guys, but you're awful listeners," Kerstin stated as the two ladies gave each other a high five and walked away. The merger and high volume production goals were not unlike Sunstream and Escher Electric. Michael knew he had ignored every opportunity offered by the women's winning 'outside of the box' thinking and wondered what was he missing in his daily work environment.

After a short break, Greg called the groups back together for a '**Group Dynamics Feedback**' assignment. Each participant answered twelve questions about the team based on their experience of the Production Game. Michael read the first eight:

1. **Which two participants could influence others and their opinions the most?**

2. **Which two participants could influence others and their opinions the least?**

3. **Which two participants had the most conflicts/disagreements during discussions?**

4. **Which participants were most accepted by the group?**

5. **With which two participants did you have the best synergy?**

6. **Which participant was the most natural as a facilitator?**

7. **Which two participants had the most desire to win?**

8. **Which two participants used questions the most to help the team get clarity?**

As Michael continued to read through the questions, he had a bad feeling that his name was going to come up quite often. He realized he'd lost focus on the big picture and got caught in the details again. He hadn't lead, he'd bullied and he hadn't listened. He hadn't made people feel understood and had only defended his point of view.

When the feedback process got under way, Michael felt his stomach acid bubble up again as the team members confirmed all his thoughts. He reflected on how incredibly quickly and easily he'd fallen into old patterns as he popped an antacid into his mouth.

> **When I am ready to learn, the teacher will appear. Getting the right person into the right role is a key part of leadership. Vision and mission come before systems, structure and strategy. I think it's time to admit that I have much to learn. This student is ready! After today, I definitely need some re-energizing.**

Michael was happy to find only a few people in the pool when he arrived. He dove into the deep end and swam several laps, clearing his mind of all visions, values, missions and Sunstream worries. After his final lap, he made his way to the hot tub and lowered himself into the steamy, swirling water next to a very relaxed Manny.

"Hello, Sunstream."

"I see you're making the most of the perks," Michael said.

"Didn't you hear what the captain said about principle 10? 'We need to *re-energize.*' Listening to my body is the first step."

"And what's your body saying?"

"Enjoy the moment. Count your Saturdays, Michael. There'll be plenty of work waiting when you get home."

"Do you know Sunstream?"

"I know your boss."

"Ralf?"

Manny looked puzzled, "Viktor Fuchs."

"Oh."

"Now there's a man with vision! You're fortunate to work with him."

Michael confessed he had never met Mr. Fuchs and briefly explained the situation.

"You missed a golden opportunity. Viktor's a real genius."

Michael thought of the many evenings he had spent reading Viktor's battery books with the scribbled margin notes and diagrams. There was a man with a mission, living his passion, a leader choosing where he could make a difference. His values and his purpose were fully aligned. As Greg would say, what he was doing was congruent. For Viktor, it wasn't just about batteries, it was much larger than that; making alternative energy more feasible and finding better storage solutions. What he had needed was a partner, a great leader worthy of his vision. What a shame Viktor hadn't met Ralf years ago!

"Are you all right?"

"Miles away, sorry. I was thinking about work stuff." Michael's mind was spinning but clear at the same time, "Please excuse me, Manny," he said as he pulled himself out of the hot tub.

"Have I spoiled your soak?"

"No, not at all, you've helped me tremendously! I just need to write some stuff down while it's clear in my head. You might say I've just experienced a paradigm shift, thanks to you!"

Why was I so critical of Viktor Fuchs, a man I've never met? Nadine Peters' negative portrayal had truth, no doubt, but did it have insight? Was Viktor more than a founder who restricted the success of Sunstream? He obviously inspired strong loyalty, not just in his staff, but also in others like Manny.

Greg asked if I could challenge my conditioning. Can I truly shift my paradigms? I'm going to talk to Viktor when I get back. Whatever the man has for management faults, he is clearly committed to a vision. He understood his mission and how to achieve it.

I'll ask him, 'What is your dream?' 'How do you determine your mission?' 'Did you discover your purpose by knowing who you are and who you want to become? Did you find it or did it find you?' 'Is change and growth part of it or is there something more, something bigger that you understand and I don't, Viktor?'

Michael's thoughts were swimming. Where was he headed? Could he achieve the nearly impossible and turn Sunstream around? Would there be a future there for him if he did?

"How do I work smarter, not harder, accomplish all that must be done on a daily and long-term basis and live a balanced life that remains 'On Mission'?"

Michael jotted down his thoughts on a page in his journal:

> **What do I need to do? Does Greg, know? Over managed, under led. Be a good manager and a good leader, not for perks, money or status, but for life satisfaction. I need to begin with a picture of success in my mind. What is my picture of success?**

His thoughts poured out much faster than he could write but, this time, they were clear and coherent even if he didn't have all the answers yet.

> **Klaus asked if I had my ladder against the right wall.**
> **Greg says we *can* choose our response, choose our future.**
> **Ralf wants me to evolve as a leader. He sees my potential.**
> **Is the student ready?**
> **I can't lead others until I lead myself.**
> **Am I finally seeing and understanding life as it could be, rather than how I've believed it is?**
> **Choose a field. Make a difference not just a living! Contribute to something larger than yourself. Be bold! Think beyond your comfort zone.**
> **Leaders need followers. People will follow someone they believe in. You need to make them curious about the journey and the destination. You must be vulnerable to be a leader. It starts with me. I need to know myself and who I am. I need to break my old self-limiting beliefs. If my life were a message, what would it be?**

It was all suddenly so clear. He would commit himself to Viktor's dream and Ralf's mission. He would be the manager, the coach and leader who achieved solar energy storage at affordable prices. He would embrace the necessary changes in himself.

> **'...the end of all our exploring**
> **will be to arrive where we started**
> **and know the place**
> **for the first time.'**
> **(T.S. Eliot)**

I've found the answer and it's no longer profound!

CHAPTER 26

On the final day of the workshop, Greg wrote the title **'My Leadership Brand'** on the flip chart and said, "Each one of you has a 'leadership brand'. It is formed by what you do, how you do it, what you say, the image you portray and the results you achieve. What you do is determined by the three intelligences I introduced to you on day one: Your **IQ**, **EQ** and **PQ**."

He then drew another diagram that looked like a propeller with three blades, one for each type of intelligence

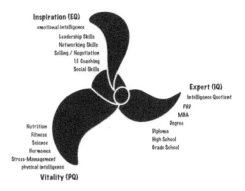

MY LEADERSHIP BRAND –
My three intelligences

IQ - EQ - PQ

"This symbolizes your **'Leadership Brand'**. We've spent a lot of time working on your **EQ** over the last two days. **Principles 6-9** are all about your **emotional intelligence**. Your **IQ** is what got you to where you are today but can't get you where you need to go. We're going to focus now on your **PQ** or **physical intelligence**; how you understand and manage your nutrition, fitness, stress and energy. The emphasis is on **Principle 10: re-energizing**, or as I call it, **I Re-energize.** This will help you achieve sustainable results." He paused and looked around the room, "So, here is the **'100 Day Challenge'**," Greg said, turning to the next page on the flipchart:

100 Day Challenge

1. F.I.T.T. Principle

2. The 4 minute workout

3. W3 - Water, Walking, Wine

4. Nutrition and The Zone

5. Vitamins and supplements

6. Immune system

7. Strength training

8. Mental fitness, mental training

9. Time for self

"Remember, you can't manage time but you can manage your energy. Each of us has the same 168 hours in a week to use in the way we see fit. You can't buy one hour more so you have to use those hours to your advantage. Do the high leverage activities that will give you the biggest return on your investment. Be ruthless with your time and invest it well. You need mental, physical, emotional and spiritual renewal. If you take what I am going to tell you and apply it to your own life over the next 100 days, I guarantee you a positive change in how you feel. I could read you so many emails from people who took this challenge and made wonderful changes in their own lives. That feedback helps me to keep doing what I do and it helps me stay 'On Mission'. These are regular people, just like you, so it *can* be done, but you have to DO IT! My main message is 'Do the Doable' because that is all you can do."

Greg turned to the flipchart and wrote,

"Resignation is the Enemy Of Vitality"

and on the other he wrote,

'Vitality is a Choice'

With that Greg turned and brought the group's attention to the first point. "The **F.I.T.T. Principle** is about doing some form of aerobic exercise. F stands for **Frequency**; you need to aim for a minimum of 3 times a week. I is for **Intensity,** being in the aerobic zone working at 60 to 80% of your maximum heart rate. T is for **Time**; 20 minutes is all it takes to make a difference. The second **T** is for **Type**, which means the type of exercise. It can be whatever you like: Power walking, jogging, swimming, whatever, but you need to get your heart rate up to where it does the most good."

"How do we know where that is?" someone asked.

"Good question. An acceptable, universal guideline is taking the number 220 minus your age, so, if you're 50, you'd be aiming for 60 to 80% of 170 beats per minute. This is called the aerobic zone where you burn fat as an energy source without producing too much lactic acid. Does that make sense?" Heads nodded. "With anaerobic training we burn more calories and this maximizes your calorie burn over 24 hours."

"Next is W^3. The first **W** is for **Water**. People tend to underestimate the importance of drinking water. It affects every part of our bodies, including our skin, organs and the way our brains function. Research shows that drinking 1.5 litres from waking to lunchtime increases mental concentration in afternoon and early evening activities. It is generally recommended to drink two to three litres of water each day for physical and mental wellbeing. The second **W** is for **Walking**. Research suggests that walking may be a preventive action against some cancers. So walk away from cancer, just start moving. Walking twenty minutes after a meal provides an additional 60 minutes of increased metabolism and fat burning. It's the lazy person's exercise program. The third **W** is for **Wine**, specifically red wine. Research shows that moderate drinkers are less likely to suffer heart attacks and actually live longer than abstainers or heavy drinkers. The resveratrol in red wine is what gives you the health benefits. So, enjoy it, but in moderation!" Greg smiled and continued, "I'll happily follow any experts who recommend drinking red wine."

It was all good learning, but Michael wondered if he could take much more in. His head was already overloaded with paradigm shifts, the **M.C.C.L.S. Model**, **Coaching Tips**, **The Ten Principles**, his **Vision** and **Values** reflections and his own thoughts, questions and notes. As Greg explained the importance of nutrition, Michael's mind drifted back to his thoughts and revelations of the night before. While he was adding to the list of questions for Viktor Fuchs, he suddenly realized that Greg had moved on from **The 100 Day Challenge**. "No worries," Michael thought, " I'll have plenty of time to work on my health when Sunstream's deadlines have been met."

The two closing activities, **'My Executive Team'** and **'One Year to Live'**, caught his attention more. "Learning is a lifelong event," Greg started. "You have been learning your whole life; from people, events and courses you've taken. This **'Executive Team'** exercise will get you focusing on those people who have had the biggest impact on your life. Alive or dead, which people had the greatest impact on you? Who has impacted, influenced and molded you into the person you are today? Which six to eight people are the most important members of your executive team? Then, write down the lessons, messages or values lived by each of these special individuals. What was their contribution to who you have become?"

Greg then shared his executive team members as an example. He drew an oblong square in the middle of a clean sheet of paper on the flipchart and wrote the heading My Executive Team. Around the square he wrote Mom, Dad, Laura, his wife, Brooks, his first coach at junior level and Tom, the Australian who introduced him to the world of leadership training.

"So, as you can see, I have my mom and my dad. I really won the Parent Lottery. Mom's message was to live every day. She modelled enthusiasm and passion for what you do, the importance of family and how to strengthen those connections. My dad taught me to live in the moment. He died when I was in my teens, taken way too young by cancer, but his love and messages impact me to this day. Coach Brooks was there for me back then. He knew the effect that losing my dad had on me, but he saw my potential. He worked with me so that I would not give up and affirmed my potential until I was finally able to see it for myself. He modelled compassion and empathy at a time when I felt very lost and alone." Michael had to swallow hard at the reminder of Klaus' similar support.

"Tom took me under his wing when I gave up my dream of professional hockey. He showed me there really was more to life than the sport I'd dedicated my life to. He forced me to take a good look at my other strengths and use them out in the world instead. Tom introduced me to the work I do now and I'll never forget him for that. He saw my potential."

"Finally, there's my beautiful wife, Laura. She has taught me to 'just be', she keeps me grounded and has been there through the roughest of times. She's taught me what love and commitment truly mean. She is my rock. She is the backbone for our family and our kids share everything with her. There is huge trust." Deep emotion poured through his words as he continued, "She stayed with me during times I could barely be with myself and kept our marriage and family strong. She gives me all the love she has and I am grateful for it every single day. I strive to find ways to make sure she knows that."

The room was absolutely still as everyone absorbed this personal and emotional revelation, "Now, I want you to put your executive team on paper just like that. You have forty minutes."

Michael drew the shape of an executive board table and tried to think. This was harder than he'd thought. Greg's vulnerability in sharing his personal story had affected him deeply and he felt the emotional weight in his chest again. He wasn't sure where to start, so he got up to get a glass of water for his antacid pill and to clear his head. After some reflection, he began to write. He wrote 'Ralf Escher'. Ralf had given him another chance to prove his leadership and had provided a challenging new direction for his life. He felt inspired by his vision to develop his company into something larger than he'd inherited, his calm demeanour, always business-like and never frantic and his intuition. His message was, "I believe in you."

Klaus and Monika were next. As a coach and friend, Klaus had been a great role model. He taught Michael to develop his physical and mental skills. He encouraged him to work hard to achieve his goals and emphasized a strong team commitment. He led his players by example, never asking more of his team than he was prepared to give himself. Michael realized that Klaus' impact went beyond what he had taught him on the field. He had shown Michael what a strong, loving marriage could look like when Michael's own parents never could. Monika had taught him to cook but he realized that she too had given so much more.

166

The unconditional support she gave Klaus and the give and take mentality that she really had in all situations was an example for him to follow. Monika was a mother figure, cheerful, supportive and loving in every thing she did.

Michael reflected for several minutes before adding his mother to his list. Contrary to Greg's experience, he had *not* won the 'parent lottery', yet his mother had modelled resilience and unconditional love. The high value she placed on education helped him make the decision to study and she had given him the incentive to make something of himself. He owed his keen ambition to her.

Michael added the final name to his list, Petra Falk. Petra had a level of elegance; a classiness that he could only hope had rubbed off on him a little. Her immersion in music, a world of sound and emotion was so different from his world, and her disciplined hours of practice were admirable. Petra demonstrated what it meant to really live your passion. Most of all, Petra knew who she was and what she wanted to become. He realized that was what had made him fall in love with her all those years ago and made him love her still. Now he had to figure out what he was passionate about.

Forty minutes later, the former teams were called back together to share their board tables and Michael, Kerstin, Saskia and Sam found a quiet place by a window. By the time they were finished, they were deeply affected by each other's stories and recollections. Their vulnerability and openness had brought their team closer together. Michael confessed, "This is the first time I have ever really thought about who has influenced me and how. It's been a real eye opener and very emotional. I could see and feel each member of my team as I was sharing. We get so busy doing what we do that we never ask why we do it. I can't believe I never even considered doing this until now." Michael's voice cracked and a tear trickled down his face. "Damn," he whispered as Kirstin put a hand on his arm.

Back in the seminar room Gregory Marks challenged the participants to look forward, "I see that a lot of you were emotionally affected by this exercise. That's good. Now, just as key people shaped your lives, realize that you are impacting the lives of those around you. Who are the people you are touching? What are those people going to remember about you? Will you be a member of their executive team? Did you make a difference? What was your message? What was your contribution? What did you model?" Michael responded to Greg' parting words in his journal:

What is my message? Part of my life's mission is to give the principles, tools and common truths to others to help them grow. I want to help them create a vision, believe in themselves by affirming their potential. You're on my executive team, Petra. I can only hope that I can earn a place on yours. It felt really good to open up and share during my executive team presentation.

The **One Year to Live** activity hit close to home for Michael as he remembered those dreadful hospital hours hovering between jumbled dreams and his painful return to consciousness.

Greg played soft, soothing music again and directed the group to sit in the same relaxed position as before, breathing in and out slowly and to concentrate only on his voice. After some relaxation techniques, he asked them to think about what they were most grateful for and happy about in their lives today. His tone became sombre, "If you knew you only had twelve months to live, what would you do? Who would you reach out to? Connect with? Make amends to? Declare your love for? Imagine, as your days neared an end, what messages would want to leave those you love? What have you learned that you could share with your kids so they could live their lives more fully and with more passion and meaning? What would you hope people would say about you after you're gone? What would be the one line you'd want them to write on your gravestone? Did you make a difference? How? With all this in mind, how are you going to live after today? What do you want more of? What do you want less of? What will you change? What priorities will you set? Which people are important to you? What legacy will you seek to leave? What's holding you back from doing those things now? My last three questions are: 'What is your real mission?', 'Why do you exist?' and 'What do you really want out of life?'"

Michael had felt really uncomfortable with such thoughts since his accident, but now they seemed less threatening. Maybe it was the calm tone that Greg used as he asked the questions, the gentle music in the background or perhaps the student was more ready than he'd ever been before. The reason didn't matter as his hand flew across the page in a flurry of words and emotions all coming from somewhere deeper inside Michael than he had ever dared to reach. Making amends. Demonstrating love. Rebuilding burned bridges. Petra flashed into his mind. There was so much he should do yet so little time. He erased *should* and replaced it with *would*. He knew that somewhere amongst this jumble of words were his values, vision and mission. He had so much to reflect upon and he was exhausted.

"What are your 'takeaways'?" Greg asked as he started to wrap up the workshop. "What's become clearer? What changes do you need to make? This is the beginning of a process, the 'inside-out' work that's necessary for you to move towards your own mission. Your leadership development journey begins now. This is all about you. Start planning your weeks, not just your days. On Saturday morning or Sunday evening, sit down and make your plan for the week ensuring that you put the 'big rocks in first'."

Michael's ears perked up. That was what Ralf had shared.

"Growing into a principle-based leader means do the right things first and making sure your health, family and leadership get scheduled into your week. Prioritize what is most important, not just what is most urgent. Focus on what matters most."

"I'd like to thank you for committing the time and energy to be here this week. Thank you for the energy you shared, your involvement and your eagerness to learn and grow. It fuels me, so thank you!" He then walked to the flipchart and wrote four L's on the blank page, and wrote in the words as he spoke,"Remember the importance of **living, loving, laughing** and **learning** and when you get back to the office make the decision to lead!" Greg looked at the group with a smile before adding '**Lead**' the list of words.

LIVING, LOVING, LAUGHING, LEARNING, LEADING

"At some point during the next week," Greg encouraged them, "reflect on the principles, share your mission and talk about your vision and your values with your life partner; think about creating a family mission statement. It's a powerful tool. Ideally try to do the vision, values, reflecting and coaching process with your partner. Pull out their thoughts, ideas and dreams and make it visual for them on a piece of paper. Then, share yours and try to bring it together and create clarity on the 'WE' level. This needs to be based on the Whole Person Model. Once you have done this on a personal level and with your partner, you can think about doing it with your team on the professional side. That means choosing to lead. Remember, it is a decision you make, an action you take. Try to put into action something you've learned within the next forty-eight hours. Take action and walk the talk. Be the lighthouse, the beacon for others to follow. Before you leave, I'd like to share with you a poem by Robert Fulghum that I hope will touch you as much as it always touches me. I want you to think about it on your journey home."

From a sheath of papers on the table in front of him, Greg read slowly, making eye contact with all of the participants. It was clear that the poem was so familiar to him, he knew it almost by heart.

"All I Ever Really Needed to Know I Learned in Kindergarten
-Robert Fulghum

Most of what I really need to know about how to live,
and what to do, and how to be, I learned in kindergarten.
Wisdom was not at the top of the graduate school mountain, but there in the sandbox at nursery school.

These are the things I learned:
Share everything. Play fair. Don't hit people. Put things
back where you found them. Clean up your own mess. Don't
take things that aren't yours. Say you're sorry when you
hurt somebody. Wash your hands before you eat. Flush.
Warm cookies and cold milk are good for you. Live a balanced life. Learn some and think some and draw and paint
and sing and dance and work every day some.
Take a nap every afternoon. When you go out into the
world, watch for traffic, hold hands and stick together.
Be aware of wonder. Remember the little seed in the plastic cup. The roots go down and the plant goes up and nobody really knows how or why, but we are all like that.
Goldfish and hamsters and white mice and even the little seed in the plastic cup – they all die. So do we.
And then remember the book about Dick and Jane and the first
word you learned, the biggest word of all: LOOK. Everything you
need to know is in there somewhere. The Golden Rule and love
and basic sanitation. Ecology and politics and sane living.
Think of what a better world it would be if we all –
the whole world – had cookies and milk about 3 o'clock
every afternoon and then lay down with our blankets
for a nap. Or if we had a basic policy in our nation and
other nations to always put things back where we found
them and clean up our own messes. And it is still true,
no matter how old you are, when you go out into the
world, it is best to hold hands and stick together."

With that, Greg moved towards the participants and started shaking hands to say goodbye. Michael felt so emotional and looking around at the others near him, saw that some were holding back their tears and some were letting the tears roll down their cheeks, unashamed. Michael couldn't believe he hadn't known any of these men and women three short days ago, yet he had opened up and shared some of his deepest hopes, dreams and fears with them. They had become a real team.

The workshop had been so much better than Michael had expected. He had gone to Davos looking for time management tips and what he had found were leadership principles. The past three days forced him to look honestly at himself for the first time. Michael used the two-hour train journey to Zurich airport for more reflection. He watched the mountainous landscape passing by his window until it became almost hypnotic and his thoughts flowed clearly. During the flight to Munich, Michael took out his journal and added a new entry:

> **Share my mission. I think I can actually do that now. I feel like a door has opened, a journey has begun. I'm committed to making a difference, to serving a cause larger than myself. When I return to Düsseldorf, I'll meet with Viktor Fuchs. Together we'll show how solar energy can be stored effectively and affordably. We'll get our new battery out into the world and make a difference.**

To do that, he knew he needed to become more effective. The pyramid of effectiveness that Greg had talked about on the second day had stuck in his mind and brought the first five principles together. Michael could vividly see the base of the pyramid in his mind with the word '**Principles**'. As he moved up the pyramid he then saw '**Values**', '**Vision**', '**Mission Statement**', '**Being on Mission**', '**Roles and goals**', '**Habits**' and '**Rituals.**' Michael quickly drew a diagram of the pyramid into his journal.

Pyramid of Effectivity

Michael thought back to when Greg was presenting the pyramid and could vividly hear his voice, "**The ten principles** form the base of this pyramid. The next step is to clarify your **private and professional values**, which strengthens your foundation. One level higher you **define and create a picture of success** by determining what you want to be, do, give and leave behind as a legacy. This means defining your **vision**. This will drive you forwards towards your vision."

"At this point, you will be able to write a clear and powerful personal **mission statement** that challenges you to be your best and truly live your principles and values. This statement is based on a whole person model. When you live this model, you will move towards your life's goal, your definition of success. Now, you need to create a weekly plan and decide which are the big rocks or the highest priorities you need to focus on.

You need to be completely clear on your roles and goals for that week. Doing this simplifies the complexity in your life. Remember, complexity blocks execution and to be effective you need to decide upon, clarify and execute your weekly goals."

"**Being on Mission** means actually executing your weekly plan and 'do the right things first'. Your **Execution Quotient**, or '**XQ**,' is an indicator of your execution discipline based on your vision and values. The question you need to consistently ask yourself is, "Am I doing what I said I'd do." This is executing based on your roles and goals. Professionally, this is your M.C.C.L.S. role and privately, your role as a partner, father, mother, son or daughter. You need to say 'no' to things that do not matter.

Identifying and executing based upon your two to three daily priorities is a big part of being on mission. This is where you have to live your values with integrity and actually do what you say you're going to do. You make a promise based on your vision and values and here is where you live it. These are **principles 1-4** working in combination. In turn, this way of living your life will lead to balance and happiness. Living these principles creates habits of effectiveness and that is what delivers sustainable results. If you do not manage to execute based on your daily priorities, if you 'know' but do not 'do', there is an execution gap and you become another busy manager with no time for anything else in life and you are not effective."

"The next step is to challenge your old habits and paradigms to ensure they are aligned and congruent with the rest of the pyramid. You need to turn down the TV in your life and turn up the one-to-one time with people you love. Re-examine your daily rituals, the things you do every day, as if on autopilot. Are they aligned and congruent with the rest of the pyramid? Athletes are very conscious of their habits and rituals, as they can make the difference between winning and losing. They know they are paid for results...but so are you. Each one of you now knows where to start on this process to become more effective and this pyramid of effectiveness will remind you of that. So, stick it up on your fridge door, your office pin-board or make it your screen saver. Whatever you choose, just make sure you remember it!"

As soon as I get home I will get started on the process of writing my mission statement and that will challenge me to be the best I can be! I am 'on mission' when I execute based on my vision and values. I will live my weekly plan with discipline and say 'no' to things that do not matter. I will change my habits and rituals to be totally aligned with the rest of the pyramid to ensure sustainable results. First, my vision and values need to become clearer before I can actually write my mission statement. I wish you were here Petra, so that we could talk and do this process together. It would be so powerful. I'm committing to 15 minutes of daily reflection and quiet time to make this happen. You will be in my thoughts often.

This pyramid of effectiveness is so powerful, I just need to keep the process going. There's still lots of work ahead. I know it's doable and I just have to 'do' it. I can change! I can become my best.

The poem by Emerson that Greg read at the end of that session has really stuck with me. I do need to start taking risks in my life because happiness really is everything. He took a moment to rewrite the poem he had already memorized:

If you do not take risks,
You cannot grow.
If you can not grow,
You cannot be your best.
If you cannot be your best,
You cannot be happy.
If you cannot be happy,
What else is there?

After finishing his journal entry, he spent the rest of the flight reflecting on his brain-writing notes from the mental training in the seminar. It was the least coherent jumble he had ever written and yet the most coherent. Nothing had changed. Everything had changed. There was a message in there for him to find. Somewhere.

He made one more journal entry:

Find your purpose based on your values and vision. Your life is not about chance, not about luck. It's in your hands. The purpose of life is a life of purpose.

Those words accompanied Michael until the taxi dropped him off at the Mertens' where Monika and Klaus greeted him warmly, "We've missed you. It's been so long. You're like a son to us, Michael," Monika said.

The **Executive Team** exercise was still fresh in Michael's mind as he hugged her, "And you've been like parents to me. I am only just realizing how important both of you have been in my life…how important you both *are* in my life and I want to say 'thank you'. I don't think I've ever told you how much I appreciate all you've done for me, especially through the tough times and there have been too many of those!" Monika laughed and patted his hand. "No, really, I don't think I've stopped to realize what an amazing couple you are," he added. "You're lucky to have each other. You have such complementary skills and there is such great synergy between you. You're a great example to many of us!" Michael talked about the Executive Team exercise and how he appreciated the people around his table.

"We've tried to be good role models, Michael. Putting us as members of your executive team is a real compliment. We're very honoured. I think it's wonderful that you put Petra as a member of your team as well. Have you heard from her?"

"No, but I think about her all the time."

Monika smiled and held Michael's hand, "She thinks about you, too, but she still needs more time. She was asking me about your workshop in Davos and she's still curious to see if you are really changing"

"I'm glad that you two are still such good friends."

"Petra calls every week and we catch up. She's doing more music teaching than before and she's loving the yoga sessions she started. I think it's been really good for her. Wait till you see her, she looks fantastic. But what about you? Tell us more about your job in Düsseldorf."

"And I want to hear about this workshop in the Swiss mountains," Klaus laughed, when I can get a word in!"

Monika brought a jug of iced water with lemon out into the garden. Summer was really in full swing now and the garden looked beautiful. They sat down to hear Michael's news. Michael admitted he didn't know what was ahead for him beyond the fall. He liked his job at Sunstream, but it could all be over by the end of September, if the company lasted that long. The leadership workshop had given him a new burst of adrenalin and positive energy to deal with whatever came. For the next hour and a half, Michael excitedly shared his leadership workshop experiences: How old paradigms limited his ability to change and grow; how the roles of *managing, coaching, clienting and leading* should all be lived; how the **Ten Principles of Leadership and Life** might guide him and how Viktor's vision could become part of his own. "At last, I know what you meant about having my ladder against the right wall!" Michael laughed.

Klaus slapped Michael's back, "I'm glad somebody managed to get through to you."

"Have *you* ever thought about becoming a leadership trainer or coach?" Michael asked, "Half of what Gregory Marks said, I heard from you first. What he teaches is what you live."

Klaus was still chuckling. "I'm a soccer coach and I try to be a good one my friend. That's my mission."

"Do you ever regret not taking that job up in Hamburg?" Michael asked.

Klaus shook his head. "When you make the right decision, there are no second thoughts."

"But how do you cope with all the stress and uncertainty? What are your trade secrets?"

"It's quite simple. I just take one day at a time, rely on the good people around me and look after myself. I still jog every day and I'm careful what I eat, except when Monika makes her famous apple pie, of course! We're no good to anyone if we burn out. Live in the moment and know what you're grateful and thankful for. It's not happy people who are thankful, Michael, it's thankful people who are happy. Spend as much time as you can living and loving, as Monika and I do."

"Funny, Greg used those same words. You're fortunate that you and Monika have each other."

"Yes, we are and we try to let each other know that," Klaus said. "It's important to say these things out loud."

"I know, that's one of the things I wasn't good at with Petra. That became so clear in Davos. I took a lot of things for granted. I thought I had everything in the bag and I screwed up. I realize now how important it is to have a meaningful relationship. I didn't have enough empathy and Petra didn't feel understood. I just couldn't share with her on an emotional level and our relationship suffered from that."

Monika announced that dinner was ready but stopped as Michael popped an antacid tablet into his mouth at the table, "Are you okay?" she asked, concerned.

"I'm fine. My stomach gets sensitive sometimes."

Once at the table, the talk shifted to Monika's work, the challenges she faced and the satisfaction she felt teaching young people.

"It's very rewarding," she said. "I know Klaus feels the same way."

He nodded. "We may not die rich," he said, "but we're doing what feels right for us. It's more about giving than getting in the long run."

"You're both leaving a rich *legacy*. Do you ever think about that?"

There was a long silence before Klaus spoke again. "Our most important legacy comes in how we live each day. I try to be an example to my players. That's easy to say, but tough to do."

"True, but isn't it also what we leave behind?"

Klaus raised his wine glass and toasted, "Then you're part of my legacy, Michael."

"Thank you," Michael said, "I won't forget you said that."

Michael helped Monika clear up in the kitchen after a lovely evening, "Don't give up hope with Petra," she said as she handed him a cloth. "Give her the chance to get to know the 'new and improved' Michael that you're showing us. Let her see the new path you've chosen."

He gave Monika a hug, "I would need to be far newer and much more improved than I am now to even begin to put right all the wrongs, but who knows. Perhaps one day. Right now I am focusing on doing the right things first and trying to be the best me that I can be, for me."

"I think I've already seen some of these changes and I'll call Petra with a friendly update and let's see where we can take it from there. If you're ok with it, why don't I suggest that the four of us get together in Munich at her next concert and go for dinner afterwards, just like we used to."

Michael grinned nervously, "Could you do that Monika? I would love it so much, could you make it happen? I'm not going to get too excited until it's a reality, but I would really appreciate it if you could try."

Monika smiled, "I'm glad you like my idea and I'll let you know what happens, okay?"

Going to sleep that night in his old room in the Mertens' house, Michael thought back to the last three days in Davos. Gregory Marks had pushed for each person to have another participant from the seminar to act as a mentor/coach to keep the process alive for the next 100 days. Greg even shared examples of participants keeping contact many years after the training. One pair even came to one of his leadership camps in Canada together, two years after meeting in Davos.

Michael and Saskia were paired together to be each other's peer coaches with the aim of supporting and challenging each other by phone, email or, ideally meeting each other face-to-face on a regular basis. Michael was looking forward to it and hoped he didn't get too busy with daily business and let it all slip away. Saskia sounded very committed to the process and Michael believed her and wasn't about to let her down. She made arrangements to call him 30 days later to keep the ball rolling. He really felt Greg had got their partnership right. Saskia's different mindset and background would create a great synergy and he was sure she would see and notice things that he didn't. Michael didn't expect this follow-up peer-coaching concept to be part of the seminar and he was actually pleased that someone would be there to keep him focused after it was over. He felt the pressure, albeit welcomed, to get things done and do the "right things first" from the very beginning.

> **"We're doing what's right. It's more about giving, than getting."** I believe I'm learning the difference between the two. It's not only about my ego. I am changing.

PART IV

"EXECUTION: DOING THE RIGHT THING"

CHAPTER 27

Hannah was waiting for Michael when he returned to work on Monday.

"Have you heard about Viktor?" she asked.

"No. Is he back?"

The look on her face spoke volumes.

"He passed away last night."

"I'm very sorry to hear that," Michael's first 'big rock', his talk with Viktor was not going to happen. "I had really hoped to meet him."

"He was a good man. We're all going to miss him," she said sadly.

Hannah's voice cracked and she quickly moved on to the more positive news that the next stage of automation was complete. Stark and his men were just running a few more checks. Michael thanked her and headed to his office in the production facility. He was shocked and a little disorientated but was determined not to lose his focus. He could see Lennard and his assistant hunched over a small monitor, intently watching a line of technical data. From the way Lennard nodded, it was apparent that both men were satisfied, "Congratulations!" Michael said, as he approached. Both men looked proud, but Stark looked exhausted, gaunt and hollow-eyed. For the past week and a half, he had burned the candle at both ends, working at Sunstream all day and overseeing annual maintenance work at Escher Electric in the evenings.

The rest of the day passed quickly for Michael as he sorted through the backlog of emails. He resolved to remember all he had learned from Gregory Marks and to apply it to his work where and when he could. However, he spent most of Tuesday anxiously watching work on the new robotic arm fully aware that it was not one of his 'big rocks', but simply too nervous and excited to do anything else. The four automated stations necessary to meet deadlines on the Hartrand contract would soon be completed!

Michael refocused and turned his thoughts to the workers' council meeting scheduled for the next day. He wanted it to be an interactive session, especially after all he'd learned in Davos. Jotting down points for the agenda, he recalled another of Gregory Marks' maxims: 'Where there's no involvement, there's no commitment'. The best place to start involving the workers might be with memories of Viktor Fuchs.

"I never met Mr. Fuchs," Michael said, as the Tuesday meeting began, "but the more I hear, the more I wish I had. I'd be interested to know how you remember him. Is there anything you'd care to say about this special man?"

The room was silent for an uncomfortably long time and Michael began to regret his choice of opening. Finally, the stories began to flow... the 'fish that got away' taking all the fishing tackle with him, Viktor bringing his dog to work and it getting into the men's lunches, but most memorably, the devotion to his solar energy battery. The final comment, "I hope those people at Escher Electric Head Office remember all he's done for this company," really resonated with Michael.

As if on cue, the boardroom door opened and Ralf Escher quietly took a seat at the table. Michael welcomed him and asked if there was anything he wished to say.

"I'm just here to listen," he smiled.

Michael turned his attention back to the team members, "I can assure you that Viktor's passion and innovation will be remembered. Last week, I talked with a man who met Viktor years ago. He called him a real genius."

"Damn right he was!" Hess interjected.

Michael passed around three photographs of Mr. Fuchs that Hannah had found. He asked the men to decide which one they would like to have made into a large picture for display in the lunchroom lounge. The consensus was a casual snapshot of Viktor Fuchs working in his lab, pipe clenched in his teeth and his face circled by a cloud of tobacco smoke. That was how they wanted to remember him.

Michael congratulated the workers on their progress with the automation project. Work on the assembly equipment had begun and would be complete a week from tomorrow. A few reporters and some of Sunstream's key customers had been invited to witness the launch on Friday morning. He was about to adjourn the meeting but was stopped by a last comment, "These past six months it's been change, change, change. I say it's time for a breather." Several others voiced their agreement.

For the first time during the meeting, Michael felt flustered and angry. The last thing he needed with his boss looking on was a revolt. What did Ralf expect of him in this situation? He needed to show he was in charge, but he also wanted to respect the employees' opinions. He glanced at Ralf, but found no help forthcoming. He just sat listening, with his inscrutable smile. Michael racked his mind, "You're absolutely right that it's been change, change, change. You've had to deal with a lot. The integration of Escher-Sunstream is a big challenge but we have to be prepared for a marathon, not a sprint. It will take time but the good news is that your automation is almost complete. In just a few days, you'll get your 'breather.' But to achieve high volume production and the profits we need to be sustainable, we've got to press on. You can't jump a canyon in a dozen small steps. It takes one big leap to make it across."

"Seems to me we'd get further if we stuck to building batteries, instead of messing about with all these robots!"

"If that were true," Michael responded as calmly as he could, "Viktor Fuchs would not have sold this company. He learned the hard way that it's not enough to build a good battery. We have to build enough batteries to make a good *profit* and, for that, we need to automate. Then things can get back to normal."

Martin Hess slammed his pen on the table, "You know nothing about what's normal! You come here out of the blue and think you can tell us all how to do jobs we've been doing for years?" He stood up, glowering at Michael, "It's Viktor this and Viktor that! But you're wrecking everything he stood for! You never even met the man!" And, with that, he stormed out of the room. Michael adjourned the meeting and the others sheepishly took their leave. Michael sat staring at the agenda on his notepad feeling angry and depressed. Would he ever get anywhere with this workers' council? What on earth had set Hess off?

"Well, that's certainly not what I expected," he said out loud at last.

Ralf looked at him in his usual calm way, "You handled yourself pretty well. Change is stressful. But don't take it personally. It comes with the territory. What's your take on Hess?"

Michael shrugged, "I can't begin to understand that man!"

"Time to terminate? Nadine recommended we get rid of him."

"Maybe. I thought somehow I could work with him but he's dead set against the automation program, he is totally anti-change and so old-fashioned."

"He's living in the past. We need people who look forward."

"Gregory Marks would say he's stuck in his old paradigm."

Ralf chuckled, "Got your money's worth, didn't you?"

"It's one of the best workshops I've ever attended."

"Greg knows it isn't about him, it's about you."

"So, what about Hess?"

Michael hesitated, "Most of the time Martin Hess is a pain in the ass. But he knows this plant like the back of his hand. If we could just get him into the same boat…"

"It's your call. But after what I saw today, I'm not optimistic."

As the two men walked together to the lobby, Ralf took a large manila envelope from his bag, "I almost forgot. Christina Fuchs, Viktor's wife, gave this to me when I visited her the day after Viktor's death. It's full of battery design notes. Apparently Viktor worked feverishly on it right until he died. He told his wife to make sure I got it."

"Have you examined these?" Michael asked.

"Just a quick look. I can't make much of them, but I don't want to judge prematurely. You're the engineer and our new expert on Viktor's handwriting!"

Back in his office, Michael dumped the contents of the envelope onto his desk and spread them across the surface. It was an untidy collection of handwritten battery notes. Most were even harder to read than the notes in the margins of Viktor's books. They would take hours to decipher. Just as he began making notes of his own, Monika called to say she had arranged tickets to hear Petra's orchestra play the next weekend, followed by dinner. It had been a long and tough day and Michael was tired but he returned to his deciphering with renewed energy and a positive smile playing at the corners of his mouth.

On Thursday morning, Michael was reading a copy of Nadine Peters' written warning detailing Hess' insulting behavior as he swaggered into his office.

"You want to see me?"

"Have a seat," Michael said.

Hess scowled but sat down.

"I have concerns about your behavior at the meeting this week. I'm not here to criticize you as a person, Martin, but your comments were way out of line."

"I say it as I see it."

"You were insulting. Nobody's been telling you how to do your job and nobody is wrecking the work of Viktor Fuchs. The only way we'll keep his vision alive is to automate this plant as fast as we can afford to and then get busy developing his newest solar battery."

Hess snorted, "You sit there, high and mighty in Viktor's chair, but you'll never be half the man he was."

Michael took a deep breath, "Martin, I appreciate that you cared deeply for Mr. Fuchs, but you're not the sole defender of his dream. From what I gather, it's much bigger than you seem to realize."

"What do you know? You never worked with him."

"No, Martin, I never had that good fortune but if Mr. Fuchs were still alive, I'd be first in line to meet him."

"He wouldn't have much time for the likes of you," Hess stood up, "Anything else? I have work to do."

"Yes, I want to come back to that last meeting. First, your comments weren't constructive. Second, they weren't smart with Escher in the room."

Hess smirked, "You can run around with your nose up your boss's rear. I'll keep my headup." And, again, he turned to leave.

"Martin!" Michael reached into the folder and held up Nadine Peters' warning letter. "You already have one of these issued for misconduct and you're not an elected member of the workers' council. You don't have any special privileges."

"Better men than you have tried to get rid of me and I'm still here."

"Martin, get this through your thick skull. I'm not trying to get *rid* of you. I'm trying to save your job. We need to find a way to work together."

"Bullshit!"

For the second time in two days, the Sunstream foreman stormed out on him. "Time to terminate" was probably right. Michael scanned Nadine Peters' letter once more then began to draft his own. It was his responsibility to 'deal with resistance to change' and he would not shed any tears when Martin Hess finally got what he deserved.

> **If I understood Greg correctly, by being responsible I keep promises not make excuses. I focus on things that I can influence. I have an important choice to make here and it's not going to be an easy one …I wish Hess had learned about paradigm shifts and heard the bit about synergy and diversity…I wonder if he can change..? Can I influence him or is it already too late?**

Michael was determined to leave his work problems in Düsseldorf for the weekend as he sat on the plane on Friday afternoon with a chest full of his own turbulent nerves. He felt as if his heart were trying to jump out of his chest. He so desperately wanted everything to go well.

At the concert, Michael watched the joy and enjoyment of the music written all over Petra's face. He'd missed that look, the one that said a million wonderful things without the need for words. Michael's eyes welled up and Monika just smiled and put her hand on his. Could he do the same and share his thoughts and feelings with her? He was frustrated that the thoughts and good intentions he had been having recently seemed to get lost as soon as he tried to verbally express them. He knew he had to work on this if he really wanted to connect with Petra emotionally.

Michael felt surprisingly at ease during the meal and, for a while, it almost felt like old times as they chatted about people they knew, Michael's new job, the Swiss seminar and, of course, the music. "I know I've heard that last piece somewhere before," Michael said, "It's so beautiful."

"I love Bedrich Smetana," replied Petra becoming animated, "It was written to sound as though you were traveling down a river."

"I could imagine that!"

"Do you know the most amazing thing of all? He was deaf when he composed it! Can you imagine that?"

Klaus and Monika had subtly excused themselves to have a drink with their friends at the bar, and give the two of them some space as they chatted. Michael decided that it was now or never. Taking his journal from his inside pocket, he slid it in front of Petra and whispered, "Klaus gave me this journal in hospital. He said it would be a good place to write my goals, to see them, to believe them and to start to achieve them. It took me awhile to use it in the way that Klaus intended but now it is the place I write down my innermost feelings. It's where I really came to grips with who I was, who I want to be and who I want to spend my life with."

Michael took a deep breath, "You had good reasons to leave me when you did and I am ashamed that I am responsible for those reasons. My journal notes gradually became letters to you when I felt incapable of putting how I feel into spoken words. I can't think of myself without seeing you by my side. I want you to read this journal, Petra, I want you to know what I've been thinking, what I'm hoping for and what I wish with all my heart will come true."

As he handed his well-worn journal to Petra, she reached out her hands and held it for a moment. "I know I've made a mistake, many mistakes, I know how much I've hurt you and I'm painfully aware that it's possibly too late but I can't let it all go without sharing my feelings with you, without telling you how I feel. I just can't live with all that bottled up inside me."

Petra opened the journal but still said nothing.

"I hope you can read my writing!" Michael laughed nervously.

Petra was quiet for another moment and then shut the journal and looked up at him, "I look forward to reading it. Thank you, Michael." She smiled at him a little nervously and slid it into her handbag as Klaus and Monika rejoined them. Greg had told them to be vulnerable and that was about as vulnerable as he had ever felt in his life. It had exhausted him and his heart was pounding so hard in his chest that he was certain the entire restaurant must be able to hear it.

A strange buzzing woke Michael, and for a moment, he was completely disorientated before he realized that he was in his old room at Klaus and Monika's and the buzzing was coming from his phone. It was pitch black. Michael nervously gropped for his cell phone wondering what kind of emergency it must be and panic gripped him as he saw Petra's number on the screen, "Petra? What's wrong? What's happened?"

He could hear her crying softly, "Petra! What is it?"

"Hi Michael. I'm sorry, I didn't mean to scare you. It's just…" She trailed off. "I just thought I'd look at your journal before going to bed and, well, I never got to bed. Oh, Michael. I don't know whether to laugh or cry, whether to slap you or hug you. Why the hell could you never say any of this to me before? Why did you keep it all in? Why did you keep me in the dark? What's the good of a partnership if we both have to guess what the other is thinking and feeling? I had no idea, Michael. I went through hell trying to accept that you would never be open and straight with me anymore. That's what made me fall in love with you all those years ago and you took that part of our love, the honesty, away. Why…" She started crying again softly.

"I'm sorry. I didn't give it to you to upset you. Oh, Petra. I'm so, so sorry. For everything."

"I see someone in this journal that I used to know, that I used to love so much, but who I haven't seen in real life for a very long time. I need to know the truth. I need to know who you really are, Michael. Does that sound ridiculous?"

"No. No, it really doesn't. It's exactly what I've been trying to get clear in my own head and now, I think I know. No... I know, I know! I'm responsible for where I go from here. I know my mission in life and I know my mission can only work side by side with you."

"No excuses? No blame?"

"No excuses or blame. I promise. You and the clear goals in my journal can hold me fully accountable!"

Petra giggled, "Don't you worry, Mr. Weber, we will!"

"Petra, let's get away!" he said without thinking, "Let's just go! I so need to be with you, I have to show you how much I love you."

"Just like that? Where? How..?

"Yes, just like that. I want the time to tell you everything. I want to share everything with you and I know exactly where, let's go back to the wine region in southern Germany, let's go to Bacherach! Do you remember how happy we were there?"

"Michael Weber! You just want to drink wine!" she laughed, "How could I forget. Yes. I'd love to. But how? When?"

"Leave that to me. Right now, you have to make me a promise; go to bed and sleep thoughts of those vineyards, the sunshine and me, okay?"

"Sounds perfect! I have concerts all next weekend but the weekend after that I'm free."

"Great. I'll make it work for then. I do love you Petra, so very much. I'm sorry I've been such an idiot."

"Good-night Michael. Let's concentrate on the future now and see what that brings, shall we?"

"Deal. Good-night."

Michael felt a tremendous weight being lifted from his soul. His head was buzzing now so he used his phone to make an online booking with the same little hotel up by the castle where he and Petra had spent so many lazy and wonderful hours. Thoughts turned to dreams as he drifted back off to sleep with a smile on his face.

The next week, Michael was kept busy checking the progress on plans for the upcoming assembly and getting the portrait of Viktor ready for display. He threw himself into decoding Viktor Fuchs' battery notes long into each evening and, hour-by-hour, page-by-page, he struggled to make sense of them. A gut feeling that this was going to be a huge part of their future drove him onwards. He understood enough of the technical parts to sense the plan was incomplete but he still had hope. Michael could make out the letters with increasing frequency, but not the meaning of the words they formed. Was there a code to crack or simply pain medication-induced gibberish?

He showed Hannah one of the mystifying pages the next morning.

"Can you make head or tail of this?" he asked.

She carefully examined the strange words and symbols, but shook her head, "It's not any shorthand I've seen. Sorry."

"Any ideas?"

"I never handled Viktor's notes," she said, "You should talk to Thomas."

Thomas Neumer had been Viktor's lab assistant and now worked with the design department at Escher Electric. Michael called him immediately and asked him to stop by the Sunstream plant on his way home. Michael got quickly to the point, "Lennard Stark told me that Viktor Fuchs was 'the heart and soul of this place.' What can you tell me about him? What *drove* him?"

"What drives any inventor? Some passion or madness the rest of us are spared. Viktor had it bad. He lived, breathed and dreamed batteries. He was trying to change the way batteries were made, but he didn't have the money and the creditors kept squeezing him. That's why he sold to Mr. Escher. He was staking every cent on the next big thing. His addiction I suppose."

"Did you work with him on this new battery?" Michael asked.

"We never got that far. There were problems Viktor couldn't solve and then he got sick. Mr. Escher put me on another project."

"Would you mind looking at some notes Viktor made after he left here?"

Michael handed over the original documents along with his typed transcripts and watched Thomas for several minutes as he sat leafing through the papers.

"Well...?" Michael asked nervously.

"This...this is amazing!" Thomas studied the page again and then looked up. "Besides me, you're the first person I've met who could make out Viktor's writing."

"But does it make sense?"

"Oh, yes. This is pure Viktor."

"I was afraid it was gibberish. *Tepo-P? Tepo-N?*"

"Viktor's shorthand. Terminal post-positive. Terminal post-negative."

It was the best news Michael had had all day, "Is it something we can build?"

"Is there more?" Thomas asked.

Michael opened the folder containing the remaining scraps of paper, all scribbled with notes. Thomas meticulously arranged them in an order only he understood, then hunched over each pile, muttering to himself and becoming increasingly more excited.

"You did it, Viktor! You really *did* it!" He finally shouted.

"But is it something we can *build?*" Michael demanded more impatiently than he intended.

"Oh, yes!" Thomas pointed to one of Viktor's sketches, "Don't you see? There's no wasted space. These connectors go over cell walls rather than through them. There's more starting power and lots more storage. He's pushed the limits at every step. This makes the Fuchs' Six Volt obsolete as well as all other batteries."

"Do our competitors have anything like this?"

"Nothing! I didn't think it could be done, but Viktor wouldn't quit, not even when he got sick."

"Can we produce it in large quantities?"

Thomas pointed to another sketch with strange symbols, "He's factored that into the design. You can build this one faster and cheaper than any of our batteries at the Escher plant but it will take another big investment to get us up to that point. But wow, this is revolutionary technology."

Michael asked Thomas to keep the news quiet until he could inform Ralf Escher. This discovery could change everything. Before he could sleep that night, Michael tried to clarify his thoughts:

For the first time I really understand what Klaus meant when he talked about an 'inner voice.' I know now what I have to do; bring Viktor's battery through its final design stage and into high volume production. It's not just about work. This is personal. This is Viktor's legacy and it may become my own.

He was so excited that he picked up the phone. He needed to talk to Petra again.

CHAPTER 28

J ust before ten o'clock on Friday morning, Hannah called to say that the customer representatives and reporters had arrived. "This is our chance," Michael thought, as he walked down the corridor to the Sunstream lobby, "to demonstrate the progress Sunstream has made. It's a shame that Ralf can't be here to see proof that his decision to acquire Sunstream was a smart one."

Unfortunately, Lennard's mood was disapproving and impatient and Michael was shocked to see how pale he looked. The robotic assembler had taken him longer than expected to program, he hadn't been home all night and he protested that he hadn't had time to do a practice run in advance. Desperate to escape Stark's negativity, Michael entered the lobby crowded with reporters, customer reps and the full Escher sales team. He took a deep breath, smiled and shouted, "Good morning!" and the din of voices hushed.

"We've invited you here this morning," he said, "to celebrate a milestone in the history of this company; the launch of Escher-Sunstream's new, automated battery assembly. The benefit for us, and for our customers, is improved quality and reduced production costs. Before we go into the production area," he continued, "I'd like to tell you about the man who created this solar battery. Viktor Fuchs was not just a gifted inventor. His vision was larger than batteries. His goal was to make alternative energy more feasible and he dedicated his life to creating better ways to store it. The result was the Fuchs Six Volt.' He strived to make alternative energy affordable, storable and widely available. A year ago, he sold this company to Ralf Escher in the secure knowledge that the production expertise of Escher Electric could take his vision to the next level. This is the reason for today's celebration."

Michael led the group into the assembly area where Stark was standing at the controls of the new equipment with the white battery casings for the Hartrand contract lined up on the conveyor belt behind them.

"In the past six months," Michael said, "our Operations Manager, Lennard Stark, and his team have automated the entire battery assembly. Launching the 'cell assembler' this morning is the final step. Automation will result in a substantial increase in our production capacity and will help us to work smarter, not harder. Now we can be a truly global company. This is a huge step for Escher-Sunstream," he declared, drawing attention towards the robotic arm. He nodded to Lennard to start the automation and as the first battery casing inched forward, the robotic arm sprang to life, picking up a lead plate and nimbly inserting it into place. The casing slid smoothly on toward the next station. There was a smattering of applause and cameras flashing as they recorded the scene.

Michael's heart sank painfully in his chest as the arm made a frightening grating sound when inserting the next plate and he saw Lennard become paler still as he stared intensely at the arm returning with another square piece. This time, the arm seemed to hit the casing askew, tipping it over and knocking the cell plate to the floor. After a moment of dead silence, a burst of laughter errupted from the crowd.

"Just a minor teething glitch, folks!" Michael assured the group as two reporters headed towards the exit, "Lennard will have it sorted out in no time."

Michael sat in his office staring at the phone. He owed Ralf Escher an explanation, but what should he say? That the promotion had been a disaster? This could not have come at a worse time and Michael couldn't see how he could help. Stark and his men were once again reprogramming the machine and running diagnostics. Every seven or eight casings, the new arm malfunctioned. Michael had overruled Lennard's objections to the premature publicity and his stonily silent disapproval was palpable. A knock at Michael's door made him jump. Lennard reported that he had the assembly machine working.

"Great!" Michael jumped up from his chair.

"That's the good news."

"There's *bad* news?"

Lennard nodded, "The problem isn't with the assembler. It's the actual battery casings. They're warped."

Michael followed Lennard to the assembly room and joined the small, dispirited group there. He took a battery casing and a square lead plate from the conveyor belt and placed the two together to demonstrate.

"How many are like this?

Lennard shrugged, "Who knows? They all *look* okay."

He threw an accusingly look at Michael as he snapped, "Didn't you use to work for that P.E.M. company?"

"I did."

"Well then, it's up to you and them to find a solution…if there is one!"

Without another word, Stark walked out of the back plant door. His job was done. Michael picked up a defective casing in each hand and returned to his office. The problem sat squarely in his lap and he had no idea what to do next. Warped casings? This was not just an embarrassing setback; it was a full-scale disaster. This put the whole Hartrand project in jeopardy.

Michael sat staring at the white battery casings on his desk with their *Guangdong* imprint. How confidently he had promoted those molds and products as a salesman for P.E.M. and now one of these very products threatened to sink his new company.

"Your company shafted us!" came Hess' accusing voice in the doorway.

"*This* is my company, Martin," he said, "and, yes…we have a complication, but so far nobody's shafted."

"Your dummies can't even make a simple casing!"

"Martin, don't make this worse than it is. I know these people. They're good and they make good products. Something's gone wrong, but we'll get it sorted out."

"Viktor must be turning in his grave," Hess muttered and stalked away.

Hannah called him to say that Ralf Escher was coming to the plant to meet with Michael. No one needed to say that it would not be a fun conversation. In the time available, Michael was determined to do as much damage control as possible and began by calling the P.E.M. office in Frankfurt. He fumbled an explanation about how the warpage was not visible and Sunstream's desperate need for quick replacement casings.

"Send your casings to Design and we can check for any possible warps. If this is P.E.M.'s responsibility, we'll help you in any way we can, but these things take some time," came the calm and professional answer.

When Ralf Escher arrived, his usual calmness seemed to have disappeared. He fidgeted with his glasses and rubbed his tired eyes.

"I guess you've heard the news from here?"

Ralf nodded.

"It's been a rough couple of days, but we're making headway. I just had a conversation with P.E.M. and they assure me they will handle our problem as soon as they can."

"I'm sure you've done what you could," Ralf answered at last, "but I'll get right to the point. Marina and I have reached a decision."

"You're going to take Nadine Peter's advice and sell Sunstream?"

"Worse than that, I think I have to shut it down. Financially, it's become almost impossible"

"But we're so close to making it! If we just get over this hump, we've got a great future ahead."

"There've been too many 'ifs', Michael..." He frowned: "*If* Viktor had not become sick...*if* the economy had not gone soft...*if* I got more credit from my banks... *if* these battery cases were not warped...I expected some ups and downs, but this time we've hit the bottom. We are totally over-stretched and we have taken on too much risk already."

Michael stood up, "Before we go any further, let me show you something."

He led Ralf down the corridor, past the front lobby and into the boardroom. He pointed to Viktor Fuchs' battery notes that still lay on the table where he and Thomas had arranged them.

"You remember the packet Mrs. Fuchs gave you? It is a game changer! It puts us in the drivers' seat with this new technology!"

Ralf walked around the table, examining each stage of the Fuchs' design before walking over and putting his hand on Michael's shoulder.

"A few weeks ago this might have made a difference. But it's too late for dreams. The reality is, we can't deliver what we don't have. I wanted you to be the first to know."

"Believe me," Michael almost shouted, panic rising, "it looks worse than it is."

"It's not all bad news. Marina and I want to offer you a permanent job with us at Escher Electric. We'll need your help planning and leading the shutdown here, of course. Then we would want you to head up the remaining Escher sales team."

Michael said nothing. These were uncharted waters and he had so much more than his own job to consider. What about all the good workers employed by Sunstream? What about realizing Viktor's dream? Could Michael let him down? He had no infusion of capital to bring to this company, but he could give it everything else he had.

"Ralf," he said finally, "your offer means more than I can say. But sink or swim, Sunstream is my *mission*. If this company goes down, I'll go with it. I just need more time."

"Sometimes, we have to choose between what our heart wants and what our head says."

"When you hired me, you said you had a hunch about my 'bringing something extra'. Now's the time to put your trust in me."

For the first time that morning, Ralf smiled, "Michael Weber, you play an even stronger poker hand than Lennard Stark. I haven't changed my mind, but you just won yourself seven days. At that point, I'll have to make my final decision."

"Thank you. I'll do my best to see that we all win."

One week. It wasn't much but, if he failed, Michael was determined it would not be for lack of trying. His next step was awkward, but necessary.

He picked up the phone and dialled the number for P.E.M.'s Vice-President, Gunnar Voss. He had to emphasize the emergency to the person at the top. Michael explained the problem and the urgency of the situation and that he had already shipped several of the faulty casings to P.E.M.'s design department for analysis.

Mr. Voss listened without interruption before promising vaguely to look into the problem. He was obviously trying to terminate the conversation but Michael persisted, "How are you handling the warpage problem with other companies? That marketing survey I put together for you last year included complaints about the goods from Guangdong."

At once Gunnar Voss was more candid and obviously mindful of his caller's inside knowledge. Yes, there had been a couple of other instances. Both were production errors and P.E.M. was working with the people in Guangdong to rectify them. Michael stated again his urgent need for replacement casings. Could P.E.M. send him another mold by the end of the week? Mr. Voss agreed, but was definitely not taking total responsibility for the problem. Clearly the warpage was a problem no one was willing to own.

One week. This was make-or-break with no margin for error. Michael closed his office door and asked Hannah to hold all calls. He needed to think, not as a salesman or even a leader, but as an engineer, step by step, breaking down the problem and considering all the angles and options.

What were the solutions? A local company could provide replacement casings if they had a new mold but they needed to identify all the usable casings they already had and start the first run by Wednesday or Thursday at the very latest. All replacements must be in stock by the time the ones they had were used up. They could extend overtime shifts to get back on schedule and complete the Hartrand contract by mid-August. The additional costs would be a hard sell with Ralf, but if they did not deliver on time, there were huge penalties built into the Hartrand contract.

Mold flaws! The warpage might occur in the production process, as Mr. Voss contended, but what if it came from the mold design itself?

They could appear again in the replacement casings and all his efforts might come to nothing.

Just unbelievable! Why on earth do all these bad things always happen to me? Why can't just one thing go smoothly? Just once in my life! And why now, when it's make or break? And why does everything always fall apart at the last possible moment? Was he just jinxed? Was this company jinxed? The weight of the problem suddenly loomed up and over him as Michael became ever angrier and more frustrated with the hopelessness of the situation. He was completely furious when phone rang. He'd told Hannah to hold his calls and then forgotten to turn his own mobile phone off.

"Hi Michael, it's Saskia. How are things going at your end?"

"Saskia, look, sorry but now is not a good time for me, I'm swamped here, okay. I'll call you back another time."

"Monkey business, Michael?"

"Wild, angry ones and more than I can handle, so if you'll excuse me..."

"Even more reason for us to talk! Take a deep breath...Now, tell me what's going on. I want the short version..."

Having to explain all his 'monkey' issues clearly and concicely helped Michael to focus his energy and he felt himself calming down. The process of talking the problems through brought clarity to the situation. He was able to pinpoint the core issues and consider them rationally rather than emotionally. Saskia asked questions from another perspective and this helped him to rethink the situation in terms of solutions rather than problems.

By the time they said good-bye half an hour later, Michael felt so much better. His problems weren't solved yet, but he felt separate from them, empowered, focused and in control of what had to be done.

CHAPTER 29

By morning, Michael had decided on the best course of action. He called an old university friend who had specialized in mold design and asked him for help. He said little as Michael launched into an explanation that the warped cases from P.E.M.'s Guangdong plant seemed totally random, sometimes in one cavity, sometimes in another.

"Could the problem be the mold itself?" asked Michael.

"Sure," came the non-commital response.

"How can we find out for certain?"

"You'll need a flow analysis and design verification."

"Can you do that for us? You're the only person I know who can give a straight answer as to whether we're dealing with a production problem or a faulty mold. Unfortunately, we have a tight timeline. A very tight deadline."

"I'll see what I can do."

"Thanks. Do you need the mold?"

"Yes and we'll need all the specs and some defective casings. Your company should have copies of everything," he added, "send me those and I'll look at them immediately."

"Brilliant. I owe you one. Thanks."

When Michael arrived at work on Wednesday morning he called for Martin Hess to come to his office as soon as possible.

"We need to talk," Michael began as Martin arrived in his oily overalls.

"More empty threats?" he muttered, looking around at the mess of folders all over the office floor. Michael took a deep, calming breath and laid the specs for the P.E.M. battery casings on the top of his equally cluttered desk. Hess sat looking at Michael with a defiant glare in his eyes but said nothing.

"The last time we met I said I was trying to save your job. I'm also trying to save *my* job."

A look of triumph swept across the foreman's face, "You royally screw up and now you want me to bail you out?"

Michael recoiled, "Martin, this may be the last conversation we have, so get off your high horse and *listen*! Ralf Escher has decided to shut down Sunstream."

Hess stared at Michael and the shock was obvious.

"He can't do that!"

"He can…and he probably has to. He took a big risk when he bought this place and now he's losing his shirt."

"So, just like that, we're all out of work?"

"The decision has been a long time coming. I've tried to tell you every way I could that the stakes were high. This problem with the battery casings is the final straw."

Hess scrutinized Michael's face, "You're taking it mighty easy."

"Mr. Escher has offered me a permanent position with Escher Electric."

"That figures!"

"That's one way the story could go," Michael said quietly, "but I've turned it down. I told you before, Martin, *this* is my company and, sink or swim, I'm sticking with it."

Again, Hess stared at Michael, "Then you're a bigger fool than I thought." But the remark sounded more like a compliment than a criticism.

"Here's something you should see," Michael said, waving his hand over the notes and sketches for Viktor Fuchs' new battery, "I think it's worth the risk. Viktor worked on this almost to the day he died. If we want to be true to his dream, we have to look to the future not get stuck in the past. All the automation we've been doing is part of his plan. Viktor believed that expanding and automating production would bring his Fuchs' Six Volt the credit it deserves and generate profits to finance this new battery. That was his plan but it might be too late."

Hess continued to stare at the papers, "I figured you guys were milking us for a quick buck."

"Who's going to care about Viktor's new battery if we can't make money with the old one? You say I'm a fool for sticking with Sunstream? I don't care. I can find another job if I have to and so can you if you learn to pull in your horns. But if the company shuts down, the new battery dies with it. Martin, who's going to build this battery for Viktor?"

Hess gave Michael a bewildered look then sat up straight and asked, "What can we do?"

"We have to get back on track and show that we can complete the Hartrand contract on time and on budget. I've persuaded Ralf to give us a week and that's now down to five days. If we can't turn this casing problem around, it's over for all of us, Martin, including Viktor."

As Hess digested that information, Michael continued, "I looked at your résumé yesterday and saw something that gives me hope. Before you came to Sunstream, you worked in plastics?"

The foreman nodded.

"How familiar are you with injection molding?"

"I've forgotten more than you'll ever know."

"Well, for your sake and mine, let's hope you can remember it all. I don't know if we can solve this problem, but I know I can't do it without you. Can we commit to working together?"

Michael reached out his hand and Hess shook it with an iron hard grip, "I'll do it for Viktor."

"Good," Michael said, "Now…what would you recommend as our first step?"

Hess thought for a moment and said, "Find out how many casings are defective and get the good ones into production."

"Agreed. Make plans to start the run as soon as possible. Next step?"

"Line up a company to make the replacements."

"A new mold should arrive on Thursday. I've been trying to find a plastics company able to help us but I'm not having any luck."

"Leave that to me. I still have some contacts."

"Good. I have a friend double-checking the mold design," Michael added.

Hess glanced at him about to say something but then nodded and headed out the door.

Early in the afternoon, Michael headed down to where Hess had assembled a small group of men. Each man had a small electronic measuring device and was inserting it carefully into the cavity of each battery casing. The stack of defective white casings was growing, but the usable pile was larger. Only one in every five or six proved to be warped, not as severe a problem as Michael had feared.

"We'll have enough done to start a run first thing in the morning," Hess called over the joking and banter. Not only was the foreman gifted with his hands, it was clear he had a strong rapport with the men.

"This is your idea of *automation*?" One of the workers teased Michael.

Michael laughed, "This is my idea of survival! I call this 'manage by panic', but it is working so let's keep going."

Michael's cell phone rang and he excused himself. Moments later he returned and took Martin Hess aside, "That was my friend in Frankfurt," he whispered. "He's run tests on those specs I sent him and he says our problem's with the mold. Are we screwed?"

Unfortunately, Hess couldn't give him the answer he so badly wanted to hear.

"I certainly hope not," Michael thought as he walked back to his office, "not if we believe in involvement, diversity and leadership. I have a committed bunch of workers here. I will not let them down. Where there's a will, there's a way."

He picked up the phone to bounce a few ideas off Klaus, who was becoming another regular sparring partner and always helped Michael to see things from a different point of view. He could now take into account many perspectives as he had Klaus, Saskia and Petra to talk to.

CHAPTER 30

On Thursday, Michael compiled his weekly report to Ralf Escher a day early, hoping to give him and Marina time to reconsider the future of Sunstream. The new battery mold from P.E.M. would arrive today. That meant they would be able to start full production on the profitable Hartrand contract. Michael remembered Ralf saying that 'in business cash is king' and he would be happy now seeing some cash flow. Martin Hess had saved the day with his solution for the mold flaw crisis: Raise the barrel heat, increase the injection pressure and extend the cooling time. In the long term, redesigning the mold would be necessary, but this temporary approach could ensure Sunstream's immediate survival.

Days ago, Michael would not have thought such dramatic turnarounds in an individual were possible. Martin had a cheeky attitude toward authority, but he was showing that his gifts could be directed to positive ends and that he, too, may be shifting his paradigms. He had even agreed to training on the new equipment once this crisis was past and had shown interest in some leadership training. Michael also realized that his own new style of leading, coaching and communication had been a factor in this as well. Martin was very grateful that Michael was showing more presence in the plant, something which Michael called 'Leadership by walking around' or LBWA.

Determined to take Klaus' advice and get back on the Gregory Marks track, Michael dug out his schedule planner and tried once again to prioritize his work tasks, a practice that had lapsed since his return from

Davos. With the death of Viktor, the planning and debacle of the promotional event, the strained meetings with Hess and the warped casing crisis, his 'big rocks' had become lost amidst the monkeys playing on a beach of pebbles and sand. He'd never been so ready for a weekend away in his life.

The sun was shining down on the vineyards of Bacherach as Petra and Michael lay on a blanket in their favourite spot. The picnic basket was empty as was the wine bottle. It had been a weekend of rollercoaster emotions and confessions that had left them exhausted yet, somehow calmer. The unsaid had been said, however painful that had proven to be. Michael had been determined to find a way forward. They had started the weekend by recalling one after the other of the countless reasons why they had fallen in love with each other in the first place. This anchored them back to the good times and the foundation they'd had when the relationship started. They talked about how they had respected each others strengths and how they complimented each others personalities. They both shared their favorite memories of the good times they'd had together. It was obvious that they were falling in love again.

The highlight for Michael was when he used the method that he learned in Davos and got Petra to open up and share for over 90 minutes about her values and her ideal picture of the future. It was apparent that she loved articulating her vision from the way her eyes shone as she spoke. Her renewed trust for Michael was evident when she shared her most intimate thoughts and expressed what she really wanted out of life. Eventually he shared his thoughts and notes from when he had done the mental training and brainwriting session in Davos. They were excited to see how much alignment and common ground they had as they shared and compared their ideas. This discussion created an emotional bond that led them to write a few thoughts on paper describing how they wanted their relationship to be from now on. It was like starting a new chapter in their relationship story:

- **We communicate our feelings openly and without fear of judgement.**
- **By accepting each other's feelings we become emotionally closer.**
- **We support and promote each other's strengths.**

- **Our relationship comes first.**
- **We are honest with each other in everything we say.**
- **We learn from our mistakes and not dwell on them.**
- **Our 1-1 time together is always a priority.**

It had been going so well until Petra made one difficult request and this led to a long stretch of silence. Michael finally replied softly, "Petra, I simply can't commit to taking a three month sabbatical with all that's going on. This year is going to be a huge challenge-IF I still have a job at all."

"Think about how good it would be for us, Michael. Think about how much this weekend has done for us already!"

"The timing's just wrong. In my new position, I have a huge responsibility and I can't let Ralf and Marina down now, not after they've placed such trust in me. Let's think about this again once things are steady at work. Please?" Petra looked at Michael and he smiled at her, "In the meantime, we will make time for more weekends away together, okay?"

On Monday, Michael met Ralf at his office with no further talk of the plant closure. Their conversation focused instead on Michael's plans for the development of Viktor's new battery. The level of excitement rose as the two men started to brainstorm and visualize their futures.

After a quick walk around the plant to speak briefly, but as positively as possible, with members of the workforce, Michael settled down at his desk to read through the file of Viktor Fuchs' scribbled speeches that he'd found. They would be valuable when it came time to market the new battery. He sent an email to the Marketing department, requesting copies of the video clips recorded months before and he knew he had to be personally involved in the new battery launch. It was now officially being called Viktor's Legacy.

In early August, before the deadline, Michael was not alone when the final pallet for Hartrand was shipped. The plant closed down thirty minutes early and all workers assembled in the shipping room. The orange and black forklift had been washed for the occasion and the workers proudly watched as the last load of cargo was transported to the waiting semi-trailer.

Ralf Escher personally thanked all of the Sunstream staff for their contribution during the challenging past year, they could see and feel his belief and confidence as he spoke, "We've seen more ups and far too many downs than any of us expected," he said, "but this company has survived and I'm confident it has a great future." He commended Michael and Martin, in particular, for their resolution of the battery casing crisis.

Michael's turn came next. He walked to the front, just as the applause for Escher's comments waned. Even before he spoke, the men cheered. Momentarily stuck for words, Michael began, "Six months ago, at our first all-hands meeting, I asked you to say thank you; thank you to Ralf, who owns this company and to Viktor who created it. I asked you to embrace change and to strive to achieve challenging goals. Working together, we have done that. It hasn't been easy and I want you to know how proud I am of you. Ralf Escher is proud and I know that Viktor Fuchs would be proud. You've helped this company not just to survive, but to thrive and become profitable. We have a future and our purpose is clear."

The workers cheered again, including Martin, and Michael almost choked up. He had two more things to say before they broke out the champagne. First, Sunstream would soon resume its work on the automation program. "Even better," Michael said, "Sunstream is now developing a new solar battery, one designed by Viktor Fuchs in the last year of his life. It will be a game-changer. It will bring affordable energy storage to everyone in the world that has sunlight. It is his gift to the future and his legacy." The room erupted once again with cheers and shouts.

"I guess my hunch about you has proven itself!" Ralf said, as he handed Michael a glass of champagne, "you're becoming quite a leader!"

Michael had no time to savor the compliment. His heartburn was back and the champagne burned all the way to his stomach. Maybe he was getting an ulcer? He thanked Ralf for his confidence and headed back toward his office to grab an antacid tablet and call Petra with the good news. He wanted to celebrate with her and he was eager to recall all that had happened with Saskia too. He was becoming a better leader but he knew where his real support and motivation had come from over this traumatic period. Those two ladies were as much a part of the team that had pulled off the impossible as anyone else. Petra and Saskia had kept him grounded through that difficult phase and he wanted them to celebrate with him too.

CHAPTER 31

Michael arrived early for his Monday morning meeting with Ralf Escher and was surprised to find Marina in his office.

"Good morning, Marina. This is a pleasant surprise!"

"Good morning, Michael. It's good to see you too but we have an issue to discuss that isn't pleasant at all."

"Oh?" Michael turned his attention to Ralf who stood up from his desk to greet him,

"I'll get right to the point; Hartrand is planning a huge expansion and have made us an incredible offer to buy our whole company. They have a very aggressive strategic plan where they want to grow by acquisitions and they have the financial backing from a venture capital organization. With the economy as is it is, we're not likely to see another offer like it."

"Have you accepted? Is it a done deal?"

"We spent the whole weekend talking about it but we wanted to talk to you before making a decision. I wasn't looking for this, Michael, but I also can't ignore it. It's no secret that our investment into Sunstream has stretched us to near breaking point these past months. It's been nerve-wrecking."

"Ralf and I have been talking and trying to come up with the best solution or a third option and we would like to hear your opinion," Marina interjected.

Michael was shocked into silence. He was fully aware that his job was not secure but, after all they'd been through, after all they'd fought for, after their amazing turn around and success? He was upset, but he took a deep breath and tried to remain calm. He fixed his gaze on the glass bowl with its rocks and sand and arranged his thoughts, "Right from the beginning, you told me my job would be a big challenge," he said, "and it's been that. But I think the opportunities ahead are bigger than ever. Sunstream has increased its production and expanded the product line. The automation is making a huge difference and our new battery, Viktor's Legacy, will give us a big advantage and set us up for an incredible future. Why sell out before Sunstream proves itself and achieves its full value?"

Ralf weighed Michael's arguments, "Of course, as you said once before, you have a *vested* interest in keeping your job."

"Yes, I have made an investment and so have you, but this is no longer just 'a job' for me. I'm fully aware that my position here was initially short-term, but I believe Viktor has left us something very special for Escher-Sunstream's future and I can't just sit back and watch his legacy be swallowed by Hartrand. They may even block, delay or prevent this new battery from ever happening as it will affect their existing business too much. Wouldn't the best course be to hold out for long-term returns? It might also be our purpose, our 'mission'. You know the importance of that as well as I do. I think we both want to make a difference and not just a profit."

Ralf nodded, "This is not an easy decision to make. It helps me to hear your commitment to Escher-Sunstream's future and I feel your emotion." He took off his glasses and rubbed his eyes, "Marina? What are your final thoughts and recommendations?"

"This company has been in your family for three generations, Ralf. I doubt that all the Eschers before you had only plain sailing, but this is your call. I know that you want security for our retirement and this sale would give that to us, but not to the people who work here. As you know, this would mean restructuring which means downsizing. Many people would lose their jobs. Whatever you decide, I'm behind you one hundred percent."

Ralf closed his eyes and they all sat with their own thoughts until Ralf broke the silence, "Based on our conversation together, your input and when I truly reflect on our vision and values, I simply have to say 'No' to the Hartrand offer."

Michael hadn't realised he was holding his breath, "You're turning them down?"

"Yes. It most certainly isn't the easiest decision, but I do agree with your assessment."

"To prevent rumors and to be transparent we need to communicate this very quickly. Our employees will be happy to hear it. Make sure all of our leadership team cascades the same message to their people. That will be mission critical and it needs to happen today. This is an example of us doing the 'right things first'."

"We have another idea that I would like your input on," he continued. "Even before this Hartrand purchase offer was on the table, Marina and I had discussed the idea of hiring a General Manager to run the entire Escher-Sunstream organization. We have spent a lot of time thinking about succession planning and our own future. Marina is right about preparing for our retirement and it is time for us to take a step back. We're not getting any younger. Michael, your dedication to this company, to Viktor's legacy and our ability to work honestly together has impressed me," he smiled for the first time that morning, "You know this business well. You think strategically and I'm confident that you will grow our brand and build presence in new markets. You have proven you can do the job and you have proven you can handle a crisis situation, multiple even! All of this has built your character and made you a stronger leader." Ralf continued, "We would like you to become the new General Manager and we think that taking this position could even open a door for you to become a partial owner of this company at some point in the future as part of your payment package. What do you think, Michael? Would you like the job?"

Michael stood up and reached out for a handshake, "I would be honored and proud to accept."

"You've more than proved my original hunch. A few months ago, I saw you as a young man with good technical training, experience in sales and management, the ability to look at the big picture and to think strategically. You were hungry for a challenge. I've watched you become a leader willing to grow, develop and drive change. You've shown empathy for others and a commitment to Sunstream's survival and you've found strengths in the most unexpected people. Martin Hess? Who'd have predicted that?" He chuckled, "that's why I'm confident you can handle this responsibility."

"Thank you," replied Michael, feeling a little awkward as such a torrent of compliments, "I appreciate your faith in me."

"Congratulations, Michael!" Marina shook his hand. "I agree with Ralf. I think you're the right man to bring Viktor's new battery to the market. We need a new Operations Manager for Escher-Sunstream too," she added, "Lennard has been quite ill and has had medical advice to retire on health grounds."

"I'd like to recommend Martin," Michael said after a moment's thought.

"I was afraid you'd suggest that," Ralf smiled. "What do you think his particular qualifications are?"

"He knows how these plants operate better than anyone and he's learned a lot working with Lennard since buying into the idea of automation. He commands respect and hard work from the men and I think it would set a good example for them to see someone chosen from their own ranks. His level of engagement brings energy to others as well."

"What would you say are the man's weaknesses?"

"You've seen them for yourself. He's often critical and temperamental, but that's changing. Much of it stemmed from his loyalty to Viktor Fuchs. Martin was devoted to the man and he risked himself to protect Viktor's vision."

"He didn't understand it."

"No, but now he does and he can communicate it and sells it well. Can you view him as you did me? Someone whose strengths can be strengthened to a world-class level and therefore will create more value for the organization in the future? We will hire for his weaknesses and put people around him with complimentary skills. I will continue to be his coach."

"As always, Michael, you can sell your ideas well, but in your *new* position, *you'll* have to live with who you hire. He will be a key member of your team, remember what Gregory Marks said before you make your final decision, 'in two to three years you will have the team that you deserve, for better or for worse.'"

"Yes, I heard that and I believe it too. I suppose this time it's me with the hunch."

"Well, for everyone's sake, let's hope you can become Martin's new Viktor."

CHAPTER 32

Martin Hess accepted the position of Operations Manager and moved into Viktor Fuchs' old office. Michael relocated to the spare office by the Sunstream boardroom, away from the rumble of the machines and the smell of Viktor's old pipe smoke. After discussing his planning options with Saskia, he tried to divide his time equally between the two plants and provide the leadership needed to turn this into one company. He created common goals and made sure they took time to celebrate small successes and communicated this throughout the whole organization. His all-employee "town hall" meetings were very well received and all employees looked forward to attending. He had made them much more interactive and people were becoming more and more involved. He also made sure that his entire team was communicating the 'why' behind what they were doing and this led to more engagement and motivation from the employees.

Michael led a one and a half day, offsite workshop for his team, including the extended team below them. The team members identified key issues and were given the time to create possible solutions. This workshop also had increased involvement, created new ideas and visually improved commitment. Another benefit of such events was that they raised the level of expectation for Michael's management team to walk the talk and do what they promised. He saw, first hand, what Gregory Marks meant. He also delegated more tasks and he worked diligently to update and fulfill his Integration Plan. Saskia was still following up with him with regular phone calls and he was always excited to update her on his progress and coaching her was also a good learning experience for Michael.

By mid-October, Michael noticed he was gaining weight again and guessed it was from eating on the run. His pants were too snug and his collar buttoned increasingly tightly. Most days he was living on caffeine and sweet snacks to maintain his level of concentration. He knew he was pushing his limits and, most evenings, he trudged up the steps to his apartment satisfied with the steady progress he was making, but ready to sleep the moment his head hit the pillow.

Driving home one beautiful autumn evening, Michael answered his cell phone secretly hoping that there was no crisis in the office, but it was Klaus chiding him for not keeping in touch. Michael explained that his appointment as General Manager for the Escher companies had him swamped with work, "I know it's the right decision," he assured Klaus, "and not just because it pays better. I know my ladder is against the right wall and I have no second thoughts."

Klaus congratulated him on the promotion and, as always, reminded him to maintain balance in his life, to eat well and get plenty of exercise. Klaus was really excited when Michael brought him up to date on the developments with Petra and reminded him to let her know how special she was to him, "Make sure you find enough one to one time with that wonderful lady and keep in touch with your old friends!"

Throughout the weekend, Michael brooded over Klaus' advice. He knew it was meant light-heartedly but it could have come straight from Gregory Marks. He loved his new position and the challenges it brought. He really felt he was seeing and tackling work issues in a more improved and sustainable way, but now he acknowledged to himself that he was only partially on the right track. Since his return from Davos, Michael had lost sight of personal planning and struggled to decide which of the many 'rocks' were actually the biggest. Without question, his scores on the **M.C.C.L.S. model** had improved: **Managing** 50%, **coaching** 15%, **clienting** 10%, **leading** 25%. He was aware that he was still being too much of 'Mr. Fix-it'. He had come so far in some ways, but in others, he knew he had made little progress. As he reflected on The Ten Principles of Leadership and Life notes he had made in Davos, he saw some huge deficits:

Principle 5: *I strive for life balance:* If he were not careful, his work as General Manager would consume his entire life.

Principle 9: I Make Relationship deposits: He needed to stay conscious of Petra's needs and keep doing the small things to make her feel special, loved and important to him. He could not take the relationship for granted as he had done in the past. He knew that and was dedicated to it. He was turning the TV down in his life but he still needed to build more quality one-to-one time with Petra into his weekly plan. He had to remember that love, like leadership, is a verb, he needed to show her that he loves her. He also had to live this principle at work and catch people doing things right and give them more recognition.

Principle 10: I Re-energize: He was finding no time for self-renewal. In the seminar Greg had said to "listen to your body" which he wasn't doing. When he looked in the mirror, he saw it was growing rapidly in the wrong places. Greg had also seen his second chin during the Davos seminar and he could see a third one coming on.

November started poorly even with all his good intentions. He had taken care to create his first weekly schedule in months and had resolved to achieve a more balanced lifestyle but the reality was that he'd hardly begun one task when another demanded his attention. Those damn monkeys again and they were really biting this time! Michael found it harder and harder to stay focused on the company's vision of better energy storage. Even with Petra gradually coming back into his life, he still felt stressed and often worked late into the evenings.

Michael was determined to get a grip on his schedule and decided to complete a Marketing and Sales report on predicted prices for the entire new battery line before leaving for the day. He was still puzzling over the figures an hour later when the sound of the vacuum cleaner in the Sunstream lobby broke his concentration. The office felt hot and stuffy, the piercing whine put his nerves on edge and the fiery stomach acid suddenly rose worse than he had ever known, surging into his throat and out to his neck and jaw. Pulling open his desk drawer, he shook out his last antacid tablet and turned back to the report, but his eyes would barely focus and the top of his head throbbed. He picked up his laptop and walked out of his office to find a more peaceful workspace. He swung open the door to the workers' lounge and flopped down in a chair to catch his breath. He was really more tired than he'd realised. This room felt even stuffier than his office, but he couldn't find the energy to open the window. The plant should not be this hot surely? The lounge door opened and a bright beam of light swept across the far wall. The custodian entered, carrying a plastic barrel, "Sorry to bother you, sir. I need to empty the waste paper baskets."

Michael shuddered, his hands felt cold and clammy and his head was suddenly dizzy. He shut his eyes, but the sensation of an icy hand gripped his throat, cutting off his breath. Another pressed hard against his chest with searing pain. Michael thrashed to and fro in his chair but could not lift his arms. Far away he heard the cutodian's voice, "Are you all right, Mr. Weber? Mr. Weber?"

CHAPTER 33

The nurse tapped Michael on the shoulder, rousing him from a maze of morphine-induced dreams. Where was he? He opened his eyes and recognized his surroundings all too well. Hospital... again. He grappled with his memories...the blare of an ambulance siren, someone holding a mask over his face and the relief the oxygen brought to the searing pain in his chest.

"Is it my heart?" he asked weakly.

"I'm afraid so. The doctor will be with you shortly."

The physician arrived a few minutes later and confirmed Michael's worst fear, a heart attack, unusual for someone under forty, the doctor said, but not impossible. He suspected Michael was one of those once-in-a-lifetime rare cases, unfortunately becoming far too common, especially in the world of business. He would need bed rest and further tests to determine the extent of the damage and the best course of treatment. It would certainly include permanent lifestyle changes.

"Any history of cardiac problems in your family?"

"My father had a heart attack when he was quite young. But I always thought I had my mother's constitution."

"Is she still living?"

"No."

The questions continued: When had Michael first experienced bouts of angina? How severe was his pain? What actions improved or worsened the symptoms? Had he ever been referred to a cardiologist?

"I always thought I had a case of stomach acid. Did my car accident last year have anything to do with this?" Michael asked.

"It's unlikely, more a matter of lifestyle and genetic disposition. You're an engineer?"

"Yes."

"Then you, of all people, should know we have a breaking point. The man who called 911 says you work day and night."

"We've been very busy."

"At the rate you're going, it'll be someone else who's busy. You won't be around to care."

"Is it that bad?"

"I hope this is your wake up call." The doctor looked at Michael sternly before leaving the room, "Unless you make some major changes, your life expectancy is going to be markedly shorter."

Michael's head spun as his thoughts ran away with him, "Lifestyle? Genetic disposition? Why me? Why now?" He struggled to get a grip on the severity of the situation, "A company depends on me. All my life I've tried to make something of myself, to learn more, push harder, serve better and now, just when I was making headway, it's all come to naught. Damn it! How many chances am I going to get before I really wake up and smell the coffee?"

The nurse returned to check his vital signs and asked if he was up to seeing visitors. Ralf and Marina Escher's visit was the best medicine he'd had all day. He told them what little he remembered of his heart attack and what he understood of the prognosis. He needed more tests and probably wouldn't be able to work for a month or two.

Ralf assured Michael that his position awaited him after his discharge and recovery, "I've shouldered the full load for the past thirty years," he said. "I think I can manage for another couple of months."

"You've been very fortunate," said Marina.

"Why is it every time I end up in the hospital, people tell me how lucky I am?"

"For some, there is no warning or recovery."

Michael could not think what to say for a moment, but Marina's gentle questioning about his life and events leading up to the heart attack kept the conversation going. She spoke as if she really cared and allowed him to open up and become very vulnerable. He had not talked so much about himself in years. It felt good.

"If I may make an observation?" she asked, gently resting her hand on his arm, "When I asked you earlier who you really are you just described yourself in terms of *what you do*; an engineer, a salesman, a manager. Can you try to think about *who you are*?"

The statement took Michael by surprise. He hadn't expected that from Marina, or anyone for that matter, and her words nagged and annoyed him through much of the evening, enough for him to realize that she'd struck a nerve. He had told Petra that he knew who the real Michael was, but he was suddenly no longer certain. Who am I then, if not an engineer, a salesman or a manager? Where do you go to find those kinds of answers?

I am a person who... Who what?
I am not my results.
I am not my resume.
Then who am I? Why do I exist? What is my reason for being...?
My real purpose? Who do I want to be?

I am a husband.
I am a leader.
Am I a rational person caught in an emotional world or am I an emotional person caught in a rational world?

So, I am...

A dozen times he started and stalled and just when he resolved to give up the riddle, exhausted, an idea popped into his mind.

"Perhaps I don't know who I am, but I do know who I am *not*. I am not a *victim*!" He recalled Klaus' visit, months before at another hospital bedside, his reassurance that such experiences make you stronger if you do not play the victim, "Now I'm a two-time survivor. Twice I've come close to death and finally, I'm learning not to mope, not to blame or feel sorry for myself. I must not surrender to depression, disorder and despair. Instead, I choose to be appreciative and grateful for the opportunities I have and to be alive. If I've learned anything from my accident and training with Gregory Marks, it's that I am proactive and I take life into my own hands. I am responsible for creating my own positive thoughts. I can do things to create a positive emotional state."

I am proactive.
I am responsible.
I pull my own strings.
I am a leader that...
This moment is the most important and this moment is the only moment.

Just as Michael arrived at that conclusion, the doctor entered his room with further test results, "With proper medication and major lifestyle changes your health can be managed. Your heart function is good. In time the constricted blood flow will find alternate pathways. I don't see any immediate need for surgery. But, be well aware, about one in ten patients have another heart attack within a year and the damage can be much worse. If you're going to avoid a fatal heart attack, it's critical that you modify your diet, optimize your weight, increase your daily exercise and reduce your stress. If you need help with that, just let us know." With that, the doctor turned and left the room.

"This is getting to be a bad habit."

Michael looked up to see Klaus' face at the doorway. He was pleased to see his old friend and motioned for him to come in and sit down.

"I guess it was more than just acid indigestion."

Klaus set a small, neatly wrapped package on the bedside table, reached over the bed rail to grip Michael's hand and stared intently at him.

"How are you, son?"

"Surviving. The doctor says there was little damage to the heart muscle."

"That's good."

"I hope you don't mind my giving your name as next of kin."

"We're honoured. Monika sends her love."

"It's kind of you to come so far, Klaus. Give Monika a hug for me."

"I will. Have they given you a treatment plan?"

"The doctor says surgery is not an option. My problem's genetic disposition…and lifestyle."

Klaus looked at him and raised an eyebrow but said nothing.

"*Lifestyle…*? That's your cue to say 'I told you so and you should eat better, take more time off and have more holidays.'"

"No I couldn't say that Michael, certainly not after postponing our sabbatical because of problems in my organization. But I am concerned. You're very young for something like this to happen."

"I will have to change my lifestyle and habits."

"Are you up to that?"

Michael nodded, "I think so. The hardest part will be adjusting my work habits. I like to be productive and there's no shortage of things to do in my new position. I've been doing a lot of thinking. I know Gregory Marks is right when he says, 'You know it, now you have to do it. You have to close the knowing-doing gap. That doesn't simply mean execution, it means execution to be productive. I know what I need to do, but I'm not sure I know how to do it."

"Don't be too hard on yourself, Michael. You've changed a lot during the last year. You have to protect yourself against wear and tear, but you know where you're going and what you want. That's a very special place to be."

"All on hold, at the moment."

"Perhaps waiting to be approached in a different way."

"You mean, now I need to start doing the right things. I need to strengthen my XQ which means to better execute on my vision, values and my goals?"

"Now you're talking a foreign language! I'll leave those lessons to Gregory Marks,"

Klaus chuckled. He picked up the package from the bedside table and handed it to Michael, "Monika and I have something for you."

Michael peeled the paper away, opened the box and lifted out an intricately designed ceramic lighthouse, about thirty centimeters high with a black base and red and white stripes. There was an arched opening at the bottom for a tea light and the round windows in the walls allowed the flame to shine through.

"This is the lighthouse from the picture in your livingroom, isn't it?"

"Yes. Roter Sand. It led the way for sailors approaching Bremerhaven in the North Sea in the late 19th century. I'm told it's a hotel now. Get yourself well and we'll visit it together."

"You guys are amazing!"

"Monika found it in an antique shop. We were going to give it to you at Christmas."

"Didn't you think I'd last that long?"

"We just thought you'd appreciate it more now."

It was the perfect gift and it occupied Michael's thoughts long after Klaus had taken his leave. Through all the storms, turbulence and darkness in his life, the Mertens' friendship had been his lighthouse. They had always been there for him. Grounded and constant, they had guided him past reefs, rocks and regrets and pointed the way to hope, whatever he threw at them.

Michael spent the remainder of the day resting and reading newspapers cover to cover, including the death notices. He had never examined them before, brief accounts that summed up a life in less than a hundred words. *Birth, marriage, death.* "Lovingly remembered by…" the stories afforded work and career only a sentence or two, if at all, emphasizing instead roles and relationships…husband, father, son, brother. Marina asked, 'Who are you?' Gregory Marks asked, 'What one line would you want on your gravestone?' He hoped his didn't say 'Died full of potential'.

Michael's thoughts made him shudder. "Since Davos, I know where I'm going and who I want to be. My vision is getting clearer, but is it clear enough? Does it get me excited and get me out of bed early? When I think of it, does it feel good? In the end, will it merit only a weak sentence or two in my obituary?" There was a light tap on the door and Michael looked up from his thoughts to see Petra standing in the doorway with a white cello case leaning against her slim figure.

Michael tossed aside the newspaper.

"Petra!"

"I was so scared when Monika called. I just cancelled rehearsals and jumped on a plane"

"I'm glad you're here. Come and sit down."

"When I heard it was your heart, I was so shocked. You sounded fine when we last talked."

"I thought it was just heartburn. I guess this makes me a typical case of denial. I won't bore you with the details but I'll survive. I will need your help to make some big lifestyle changes," He admitted. "You brought your cello?"

"I didn't want to leave it out in the car in the cold."

"Would you play the Bedrich Smetana piece again for me? The Moldau? I can't tell you how much it would mean. I've been dreaming about you playing it that evening. Your passion for what you do is an inspiration to me."

"Don't you think people will mind?"

"How about we close the door, you come as close as you can and we'll call it special therapy."

Petra smiled and shut the door, seated herself with the instrument cradled between her knees and softly drew the bow across the strings, closed her eyes and began to play. Michael gazed at his long lost soul mate, her body swaying, her fingers caressing the strings and that look on her face that he loved so much. She was passionately in the moment, lost in the sound and emotion. He closed his eyes and let the music carry him away.

Michael opened his tear-filled eyes as she stopped. For a split-second, Michael was back in the wine-region of France with Petra, feeling all those same emotions of pure joy and love again. Petra must have felt it as well and, at that moment, she glanced up at Michael and leaned over the edge of the bed and kissed him softly on the forehead.

"Look after yourself, Michael and let's talk properly as soon as you're up to it. We need to discuss the living arrangements some time soon." They were still working in two different cities and it wasn't the most convienient of set-ups, especially with Petra's weekend concerts, "In the meantime, concentrate on getting well, I don't want to lose you again."

CHAPTER 34

Michael walked the long corridor of the cardiac ward many times during the weekend until he was finally discharged. Michael rode home in the taxi wrapped in a hospital blanket he had promised to return. He hoped his winter coat still hung in the office at Sunstream.

His rehabilitation began at the clinic three days later. The doctor presented Michael with a detailed exercise plan that required three visits to the therapy clinic each week with vigorous workouts for several months. The nutritionist gave him another detailed plan filled with dietary advice about carbohydrates, protein, good fats and bad fats. It was a steep path to lifestyle change, but Michael was determined he would not stumble again. He felt motivated and focused, yet his hours at home passed slowly. Much of the time he was tired and weak. On good days, he only managed a short daily walk around the block.

After a demanding workout at the clinic one afternoon, Michael returned to his apartment and reread his report chronicling the discovery of Viktor's cryptic notes and the new battery design revelation. It was a new paradigm and it totally changed the rules of the game for solar energy storage. He had committed to bringing the new battery into full production and ensuring the legacy of the Sunstream founder. It would impact people all around the world, as people would be able to turn the sun's energy into stored power.

Through thick and thin, I've worked toward this goal. It's part of my legacy now too. Escher says, 'Work smarter, not harder', but beyond my work, what am I living for? Who am I living for?

That reminded Michael of a flipchart that Gregory Marks had drawn at the seminar and he flipped back through his journal until he found the appropriate page of notes:

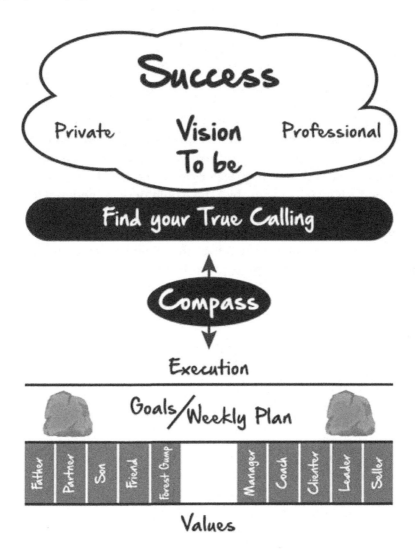

As he reflected on the page, it became very clear. He needed to re-think his values, both privately and professionally, and define the roles that he wanted to live. Professionally, this would be his M.C.C.L. roles and privately it would be his role as a partner and perhaps some day as a father. On the flipchart he saw 'brother', 'father', 'son', 'friend' and even Forest Gump, which referred to the role of re-energizing weekly. His vision up at the top needed to become clearer and exciting enough that it would pull him in the right direction. It would then get him out of bed early and give him a sense of purpose. His vision and values would be like a compass, they would help him to identify the priorities that he wanted to live each week, like an internal GPS.

Greg's 'clear vision and clear values lead to clear roles and goals' message really made sense now. He needed clear values, defined success and goals for each role in his life. Before now, he thought Greg's message only applied to companies who needed a clear vision and values, but Michael realized that it starts personally. For the first time he really understood what Greg meant by **'The whole person model'**. He was so much more than just a manager. Now Michael just had to be strong enough to execute his weekly goals for each role, his execution quotient. This was the key to living principle 4 and **'Being on Mission'**; the **principle of effectiveness**, **discipline** and **execution**. Doing **'the right things first'** and **saying no to what is not important**. This model would help him to simplify the complexity in his life, and "complexity blocks execution!" He thought jubilantly.

On that thought he picked up the phone and dialled Petra's number. He knew that she appreciated these regular calls as much as he did and it was a good place to start.

By early December, Michael felt ready to stop by Ralf's office for a visit.

"It's good to see you upright!" Ralf said, rising as Michael entered the office. A thick layer of papers covered his desk.

"It'll be great to be back and relieve you of some of this lot."

"All in good time," Ralf shook Michael's hand and gestured for him to take a seat. "How's it going with your lifestyle changes?"

"Slow and steady. The hardest part is deciding what to eat and changing my old nutritional habits."

"Maybe our friend Gregory Marks can help again. He does a lot of personal coaching, including energy management and helping people in making better food choices. Why don't you book a one to one coaching session with him? Consider it your Christmas bonus. Now, let's get down to business."

"I heard there was another parts mix-up on the automation order for Sunstream."

"Martin sorted it out before it even became a problem. He's become very proactive and has expanded his area of influence tremendously."

"Good for Hess!"

"You were right about him, Michael. The man has some rough edges, but he's working out well."

"He just needed someone to believe in him."

"And someone to believe *in*," Ralf added.

Michael smiled at the compliment.

"Since I turned down the Hartrand offer, they have become very aggressive and bought a company with a plant in Cologne so they can compete directly against us. They are investing big money in new production technology," Ralf continued, "They've cancelled all their orders from us. But that's not all they've done." Ralf stared out the window at the leafless trees.

Michael waited as long as he could bear before asking, "Well, what else?"

"Three of my sales team have given their notice, effective at the start of the new year. They're joining Hartrand. We might have the best battery, but they've got tons of cash and they're hitting us where it hurts."

"Anyone else?"

"The rumours aren't good. They've even approached our head of sales, Walter Fischer, and two guys on the Research and Development team!"

"Damn!"

Ralf turned to face him, "Do I take it from your response that *you're* not 'in play'?"

"Are you asking if Hartrand has approached me?"

"It'd be a smart move on their part."

"Ralf, the answer is no. No, they've not contacted me and no, I'll not consider it. Not a chance! My future is here with you…and Viktor."

"That's the best news I've had all week," he said before lapsing back into silence. Michael had no idea what he might be thinking.

"They're after the whole sales team?"

"Apparently. It isn't so much what it'll do for them as what it does to us. They can cripple us and then pick off the assets."

"Over my dead body!"

"I just found out this morning. Our budget's stretched to the limit and I can't fight Hartrand on salary or incentives."

"Do you mind if I talk with Walter and find out what he knows? We really need him to stay with us because if he leaves, other top sales and marketing people will follow with him."

"Go ahead. But I don't see what we can counter offer."

He turned to go and Ralf followed him to the office door, "That offer of more time with Gregory Marks is still an option, Michael. I don't want to lose you too."

Michael continued to brood on the assault from Hartrand long into the night. It was not a happy prospect. Hartrand had strong advantages, particularly the financial reserves to make big investments and cover short-term losses. But smaller companies also had their strengths. You could field a flexible, nimble team and not get bogged down the way big corporations sometimes did. At Escher-Sunstream, decisions were still made by the people, not by 'company policy' and this could be their advantage as this lead to quicker decision making. The employees were clear on the company's goals and vision and were more involved and empowered.

As he relayed the details to Petra that night, during one of their now daily phone conversations, he knew that they could compete against an aggressive, large company but he just didn't know how to do it without working long, hard hours. Perhaps Greg could help on that front. He had spoken about **Life Balance and Re-energizing**.

After saying goodnight to Petra, Michael sent Greg an email, asking for a one to one session early in the New Year, explaining it would have to be in Düsseldorf as he wasn't permitted to travel for some time yet.

The doctor finally approved Michael's return to work halftime, provided he was able to do so, "Without significant additional stress." He woke early on the morning of the 15th and found two email replies in his inbox: A short message from Gregory Marks suggesting they meet on the third Friday in January at the Dutch Hotel near the Düsseldorf airport, the other, and equally brief, came from Walter Fischer. After his holiday he would be returning to Düsseldorf on the second week of January and would be happy to meet.

Michael timed his arrival at Sunstream so he could greet the workers during their lunch break. Hannah happily accompanied Michael to the workers' lounge. There were trays filled with cookies and chocolates and, most prominently of all, was a long "Welcome Back!" banner on the wall.

"Hey, fellows, look who's here!" someone called out.

The men cheered loudly and one voice shouted, "We just got you broken in and you broke down."

Michael grinned, "It's good to see you all. Thank you for this welcome back. You'll never know how much it means to me. We've all faced some challenges lately and, like Sunstream, I'm still alive and still moving forward. I appreciated your card and all your support and hard work during my absence. If I've learned anything these past weeks, it's not to give up hope."

There was another cheer and one of the men pushed Martin Hess to the front. He had a serious look on his face and a blue 'Vacation Request' in his hand, "You're a newcomer here, Weber, so let me explain. Next time you need a vacation, there's a simpler way." He waved the paper over his head, "See…you fill in this form here …and then you send it to yourself."

Everyone laughed, including Michael, "I'll be sure to remember that!"

The lunch break was over and the ice was broken: Michael had returned to their world, his world. Minutes later, he unlocked the door to his office and surveyed the scene. The surface of his desk had been freshly dusted and polished and he set the ceramic model of Roter Sand, on the corner. He struck a match to light a small candle inside and sat watching the flame flickering through the tiny portholes. Looking at the lighthouse instantly reminded him of the **10 Principles** Greg had drawn on his own lighthouse in Davos. He reviewed the **Ten Principles** and the key notes he'd made in his journal about his own **vision** and **values** reflecting on how he was living these principles and what progress he had made. After these moments of reflection, he realized that the storm was past, his direction was clear and Michael was, finally, back **On Mission.**

CHAPTER 35

Michael found it hard to concentrate at the budget-planning meeting with Ralf during their next session. His thoughts continually slipped back to the employees who were deserting them for Hartrand. It was now up to eight employees, including some of their best. Was it really possible that they believed their best opportunities for career advancement lay with their opposition? Or were they leaving just for the money?

"Thomas in R&D won't leave," Ralf said, "he's assured me of that and I've just approved the permanent appointment of Martin as Operations Manager. That should hold him."

For the remainder of the meeting, the talk revolved around budget projections for Sunstream. Michael was confident that revised data collection procedures at Sunstream gave a more accurate picture of its productivity and profits.

The following Tuesday evening, on his way home from work, Michael met Walter Fischer at a small restaurant for an 'off the record' chat.

"I know that you've been talking with Hartrand," Michael said after the small talk, finally introducing the topic they both knew was coming.

Walter made no reply. He seemed hesitant to reveal his thoughts.

"As you know, a couple of our sales guys have already gone. And you? Any decision?"

"I have some things to consider. The salary would be better."

"What about the rest of your team?"

"That's not for me to say," Walter eyed Michael carefully. "I know the people at Hartrand would like to talk with you. They'll make you a good offer."

"I'm not even slightly interested. I wouldn't want to become just a number and become lost in a huge company. You know what Hartrand's trying to do to at Escher-Sunstream. Ralf deserves better."

Walter shrugged, "It's just business, Michael. If you play your cards right, Hartrand can put some real money in your pocket. A big organization also offers more security."

Michael persisted, "Walter, there's no such thing as security. We are all replaceable at any time. I'm serious. Sure, I used to think it was all about dollars, climbing the corporate ladder, showing off the perks and all that stuff."

"You've lost your drive?"

"I've found a better vehicle. Look, the best work of my career is ahead of me. The launch of the *Viktor Legacy* may be the most important thing this company ever does."

"Don't lose perspective, Michael. It's still just a battery, however good you might think it is. Working for Hartrand will give you a global scope. It could be the move that makes your career."

"Walter, I'm an engineer and you're a great salesman and I *know* that if we work together we can get great synergy. This new battery is a game changer and I don't want to miss the action. And, frankly, I don't think you do either. Think of the impact that our battery will have for people around the world who currently have no access to electricity!"

Michael saw a glimmer in Walter's eyes and knew he had connected.

"If you stay, we'd like you to be head of the Sales and Marketing for the whole company. So, can I tell Ralf you're still in the fold?"

"Can I tell their CEO, Dave Larner, you'll talk with him?" Walter countered.

"I'm not interested."

"That's brave talk, Michael, but we all have our price."

"No, Walter, some of us have our principles."

After a little more small talk, Michael said good-bye to Walter, feeling more clear-headed than he had before. He had a gut feeling that he got through to Walter and he would stay.

Professional relationships are built through one-to-one time. People need to feel that they are valued and respected. If we can make them part of our exciting vision it will hopefully become part of their purpose, their reason for being and give meaning to what they do. I choose to lead and therefore need to increase their involvement in this process. Now I need to communicate this so clearly that everybody in the organization will become more engaged and feel a sense of urgency. I think my leadership team is strong enough and ready to help me with this challenge.

Saskia is a great help. Our phone calls keep me focused. She was very happy to hear about all these challenges in my professional life, but she keeps reminding me to make more one-to-one time with Petra. I have been trying, I see her on the weekends, when she's not performing, and we go to yoga and for walks together. Fancy me doing yoga! Since the weekend at the wine region it is clear that things are getting better, but I still sense some hesitation on her part even though she mentioned 'living arrangements'. Hopefully she appreciates my daily phone calls and sees that I am committed to her. I don't want to push her about moving to Düsseldorf but we need to find some sort of solution together in order to move forwards.

PART V

"POWER OF ONE – TO – ONE COACHING"

CHAPTER 36

Gregory Marks was waiting for Michael in the Van Der Valk Airport Hotel restaurant on Friday morning. The two men greeted each other warmly. "That's a healthy change," Greg commented as Michael ordered a cup of green tea, "Not drinking 6 cups of coffee a day anymore? One of your takeaways from Davos?"

Michael laughed, "Among many! The heart dietician at the hospital recommended it too. I'm glad you approve. I'm afraid I missed most of your health tips in Davos. A bad case of 'information overload' I'm afraid, but the student is ready and eager to learn now. I've had my wakeup call. Focusing on the topic of energy management will be interesting."

Greg smiled, "Well, today you can hit the 'Reset Button' and move forward from here."

"I have some pressing questions," Michael said, flipping open his notebook.

Greg nodded, "I'll do what I can to assist. But first, bring me up to speed on what's happened since the workshop."

Michael recounted all that had happened since then: His Sunstream start, Viktor Fuchs' dream becoming his mission and the roller-coaster of events that followed, ending with his heart attack. Without question, his time at Escher-Sunstream Electric had been the most demanding, yet most exhilarating, year of his life.

"Ralf tells me you've worked wonders," Greg said: "You've turned around a contentious employee, you've increased the involvement of the workers'council, you've recognized a break-through innovation and you've persisted even when the outcome seemed doubtful."

"You've been talking to Ralf?"

"Yes. He's proud of you."

"He's a good boss. He has strong values and he lives the ten principles. Ralf 'walks the walk' just like you say we should. I see him doing that and it makes me respect his integrity and I know that's the number one thing employees want from their boss."

"He's also afraid you may burn out."

"That's why I'm here," Michael said.

Greg waited a few moments as if digesting the information and then asked, "So, what is the goal of our coaching session today?"

"Ralf probably told you that we have the prototype for a much better battery with revolutionary technology. It seems our launch will be more complicated than I thought, but I'm confident it's a great leap forward. What I don't know is how to bring the project to completion without working even longer and harder. I'm dedicated to following whatever time-management advice you can give me."

"Michael, I think you have the same view of coaching as many people do, that the coach is someone who has lots of recommendations and a solution for every problem. That isn't what this is about. I am not a consultant and I do not give advice. What I do have are thought-provoking questions. You have all the answers you're searching for within you, Michael. My role is to help you draw them out and help you gain clarity. Perhaps I should have asked, 'What are you expecting from *yourself* in today's session?'"

Michael couldn't hide his disappointment. If he was going to succeed as a leader, he really did need to learn more about managing time.

"Ralf showed me the 'Big Rocks' activity and said he got it from you. You must have more stuff like that?"

"Of course there are tools," Greg said. "If you've done the Big Rocks, you already know about weekly planning, goal setting and prioritizing?"

"Yes."

"So you know, but…"

"Knowing and doing are two different things," Michael cut in, "I know, I know. That's the execution gap. You're right."

Greg smiled at Michael, "Some of my most successful clients have built the habit of having their own **Personal Strategic Planning** session on a weekly basis. They take twenty minutes late on a Friday afternoon or a weekend to reflect on their vision and values before planning for the coming week. Those twenty minutes bring them back to what is most important. Remember this, Michael: Each week we receive a gift of 168 hours and our biggest challenge is to do the right thing with those hours. You know my message: Be ruthless with time. It is always about doing the 'right things first' and most of the time, you know what you should do. It's now time to close the 'knowing/executing gap'. Think about which 'high leverage activities are going to give you the best return on your investment. Constantly ask yourself two key questions: Why am I paid? What is the most productive thing I could be doing right now? When you contacted me in December, you were concerned with **Life Balance** and **Re-energizing** and wanted to re-focus on your **vision and values**."

"Yes, all of that and I need your recommendation for a heart-healthy diet too."

"I don't recommend diets. What I talk about is 'nutrition for sustainable performance'. Without energy, living the other principles will not be sustainable. The secret to leadership is energy. Remember, you can't manage time, but you can manage your energy. Managing your energy definitely involves doing the right thing first, especially for leaders. Tell me Michael, why did you choose these principles to talk about today?"

"They were my lowest scores on the **Self Evaluation** I did in Davos and your feedback agreed with that. You said **Life Balance** and **Re-energizing** were the key to all the other principles."

"Another 'takeaway', that's good! We can spend time this morning talking about **Principle 10, Reenergizing**, we'll talk about nutrition at lunch and we'll focus on **Principle 5, Life Balance**, this afternoon. I see you've brought your notes from Davos so let's start by reviewing the **M.C.C.L.S. Model** and the **Ten Principles of Leadership and Life**, where you were then and where you see yourself now. I would also like to focus on your **Leadership Roadmap**. That means we'll create a plan for developing your team over the next eighteen months. This plan will help build trust, increase involvement and improve team spirit through team building. This is choosing to lead and living the 'L' in the M.C.C.L.S. model.

We'll also try an activity I love called **'Your True Calling'**, it connects and aligns with **Principles 2 & 3.** It's about leading yourself to where you're meant to be. Let's head up to the room I've arranged."

Greg seated Michael at a table in the corner of a long room with large, panoramic windows overlooking a beautiful view of the city. There was a pitcher with water and two glasses on the table.

"Don't underestimate the benefits of water," Greg said, pouring a full glass for each of them, "I recommend you drink two to three liters every day."

"I remember you saying that in Davos," Michael said, "but, once again, to know and not to do…"

Greg took a pen and some paper and pulled up a chair to the left side of Michael, "Don't beat yourself up about the past. Press the Reset Button today and move forwards."

They started with Michael sharing some of his successes over the past few months and then they moved into the M.C.C.L.S. and created a **Leadership Road Map** for his team development process. He shared that his coaching had improved, especially the quality of his questions. He was now much better at challenging people to become clearer and he was also giving fewer tips than before. It was now clear that leadership was a decision he had to make *and* actions he had to take. Creating a vision and mission statement and clarifying values for the whole organization was a major part of his plan. This would take him way out of his comfort zone. It would also mean that each team would take part in a workshop on the topic, create action plans and drive the change necessary on every team and in every department. It was clear to Michael that this process would help his organization to become more aligned. An hour later, Michael was excited to see his leadership roadmap on paper as it stretched over the next eighteen months. Now he would just have to sell it to his team. At that point Greg sketched a propeller shape on a new sheet and filled the empty spaces with words, just as he had in Davos.

"Do you remember this from Davos? Today the majority of our focus is going to be on **PQ** or physical intelligence. In Davos, we focused mostly on **EQ**, your emotional intelligence. As you know, you have lots of **IQ** but it's your lack of **PQ** that landed you in hospital."

Greg drew a line across the bottom of the pad. On the far left end he wrote the word Death, then, working across to the right: Disease, Dying and Sickness. On the far right side he wrote Vitality, Full Engagement and Optimal Health.

The Vitality Line
"Move to the Right"

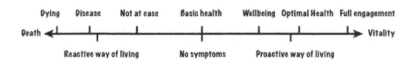

"Each of us are somewhere on this continuu Michael," Greg handed him the pen. "Where would you place your X right now?"

Michael stared at the line and suddenly found it hard to swallow. He placed a small x near the words Sickness and Disease. He handed the pen back to Greg in silence.

"What do I need to do?" he asked in a solemn voice.

"First, you need to know that you *can* hit the Reset Button and you *can* work your way up from where you are, Michael. But you also have to realize that YOU are the only one who can do it. No one else can do this for you. **Re-energizing** is something you can't delegate. I can advise, coach and support you, but people who live **Principle 1** strongly accept **Responsibility** for their health and take it into their own hands.

"If it's really going to be, then it's really up to me," Michael almost whispered.

Greg nodded and looked at Michael seriously, "Too many people define 'health' as the absence of unhealthy symptoms. They like that definition because it means they do not have to change their habits. A reactive person waits until they get a symptom and then takes action to try to get rid of it. A proactive person knows vitality is a choice and tries to move to the healthy end of the spectrum every day. Edward Stanley, who was the Earl of Derby in the 1800s, was insightful enough in the late 19th century to say, 'Those who think they have not time for bodily exercise will sooner or later have to find time for illness.' You learned that lesson the hard way. That's the time management tip you've been looking for: You can't manage time, but you can manage your energy. Remember, it's the choices you make and the actions you take that determine your future."

Michael opened his journal and quickly noted:

Vitality is a choice.

This really hit home as Michael remembered the words Klaus had written at the front of his journal and the considerable recovery time he'd needed after his heart attack. Up until now, he had only been reactive in managing his health and had taken it for granted. This brought him back to the saying 'what you take for granted often disappears' and was now motivated to make some real changes.

"Do you remember '**The 100 day Challenge**' from Davos?" Greg asked.

"I remember what you said about water consumption, the **F.I.T.T. Principle** and some of the core exercises. I even remember you recommending drinking red wine. I liked that part! Beyond that? If only I'd I paid closer attention, the last couple of months may have been quite different."

"Don't beat yourself up, remember? It often takes a crisis for people to decide to make changes. Illness hits, partners leave, kids rebel...what causes the change to start is less important than the fact that it does start and I believe you're ready."

Greg began a review of what Michael did remember, beginning by focusing on physical exercise, "Why is it important for *you?*" Michael considered the most obvious reasons: Losing weight, building muscle tone, relieving tension and then suddenly said, "My life's at stake and I want to be happier."

"Those are some pretty good reasons to make changes. People make changes to receive benefits or avoid pain. It helps when you are mentally aware of those benefits before you start and you will only benefit from them physically if you take action."

Michael mentioned the three, weekly aerobic training sessions he attended as part of his physiotherapy and Greg nodded his approval, "Good start. These actions are going to reduce heart rate, improve blood pressure, increase your good cholesterol and produce endorphins, the body's natural pain and stress fighters. You'll feel so much better. Build it into your weekly plan and make it consistent. I want you to email me at the end of next week with an update on how you're doing and then again at the end of the month. Can you make that commitment to keep yourself accountable?"

Michael assured him that he would.

For the next ninety minutes they focused on other parts of **The 100 Day Challenge**. For Michael, the two most interesting points were: **The Most Important Four Minutes** daily exercise and research findings concerning the immune system. Greg shared that some of his clients take four minutes just before entering their house at the end of the working day where they reflect on their vision and values. This short, daily habit helps get them mentally prepared to be the person they want to be as they enter the house. Michael was also fascinated by research to prove that 140-240 minutes per week of aerobic training had a huge impact on the body and rebalanced naïve and memory cells in the immune system to become balanced again. This, in turn, prevents most common illnesses and, perhaps helps protect against long-term health issues. Michael wondered where he would be able to find 140 minutes a week to move aerobically.

CHAPTER 37

G reg automatically headed towards a window table in the restaurant. Both men ordered salads to start and then a plate of grilled chicken and Mediterrean style vegetables for the main course, "No dressing please. Just oil and vinegar on the side," Greg added. "Will it bother you if we talk about nutrition as we eat?" he asked.

"I think I can digest it," Michael smiled.

"Good. The concept I recommend is called **'The Zone'**. It's derived from research by Dr. Barry Sears and you can read about it in a number of books he's written. If you're into sports, you know the term. It's that euphoric state when you're totally focused, full of energy and everything is working in your favor."

"What makes this diet so special?"

"It's not a diet, it's a nutritional lifestyle. Sears is a medical researcher and his genetic disposition to heart attacks is much like yours."

"Now you've got my attention."

"What first interested me about **'The Zone'** was its use by Olympic athletes for medal-winning performance. By following it, you're ahead in two areas: It's good for heart health and for enhanced performance. You'll find that 'The Zone' is a balanced program based on science. Plus, it's the foundation of **Principle 10, Re-energizing**. Once you start making changes, you will feel the difference: Increased energy, concentration and vitality and when you feel like that, you will never go back."

The waitress arrived with their order and Michael found the talk of food had stimulated his appetite. "Decreasing the amount you eat can increase the number of years you live." Greg said with a grin. "That's one of the few things that has been proven about nutrition and longevity. Don't get me wrong, I *love* to eat and I still eat too much sometimes, but it's the ratios and timing that are important. You need to consume 40 percent carbohydrates, which are low glycemic. This means lots of fruit and vegetables because they are full of fibre and break down more slowly to create glucose. The remaining energy should come from 30 percent protein and 30 percent un-saturated fats. There are healthy, cleaning fats and there are unhealthy, clogging fats. Healthy fats include olive oil, coconut oil and nuts. Unhealthy fats, the clogging ones, are animal based. Good sources of protein are chicken breast, turkey, fish, eggs and sometimes red meat. Without the protein and good fat, you will be hungry constantly and not a high-performer. If you eat right, you will maintain ideal levels of glucose, you'll be burning your own fat and be able to maintain your concentration."

"This is all new to me."

"It's all explained in detail in Dr. Sears' books. My two favorites are called *The Zone* and *Maintaining the Zone.* Here's my main point; this meal has the right 'zone' ratios of carbohydrates (in the vegetables and salad), protein (in the grilled chicken) and fat (in the avacados and seeds). It's low glycemic and won't trigger a surge of insulin, meaning it won't cause an energy peak and trough, and it will sustain us for a long time. So, Michael, let's enjoy our lunch, slowly," Greg added with a smile.

After lunch Greg said, "I could tell you about my own experience or about that of hundreds of high performance athletes who use the 'Zone', but maybe our best example is Ralf. He's no longer the overweight, stressed executive I first met."

"Ralf? Stressed?" Try as he might, Michael could not assimilate that image with Ralf's placid demeanour.

"Once upon a time he certainly was, but his levels of energy are now consistent. He dramatically reduced his white bread, juice and pasta intake. I don't think he eats anything like that any more. He doesn't talk much about himself, but if you ask him, I'm sure he'd be happy to share his experiences. The key is three balanced meals and two snacks a day with that 40-30-30 ratio and a maximum of five hours between them. That evens out our energy peaks and valleys. This allows you to hit the switch and become the fat burning person that you were designed to be at birth. Losing weight and creating energy becomes easy."

"So, if we're finished here, it's time for a walk and some fresh air," Greg said, standing up and putting on his coat. "Twenty minutes of walking in the one hour window after lunch is an excellent habit. These twenty minutes give us an additional sixty minutes of increased metabolism and fat burning. I call it 'the lazy persons's exercise plan'"

"I'll meet you downstairs in a few minutes, I just want to write down a few notes while they're fresh in my head."

Optimal Nutrition and Energy Management

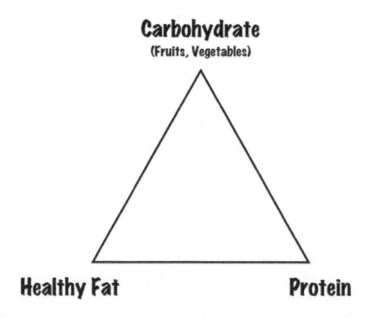

Carbohydrate
(Fruits, Vegetables)

Healthy Fat   Protein

Healthy fat: Olive oil, coconut oil, canola oil and good nuts.
Protein: Chicken, turkey, fish, eggs, some red meat.
Carbohydrates: Lots of fruit and vegetables – berries are the best.

- This allows me to burn my own fat and provides constant energy.
- Reset the engine five times a day.
- Use energy shakes with this balance as breakfast or a snack.
- 140-240 minutes of aerobic training per week to strengthen immune system.
- The most important four minutes: Take four minutes to reflect on vision, mission and values to refocus on what matters most before the transition to your private roles at home. If these four minutes could help me let go of work, wow, what an impact that would make!

Michael scribbled the last sentence, grabbed his coat and dashed out into the early winter sunshine.

CHAPTER 38

B ack in the room and fully refreshed, Greg showed Michael a **'Life Balance Analysis'** sheet.

Eight lines radiated from a center point, each representing aspects of a balanced life: **Business, Hobbies, Health, Mental, Social, Family, Financial** and **Spiritual**.

Life Balance Analysis

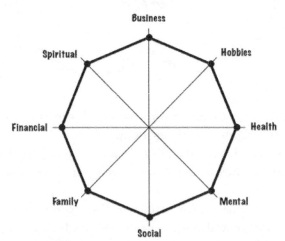

- Where am I today?
- What is important? What do I value in each area?
- Where do I want to be?
- My motive? Why do I want to change (benefits)?
- My actions within the next 100 days?

  What do I have to start doing?
  What do I have to stop doing?
  What do I have to do more of?
  What do I have to do less of?

"First, think about what each of these words means to you, create a definition and put it onto paper. Show how much time you devote to each one by putting a point somewhere on each line. That means the further away from the center point is more time, closer is less time. Then, reflect on what is important and write what you value under each. I'd also like you to reflect on what success means to you under each heading."

For **Business**, **Mental** and **Financial**, Michael's were close to the end of each line. **Health** did not extend as far, but was much better than it would have been before his physiotherapy program had begun.

Hobbies, **Social** and **Spiritual** were clear areas for improvement. **Family**, which to him meant the relationship with Petra, had improved but was still an area he needed to work on and that meant getting more one to one time with her. Connecting his points, the shape was not the balanced octagon he would have liked it to be.

"Not so good, is it?"

"Knowing your values and living your values are two different things entirely. Your results aren't unusual and they show us where to focus our attention this afternoon."

The next 60 minutes were spent with Michael articulating what was important, what he valued and what he wanted to be under each heading. Greg kept challenging him with thought provoking questions and it helped to bring him clarity. Sharing his values was easy but defining success and sharing his picture of the future was extremely difficult. He really enjoyed the process though, especially with a sparring partner like Gregory Marks to work with.

"By looking again at what you wrote beside each word I think your values are very clear. You know what's important. Your challenge now is to consistently live those values. When I asked you to rate each value on a scale from one to ten on how you lived them, some of your scores were shockingly low. What's the message for you? When we focused earlier on **Principle 3, 'I have a clear vision'** you were not really clear and you'll need to invest much more time in this process. You need to see the unlimited possibilities you have if you can strengthen your strengths to a world-class level. I believe that's not only possible but it'll make all the difference. Imagine your possibilities, Michael." After a few minutes of silence Greg continued, "Now, what do you remember about the **Principle of Life Balance** from Davos?"

"That it's all about happiness and there are twenty-two muscles in a true smile. That's missing in my life because I was a workaholic, but doesn't financial security depend on my work?"

"On work, yes. On overwork, definitely not. Focus on the highly rich activities. That means your weekly priorities on your **M.C.C.L.S. Model**. Think back to paradigm shifts. There are different ways of getting things done. I believe 75 percent of our satisfaction in life comes from the relationships we have with others. So, the challenge for all of us is to make more time for those relationships. Building more one-to-one time for our significant people and doing the small things to make those people feel important and loved is the key to living **Principle 9: Relationship Deposits.** By doing this you will also feel love, which makes you feel happy and that leads to those 22 muscles contracting to form a real smile. When you're happy, you are more productive. It's a win-win."

"Doesn't that bring us back to where we started?" Michael asked, "Time management?"

Greg shook his head and laughed, "You're very persistent, Michael, I'll give you that. I'll say it again, 'We can't manage time....'"

"We can only manage our energy."

"We've talked about fitness and nutrition and we've looked at your values and life balance. Now, we're going to move in a different direction to help you get more clarity on your vision. It's an exercise I call your **'True Calling'.**"

Michael nodded.

"Each one of us has a 'true calling' in life, a clear, defined place where our gifts, skills and passions come together to produce value and drive our economic engine. This is what you're being called to do, it's what you love and what you're good at. If you can find it you really never work another day in your life, because doing what you love isn't work and it won't feel like work. It becomes part of your purpose, your passion and your **'True Calling'**. It's finding what you're really meant to do. It's finding why you're here. Do you know anybody living like that Michael?"

Michael immediately thought of Petra and the pure joy on her face every time she performed.

"Look at this diagram." By the top left circle was written, 'Passion: What I love to do' The top right said 'What drives my economic engine / what can I do that creates value.' "My strengths and core competencies' was in a circle towards the bottom. "Remember, the more value you create for others, the more you will earn. It's the law of business."

My True Calling

Passion:
what I love to do

My Economic Engine
Things I can do to create value

My Strengths and core competencies
Where can I be best in the world? (10,000 hours)

Greg pressed play on a small stereo system and soft, meditative music filled the room as it had Davos. "Michael," Greg said softly, "I want you to relax…" and he lead Michael through the same breathing and relaxation techniques that they had practiced in Davos. As Michael's body and mind become still, Greg asked him to reflect on each of the three circles he'd drawn. After about ten minutes of deep reflections to the many questions that Greg asked, the exercise then moved into the brain-writing phase.

"Now, pick up your pen and start writing in your 'strengths and competencies' circle. What are you good at? What have other people said you're great or 'a natural' at? What could you become the best in the world at if you had 10,000 hours to dedicate to it?"

'Analytical thinking, creative problem solving, visionary thinking, great with numbers, written communication,' flowed from Michael's pen.

"Keep writing Michael. What is at the core of who you are? What are your strengths? What parts of your job are you really good at?"

Michael continued to write, remembering his many speeches, presentations, his ability to sell and his strength in mathematics. When Michael had filled the circle with as many words as he could, Greg asked him to find two more before moving on.

"Now we're moving from your strengths to your passions. What are the things you love to do, things you are deeply passionate about? What are the things you do when times really flies by? When do you become lost in the joy of spending time on that activity? When are you at your best? When are you 'in flow'?" He could see that Michael was struggling, "It's okay, Michael, we all get so busy working and climbing the ladder that we often focus all our attention and energy on the demands of daily life and forget about our real passions. Sometimes, we have to go further back into our memories to when we allowed ourselves to live our passions. As a child, as a teenager...what was it you loved to do most? What were your passions in life?"

Michael's pen hovered over the page, what do I really love to do? This was much harder. He had driven himself so hard for so long that he had pushed these things out of his life. Slowly, he began to write: Cooking, spending long hours in Monika's kitchen. Soccer, he might have been great if he'd focused more. Travelling, hiking and camping in his college years. He couldn't get enough of that back then but couldn't find a weekend for it now. The circle began to fill with things he hadn't thought about in years.

"Now Michael, make a list of the things that you could do to create value, things that would produce income and drive your economic engine. Put your job title in the center of that circle. What else could you do to create value for others? Which favorite hobby or interest could you convert into a career or a profession? If Ralf said, 'Sorry, the business is gone', what else could you do? How could you pay the bills? Think beyond your present job to what else you could do? Maybe it's something you've always wanted to try; you have the skills for it, but never took that leap of faith. What does the world need today or in the future? What business would you love to start? If I meet you ten years from today, what would you love to be doing? If you knew you could not fail, what would you do? Why are you here and what are you being called to do? Dig deep Michael, what is there? Keep digging and, when you're done, dig a little deeper..."

Michael began to let his mind become open to possibilities. Writing down his passions and remembering the joy those past experiences had brought him kindled his fire. What if he had acted on those interests, those passions? His ideas continued to excite him as he filled the circle.

"Look at all three circles. Is there something that plays to your strengths, that you are really passionate about and could drive your economic engine? If so, you have found your 'true calling'. It's what you're being called to do. It becomes your life's purpose, your vision, the reason you're here! Moving towards it becomes your mission. Build it into your mission statement knowing that when you get there, your 'working days' are over. Imagine how that would feel."

Michael studied the circles. He was sure he was close, but was just not quite there quite yet.

"That's okay, some people are able to do this exercise once, what they should be working towards becomes instantly clear and it develops into a powerful pulling force. For others, it takes more time, work and self-reflection. It's in you, Michael, you just have to really want to find it. Quite often, that search takes us outside of our comfort zone. Think back to the poem from Emerson about taking risks and remember, if you do not take risks, you cannot grow and if you cannot grow you cannot be your best. If you cannot be your best, you cannot be happy. When you are ready, you will find it. Your 'true calling' is waiting to be discovered. Part of your purpose is to find it and you don't want to feel the pain of regret later in your life if you don't look for it. Do what you're really called to do Michael."

Greg stood up and gave Michael a few minutes for a thinking break.

Greg then looked again at Michael's **Life Balance Analysis**, "Your analysis shows that all your time and energy is dedicated to your work. Your hobbies, relationships and vitality are suffering because of how you spend your time. At the end, no one wishes they'd have spent one more day in the office. No one regrets new things they *did* do. They wish they had done more: Loved more, laughed more, found more one-to-one time with key people and spent more hours doing the things they were passionate about. They wish they had spent more time making a difference in the world, to know they'd contributed, that they had mattered. What if your heart attack had not been a warning, but your death?"

Michael felt incredibly uncomfortable as he thought about that, "I'd have died alone. I'd have died never seeing Australia, India or Bali. Hardly anyone would notice I was gone. There would be a stone with my name, date of birth, date of death and it would say, 'Never found his true calling. Hadn't quite got around to living yet…'

Michael's voice became more hushed as the realization hit him.

"How do you feel right now?" Greg asked.

"I am more ready than I've ever been to get my life on track. I feel motivated to change and committed to seeing it through."

"That's good to hear. So, what is clearer for you after today?"

"I need to get more living in my life."

"What are your next steps? What are you going to do more of? What are you going to do less of?"

"I'm not certain, but Petra and I recently spent a weekend together in the wine region. I did a similar exercise with her as you did with us in Davos. She got very excited as she shared her values and vision with me. I made notes as she talked and she loved it. That's when she came up with the crazy idea that we both take sabbaticals and spend three months in Australia. She thinks it would be a reset for our relationship and would give us time for love and cementing our relationship without interruption."

"Great idea! Do it now! I've had two sabbaticals and they are life changing experiences," Greg exclaimed. "I'm sure Ralf would support it because he is counting on you in the future and would understand how important this is for you. I think sabbaticals to re-energize key employees will be part of the new culture that Escher is trying to create."

"I just can't see how it would work. The company needs me, especially at this crucial point. I will make the effort to organize more romantic weekends away that really is all the time I can commit right now."

Do I want to see my true calling?
Am I willing to take the necessary risks to get there?
Is my life balance important enough to make the necessary changes?
How can I live my values more and be more congruent?
Am I ready to leave my comfort zone?

PART VI

"LEAVING A LEGACY"

CHAPTER 39

N early a month after the coaching session with Gregory Marks, Michael had progressed with his leadership roadmap and had been on a two-day offsite workshop with his team. They started the workshop with team members giving him feedback on where they saw his M.C.C.L.S. percentages based on the pre-reading and the model he had taught them. They identified how he was spending his time the last month and what they clearly expected in the future. This specific feedback had definitely helped Michael and he was dedicated to becoming more aware and effective moving forward. He explained to them how important it was for the entire team to understand and live all the roles of the M.C.C.L.S. model in order to create a new leadership culture. Michael had shared one of the key messages of the workshop in bold letters on a flipchart:

We are over managed and under led. This needs to change.

At this point the participants did some one-to-one peer coaching with each another and shared and compared how they had invested their time on the M.C.C.L.S. They were very intense in this phase and helped each other set goals for the next 100 days. This phase ended with Michael reminding them that they were paid to lead and coach and not just manage.

They focused on vision and values and produced a rough draft that would be reworked in the next two months. A small team of three was elected to be the taskforce responsible for taking the rough draft further. He found that the session created a new level of trust and increased involvement amongst all members and the team got really excited during the vision creation process. Michael could actually feel the energy and was impressed by the concentration in the room.

Greg had sparked a major change in Michael's management style. He was making headway in his efforts to delegate. Coaching, training and monitoring were necessary before significant delegation and full empowerment could take place and there seemed to be no immediate time benefit. However, Michael was confident it would eventually relieve his workload. Working full days again was making him feel more productive and scheduling time into his days for regular fitness was boosting his energy levels. He even realized, happily, that he was losing weight.

Michael was enjoying the positive energy in the room when he noticed his phone vibrating and was startled by Petra sobbing so hard he couldn't understand what she said. Then he slowly understood, 'accident', "Take a deep breath, Petra. Who's had an accident?"

Michael waited as she stifled her sobbing enough to stutter, "Klaus. He was out jogging and a car hit him."

"What?! How bad is it?"

Michael waited, hardly breathing, as Petra sobbed again, "He didn't make it, Michael," she almost whispered.

Michael stared at his journal in his hand. Klaus's visions and values: Walk the talk, be a role model, keep your thoughts positive, live the dream. How could Klaus' dream be over?

"Michael?"

"Are you sure, Petra?"

"Monika just called. She said she couldn't reach you. She asked us both to come."

He was stunned into silence.

"Michael, can you come?"

"Of course, sorry, yes, I'll come," Michael cleared his throat. "I'll catch the next flight. Where should I meet you?"

"Come to Monika's."

Michael made his apologies to his team, explained about the emergency and headed back to his office to gather his things.

He flopped down in his chair and his eye fell on the lighthouse Klaus had brought to him in hospital on the corner of his desk. Klaus didn't make it... the beacon was gone, his guiding flame snuffed out in a moment. Michael stood up shakily then whirled around and dropped back into his chair. He sat for several minutes, numb from head to foot, trying to control his breathing before calling Ralf to explain the circumstances. On impulse, he reached out and clasped the ceramic lighthouse with both hands. It was the last thing Klaus had given him. Michael sobbed as he realised that he had taken Klaus' guidance for granted. They would not be visiting Roter Sand together now.

It was almost dinnertime as the taxi dropped Michael off at the Mertens' house. Michael had tried to think what he should say to Monika during the entire trip from Düsseldorf to Munich. He paused at the door, still without the words. He knew that the moment he entered the house, his real home, it would all become real. Petra answered the door when he finally pushed the buzzer. She hugged him fiercely, her body quivering with suppressed sobs.

"Oh, Michael," She groaned.

"How's Monika?"

"As well as you can expect. It's been a horrible day."

Michael could hear Monika crying softly in the bedroom down the hall and they both stood looking at her door.

"I should go to her," Petra released her grip on Michael and wiped her eyes. "The priest just left. He told her not to hold back her tears."

"Should I go in?"

"Let me tell her you're here."

When Petra returned from the bedroom she joined a stunned Michael at the kitchen table.

"Do you know more about what happened?"

Petra didn't know much more than she'd already told him, just that the accident happened early in the morning as Klaus was jogging. A driver had lost control and hit Klaus. Apparently, he had tried to sit up afterwards, saying, "It's okay. I'm all right." Moments later he was dead.

At that moment, Monika emerged from her room, looking sad and red-eyed, but composed and with a sense of strength and acceptance that struck Michael. She walked straight over to him and wrapped her arms around his strong shoulders, "Oh, Michael," she began, "I was not prepared for this day. You always know it will come, but somehow you believe it never will. I'm going to miss Klaus so very much. He was part of me. I'm greatful that he always insisted we live each day to its fullest. He used to say that you never knew which day might be your last." Monika struggled to hold back another flood of tears but then Michael hugged her tighter and she let them flow.

"Monika, I'm so, so sorry. You and Klaus are my true family and I owe you so much: Your friendship, your confidence, your trust in me, even when I made mistakes…and I made big mistakes."

Petra, joined Monika and Michael. The three of them held each other close, sensing the warmth and love of the man who was missing. They reluctantly moved apart and Monika picked up an envelope from the table and handed it to Michael, "Klaus said he wanted you to have a copy of it…to help you face new challenges. It always helped him and he wanted to frame this for you. Read it when you have a quiet moment." He put the envelope in his pocket.

The priest returned and the four of them took their places at the dining room table to begin the funeral planning. At each suggestion the priest made, Monika simply nodded and said, "Thank you." She had only two requests: That Petra play her cello at the service and that Michael offer words of remembrance. Michael had never spoken at a funeral, but finding positive things to say about Klaus would be easy: Klaus fulfilling his potential, living a life that was disciplined, balanced, loving and principle-centered.

Knowing how difficult it had been for Monika to call Klaus' mother, Petra phoned the Mertens' closest friends in Munich. Most of them had already heard the news on TV. She asked Michael if he would contact some of the out-of-town people while she returned to comfort Monika. He did his best to communicate the basic facts: Klaus was dead. His funeral would be held at his parish church at eleven o'clock, next Friday morning.

Later in the evening, as he switched on the TV, there was the news: "The sports community is in shock tonight over news that a well-known soccer coach has died in a tragic accident. Klaus Mertens, 52, was struck by a car while out jogging this morning. No member of the family has been available for comment at this time. Dirk Möller, manager of the Munich soccer club where Mertens worked for the past 18 years, described him as a 'good friend, a great coach and a real developer of talent.' While police are still investigating the accident, witnesses say the road was icy and the driver skidded, striking the victim from behind. No drugs or alcohol were involved and speed does not appear to have been a factor."

How often had he heard such newscasts and paid little attention? And now, when it mattered most, the report seemed flat and empty, factually accurate but containing little of who Klaus really was, only that he had met with a tragic and sudden end.

Michael turned off the TV, sat down and tried to gather his thoughts and put them on paper as Klaus had taught him. The process was so much harder than he'd imagined and he was really struggling to attain clarity. How could he convey who Klaus really was? Did he even know? 'You are my legacy.' 'It's always more about giving than getting.' The ideas that he had expected to flow so freely were now slow to come and he wrung them out drop by drop. The eulogy must have finality and must cut to the essentials. If he could find a theme, he might get a decent start. Perhaps he could use **The Ten Principles**. Klaus had teased him, saying he would continue to be a coach, not run off to the mountains to become a leadership coach. But somehow, without having gone to a workshop with Gregory Marks, Klaus knew and lived the principles: **I am Responsible, I clarify my Values, I have a Vision, I live my Mission and I strive for Life Balance**. How had he learned that? For the next few hours Michael was lost in reflective thought of how to effectively convey Klaus' message.

The funeral chapel was filled with wreaths and floral arrangements. The pews on both sides of the church were filled to capacity and there

265

were people standing in all the available space at the sides and back of the church. The priest took charge of the commemoration, leading the opening hymn and reciting prayers, "I have fought the good fight to the end," he read, "I have run the race to the finish. I have kept the faith." The text suited Klaus well.

Petra had told him she would accompany a soloist singing 'Ave Maria' after Holy Communion and then it would be his turn to speak. Michael felt like he was fifteen again, sitting on the bench, waiting for Klaus to call him into the game. The palms of his hands felt clammy as he fiddled with the softly worn, burgundy leather journal Klaus had given him. It had seemed the right place to write these words. He hoped they were appropriate. He wanted to speak well, for Klaus' sake but his mouth felt so dry.

As the last strains of 'Ave Maria' turned to silence, Petra laid her cello on its side and gave Michael a smile of encouragement. He walked slowly to the front and rested his hand at the head of the casket, feeling momentarily that his hand was on Klaus' shoulder and wishing Klaus' hand was on his before taking his place at the lectern. He stood for a moment, looking at Monika and surveying the crowd of expectant faces. He no longer felt nervous. This was not about him. It was about Klaus. He could and would do this well for him. Michael cleared his throat and began.

"My name is Michael Weber," he began, "and I am deeply honoured that Monika has given me the opportunity to share some of my memories and thoughts about our dear coach, mentor, friend and my Father-figure, Klaus Mertens.

Each one of us is still reeling as we try to come to terms with our sudden and tragic loss. We repeatedly ask the questions, 'Why? Why now?' and along with the questions, come a sense of guilt and a heightened sadness at the suddenness of it all; of the missed opportunity to say goodbye to Klaus and perhaps, more importantly, 'Thank you'. Maybe, like me, you're wishing you had picked up the phone more often just to chat, wishing you'd made the effort to spend more personal time with the man who gave so much of himself to us...wishing you'd made a greater effort to stay more closely connected. Sadly, those opportunities

are now gone. I believe that, while we are no longer able to see Klaus, he is, nonetheless, still here with us listening to the words we are trying to say. Knowing that, is giving me the strength to continue.

Michael felt his throat catch, but he was determined to make his friend proud.

Klaus was a great coach, a loving husband, a role model and so much more. He was a man whose values were clear. He truly knew what mattered most in life. He and Monika lived that truth every day and they worked tirelessly as a team to move towards their vision.

Each of us has so many wonderful memories of Klaus. It is these recollections that reach beyond the dry facts of a man's life and give it meaning. Those memories are the true threads that create the fabric of a person's life.

Many of us here knew Klaus as our coach and we can attest to his love and passion for soccer and for life. He could talk at length about our games and remembered all of our plays, even though most of us may have forgotten them. But, as important as the game was to Klaus, his mission was bigger and broader than soccer and it has taken me a long time to understand that.

After a training workshop last June, I visited Klaus and asked him about his legacy, a question that had been asked of us and, without hesitation, he told me that we are his legacy; the people we have become and the work we are doing in the world. Life, he often told me, was more about giving than getting.

When Klaus was offered a better job—at least what I thought was a better job; one with more prestige and great pay—I was shocked that he turned it down. Instead, he stayed dedicated to his old club, despite its many troubles. I attributed his decision to a lack of ambition, a reluctance to change. I failed to see that Klaus was a man 'on mission,' that his vision was clear and that he was being true to his values. 'I may not die rich,' he told me, 'but I'm doing what's right.' I know that my lack of understanding at that time hurt him deeply but, he forgave me and moved on as he always did. Klaus, please know that now I understand. It is not too late to say how grateful I am.

Klaus, I'm beginning to see what you really taught us. In everything you said and in everything you did, you showed us that an effective leader gives direction, encouragement and hope. As young as we were, you affirmed our potential, not just on the soccer field, but on the playing fields of life. You offered us friendship and support and despite our growing pains and sometimes, thoughtless actions, you persisted with us through whatever difficulties we faced. You and Monika provided so many of us with a clear, true picture of what a deeply committed relationship looks like. You provided a consistant example of real love and you demonstrated how the small, daily gestures build the foundations of deep, committed relationships. I now know that it was true love we witnessed. Monika, I thank you for that. You and Klaus set the standard for what I hope to achieve in my own life one day.

As the words poured out, Michael set his gaze on Petra and her gentle smile made him know he'd been heard.

Most importantly Klaus, you pointed the way to hope, like the lighthouses you loved so much. You believed in positive outcomes and believed that the start you gave us would lay the foundation for our future successes in life.

Addressing the congregation now, Michael continued with a personal story of his own.

I had been in a car accident and had been feeling very sorry for myself when Klaus brought me the journal I now hold in my hands. He had written on the first page, "Goals: See them, believe them, and achieve them." At first, that made little sense to me but as I began to use this journal, those words helped me to deal with my confusion and make better decisions during a very difficult time in my life. He also wrote a beautiful Mahatma Gandhi quote about keeping your thoughts positive as they, in turn, keep our behavior, habits and destiny positive. Thinking back, I don't ever remember anything that came out of his mouth that was not positive.

Just a few months ago, Klaus visited me in the hospital once again and brought me a ceramic model of a lighthouse we had talked about: Roter Sand. This gift was, and will continue to be, a beacon of hope for me. I have come to realize that Klaus was, in fact, the lighthouse for many of us; offering direction, a place of safety and a beam of light on the darkest of nights. Klaus was grounded in the truest sense of the word. When offered an attractive alternate job, he didn't waver. When faced with difficult circumstances at work, he didn't waver. And, when younger friends, like me, failed to appreciate his friendship and generosity, he still did not waver.

Even in the darkest hours, Klaus did not give up hope and in our grief, we too must not give up hope. If we are in fact his legacy, as Klaus so strongly believed, we have a responsibility to see the potential within ourselves, to keep our thoughts and goals positive, to see them, believe them and achieve them in a way that makes a difference in the world. May we each strive to be like Klaus, a lighthouse showing others the way. Let us be people with solid core values and clear visions, who lead by example and leave positive imprints on the hearts of those we touch.

Klaus, we are here today to honor your memory, your legacy. Thank you for playing such an important role in our lives.

As Michael neared the end of his eulogy, he also reached the end of his ability and resolve not to let his emotions get the best of him.

So, I offer my gratitude to you, my dear, dear friend.

Michael's voice remained strong and clear, but tears streamed down his face.

Thank you for your love, your understanding and your never-ending faith in me, in each of us, here today. Thank you for the example you set and all the promises you kept. You made a difference, my friend and those of us whom you leave behind here today, will continue to share all that you taught us as we move forward in life with your beacon of hope, your lighthouse, in our line of vision. We are your legacy. You will never be forgotten. Rest in peace, Klaus and good-bye, dear friend.

The next day Michael remembered little of what else was said at the service but, strangely enough, he was filled with a sense of peace. The past few days had truly brought Petra and him together again. They had offered solace to one another and felt so comfortable in each other's presence. As they held each other in a strong embrace, Michael and Petra heard the soft footsteps of Monika approaching in the hallway. As she entered the room, a gentle smile lit up her face and a single tear rolled down her cheek, "Klaus would be so happy," she said as Michael and Petra welcomed her into their arms. "We always knew you two were meant for each other."

"Looking back, the only regret Klaus and I had was not going on our sabbatical to Australia. We talked so much about that but never made it happen. So, I have decided to commit to doing it this year," she smiled.

CHAPTER 40

Michael was quiet for a moment after Petra had finished reading aloud the rough draft they'd been working on. "Wow!" said Michael when he finally spoke, "those are powerful words that exactly describe our mission. I love it Petra."

"I think we're there too. It brings together all our thoughts and issues from the last two years. It felt so awkward to write something like this at first but, after all our discussions and then actually writing down our vision, I realize how glad I am you encouraged us to write this."

"This is going to help us keep on track, committed and accountable, that's for sure," agreed Michael.

He thought of the challenges and disagreements that they'd both worked through to get them where they were at this moment. It had taken time, effort, commitment and forgiveness from both of them for the mistakes they'd made, "We've worked hard and come a long way, haven't we."

"Yes we have Michael, and it has been worth it. Our relationship will never be perfect, none are, and life will always throw things at us, but if we keep working at it with more awareness and just keep living and loving, I know we will continue to grow and get stronger as long as we live the words in our mission." Petra leaned back on the sand of the beach they sat on, "This sabbatical has been such a rewarding experience already. I'm so glad we settled on Australia."

"Monika's photos were pretty convincing though, weren't they?" Michael laughed.

"I know. I'm so glad she went through with the trip. It's such an amazing place! I can't believe how much we've already seen and experienced and our three months here aren't over yet." She sighed happily, "I think this spot is my favourite so far. What a hidden gem!"

"Smokey Point is very special. It was one of the places Klaus wanted to take Monika on their Australian sabbatical so she was determined to come here. He showed me so many pictures of that lighthouse over there but he never got the chance to see it for himself. I couldn't bear the thought of that being us Petra, of dreaming about something but it never happening and the timing is so right just now. It is perfect."

The thought of his old friend, Klaus, stirred a memory in Michael, as he thought about all that had happened in the two years since Klaus's untimely passing. "You know how much he loved lighthouses. I apologized once to Klaus for taking so long to hear his message. Do you know what he said? 'Lighthouses don't thrash around shouting out warnings and searching for souls to save. They remain firmly grounded and send out a constant message for all who need it. Michael, you heard the message when you were ready for it. That's exactly how it's supposed to happen and I'm glad I was there for you when you needed me.'" Michael's voice cracked.

"He was a guiding light for so many of us," Petra said as she took his hand.

"That's who I want to become, a guiding light for others, a real leader, a role model, a lighthouse."

"But Michael, can't you see, you've already become that in so many ways! Look how you've turned around the team at Sunstream, how they came together, how they've seen Viktor's Fuchs' Legacy completed and the impact it is making around the world. Only a true leader could have brought those men and women together they way you did."

"Yes, I know but it feels like there is so much more yet to do."

"There will always be more to do. That's life. We keep growing, learning and reaching. We get somethings right, and we make our mistakes. The important thing is that when we do get off track, we hit the reset button and start again...isn't that what you tell me?" Petra smiled, having turned one of Michael's favorite sayings back on him.

"You're right. But to be honest, I needed this sabbatical more than anyone could have imagined, especially me. The pressure of finalizing the Legacy, the pressure of the competition...I was afraid that business was going to destroy me like it did before." Michael thought back to some of the long days he'd put in getting the Legacy to market. "After Klaus died, I was so determined not to get swallowed up by business again. Death can be a good teacher. It taught me to live my values, to live all that I'd learned every day. But it's so hard on a day to day basis."

"It's hard, but the important thing is that you are consciously aware and making adjustments that are making a big difference. I know in a perfect world you'd be at the gym every day, but you still never miss a week do you? You're maintaining your weight, you're watching your health. You are conscious of it all Michael, that's the most important thing. And you know what else?" Petra asked, looking deeply into Michael's eyes, "You promised me when we started over that I would feel your love every day. I do Michael, in spite of all the challenges and the stress, I always do."

Petra leaned over and kissed him, then pulled a beautifully wrapped package out of her handbag and handed it to Michael. He smiled as he unwrapped a new journal.

"Your old one is crammed so full. This one is to celebrate our new start together. Our mission statement can go on the very first page and we'll move forward from this moment."

Michael thanked her with a long hug, "How can I thank you. I didn't think to bring a gift for you."

Petra smiled and sat up, "Don't you see? This is your gift to both of us. We are living our dream. This quality time together, this old motorhome, sleeping under this amazing sky with no schedule, no commitments, just living and loving. That's about the biggest gift we can ever give ourselves."

"I never thought I could let go, just be and enjoy just being, but these three months will allow us to invest some renewal time into our bodies, hearts, minds and spirits. It's just what we need right now. Klaus is definitely looking down on us and smiling." Michael said.

"Speaking of Klaus," she smiled, reaching for his old journal and taking Michael's crumpled copy of the poem that Monika had given him the day Klaus died, "I'd say this is something else that will need to find a home for in your new journal."

"I always saw myself as that boy who fell down," Michael said. "We had that poem, The Race, up on the wall in the club's changing room as a source of inspiration. I wish I could become an inspiration."

"As long as you live what you believe every day you will be an inspiring leader and a lighthouse for many."

Michael became quiet as the tears in his eyes blurred the words to the poem he knew so well.

"Read it for me, Michael?" she asked gently.

Michael looked at her, nodded slowly, then cleared his throat and began in a quiet voice that gained in strength as he read. He didn't need to look at the words often as he began:

THE RACE

By Dr. D.H. (Dee) Groberg

Whenever I start to hang my head in front of failure's face,
my downward fall is broken by the memory of a race.
A children's race, young boys, young men; how I remember well,
excitement sure, but also fear, it wasn't hard to tell.
They all lined up so full of hope, each thought to win that race
or tie for first, or if not that, at least take second place.
Their parents watched from off the side, each cheering for
their son,
and each boy hoped to show his folks that he would be the one.

The whistle blew and off they flew, like chariots of fire,
to win, to be the hero there, was each young boy's desire.
One boy in particular, whose dad was in the crowd,
was running in the lead and thought "My dad will be so proud."
But as he speeded down the field and crossed a shallow dip,
the little boy who thought he'd win, lost his step and slipped.
Trying hard to catch himself, his arms flew everyplace,
and midst the laughter of the crowd he fell flat on his face.
As he fell, his hope fell too; he couldn't win it now.
Humiliated, he just wished to disappear somehow.

But as he fell his dad stood up and showed his anxious face,
which to the boy so clearly said, "Get up and win that race!"
He quickly rose, no damage done, behind a bit that's all,
and ran with all his mind and might to make up for his fall.
So anxious to restore himself, to catch up and to win,
his mind went faster than his legs. He slipped and fell again.
He wished that he had quit before with only one disgrace.
"I'm hopeless as a runner now, I shouldn't try to race."

But through the laughing crowd he searched and found his fa-
ther's face
with a steady look that said again, "Get up and win that race!"
So he jumped up to try again, ten yards behind the last.
"If I'm to gain those yards," he thought, "I've got to run real
fast!"
Exceeding everything he had, he regained eight, then ten...
but trying hard to catch the lead, he slipped and fell again.
Defeat! He lay there silently. A tear dropped from his eye.
"There's no sense running anymore! Three strikes I'm out! Why
try?
I've lost, so what's the use?" he thought. "I'll live with my
disgrace."
But then he thought about his dad, who soon he'd have to face.

"Get up," an echo sounded low, "you haven't lost at all,
for all you have to do to win is rise each time you fall.
Get up!" the echo urged him on, "Get up and take your place!
You were not meant for failure here! Get up and win that race!"
So, up he rose to run once more, refusing to forfeit,
and he resolved that win or lose, at least he wouldn't quit.
So far behind the others now, the most he'd ever been,
still he gave it all he had and ran like he could win.
Three times he'd fallen stumbling, three times he rose again.
Too far behind to hope to win, he still ran to the end.

They cheered another boy who crossed the line and won first place,
head high and proud and happy – no falling, no disgrace.
But, when the fallen youngster crossed the line, in last place,
the crowd gave him a greater cheer for finishing the race.
And even though he came in last with head bowed low, unproud,
you would have thought he'd won the race, to listen to the crowd.
And to his dad he sadly said, "I didn't do so well."
"To me, you won," his father said. "You rose each time you fell."

And now when things seem dark and bleak and difficult to face,
the memory of that little boy helps me in my own race.
For all of life is like that race, with ups and downs and all.
And all you have to do to win is rise each time you fall.
And when depression and despair shout loudly in my face,
another voice within me says, "Get up and win that race!"

They were both quiet with their own thoughts as Michael finished the poem. After a long silence, Michael verbalized the powerful question in his head, "So, what's the message for me?" He stared intensely at the Smokey Point lighthouse. As he glanced from the base to the top he reflected on The Ten Principles and answered his own question. "To rise each time I fall, to take risks, to grow, to choose, to live my principles and to stay 'on Mission.'"

AFTERWORD

I know that some of you will want to come back to the core content, the models and the key messages again and again to support this process of whole person development so I have written the following pages as a summary of the story's key content.

Paradigms and paradigm shift:

Your paradigm is the way you see the world. It's your mental model, your frame of reference or the lens through which you see the world. It has been formed by your conditioning and your experiences and creates your perception of reality. You paradigm is made up of your assumptions and the old rules you picked up along your journey. You need to make a paradigm shift if you want to change your habits and behaviors. Your behaviors and habits are always aligned with your paradigm and that is why change is so difficult. If you do not change your paradigm, you cannot change. All revolutionary change is, by definition, an example of a paradigm shift.

Being on Mission
Brainstorm 12 words

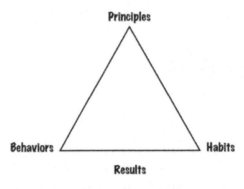

Principles

Behaviors

Habits

Results

Private – Professional

Define what each of these words mean to you. Brainstorm ten or twelve words that you associate with 'Being on Mission.' Think about how this pyramid influences- or is connected to- the results that you get in your private and professional life.

M.C.C.L
Coaching Proccess

	Past	Today	Future	Strengths	Weaknesses	Role Models	Values
Managing	85	75	20				
Coaching	0	2	15				
Clienting	0	3	15				
Leading	5	5	20				
Selling	10	15	30				
	100%	100%	100%				

THE M.C.C.L.S. MODEL

There are four or five roles that you need to live to be effective in your professional life. I believe that most companies are over managed and under led. Remember, you manage things but you lead and coach people.

Managing

Administrative work, paper, fire fighting and getting caught as Mr. or Mrs. Fix-It. You are actively involved in the execution and the details and you take ownership of the problem. Most people spend 80% of their time managing. This is more top-down telling; the old fashion boss.

Coaching

The one to one time you invest with your employees. It involves empathy and understanding. A good coach leads with quality questions to bring clarity and help people create action plans. Most employees feel their boss does not find enough one to one time for them. This means affirming people's potential so that they can clearly see it in themselves.

Clienting

Networking with a purpose where you find time to manage the relationship and get more closeness to your internal and external customers.

This could be golfing, having dinners or drinks and eventually getting to know people on a private level.

Leading

Involves creating a vision, selling and communicating that vision so clearly that other people can see it as well. Creating a clear mission statement and defining clear values for yourself and your organization is an important part of leadership, as is the development of strategy and getting people involved in this process. Most senior leaders need to do a better job of team development and selling the 'why' behind what the company is doing. Change management and the ability to facilitate a good workshop are also parts of leadership.

Selling

This role is lived by people who really go out and sell the products or services to the real customers. This role includes: Understanding needs and the customers business, finding the pain point and what keeps customers up at night, selling solutions by creating benefits, not just selling features, negotiating win-win agreements and closing the deal. A sales leader would perhaps spend 15% of their time in a selling role dealing with their key account customers.

M.C.C.L.S.
1 to 1 Coaching Proccess

Phase 1

o   Where do you spend time now? M.C.C.L.S. %
o   How was your time spent two years ago? M.C.C.L.S. %
o   What are your strengths and weaknesses in each role?
o   What are your values in each role? What is important in each role?
o   Who are your role models in each role? What do they do well?

Phase 2

o   Where do you want to be 18 months from now? M.C.C.L.S. %

Phase 3

o   What is your motive for changing your M.C.C.L.S. %?
    What is your reason for changing?
o   What are your benefits privately and professionally?
o   WIIFM → What is in it for me?

Phase 4

o   What is your action plan?
o   The next 100 days?
o   What do you need to:
    · Start doing?
    · Stop doing?
    · Do more of?
    · Do less of?

CREATING A LEADERSHIP ROADMAP

Y ou should create your team development plan over the next eighteen months. This plan will help to build trust, increase involvement, improve team spirit and will help with the team building process. This is choosing to lead and part of living the 'L' in the M.C.C.L.S Model.

- When are your operational or management meetings going to happen? Remember: These are management meetings and management tools. Put them on your road map:

My Leadership Roadmap

Today   9 Months   18 Months

My Plan to Develop my Team /Extended Team

When are your leadership meetings going to happen? Remember: These are leadership meetings and will include the following points:

- How often are they going to happen? Mark this on the road map.
- When are you going to do a strategic workshop?
- When are you going to do some team development or team building?
- When are you going to work on vision and values?
- When are you going to do some leadership development and training with your team?
- What are you going to do to increase trust?
- What are you going to do to increase involvement?
- What are you going to do to create a feedback culture within your team?
- When are you going to create or come back to your mission and mission statement?
- Remember good teams spend 3-6 days per year on offsites. When are you going to build those in and what are you going to do?
- What could you do in an offsite to simplify complexity and get your team more focused on priorities?

This is living the L of the M.C.C.L.S Model. It's choosing to lead.

Coaching tips #1

- Clarify the goal
- 20/80
- Leading pen
- No home movies
- Pacing/leading
- Positioning
- 8/38 second rule
- More of, less of
- No tips

- SMART goals
- Follow up plan

- **Initial Coaching Phase**
  The coach and the executive should agree on the goal of the session. What do they really want to take away or focus on?
- **The 20/80 Rule**
  Talk only 20% of the time, 80% of the time you should be listening to what your executive has to say.
- **The Leading Pen**
  Use your pen to bring your client's attention back to something important or to highlight something on the page. It helps to focus their attention and lead the conversation. It refocuses them on that key word or phrase.
- **No Home Movies**
  Don't share your personal experiences too often. This is about the client, not about you. Keep yourself out of it.
- **Pacing and Leading**
  The two phases of coaching. In the 'pacing' phase, make a connection by matching the tempo, tone and body language of the person you are coaching. In the leading phase, begin to lead the conversation by asking the right questions and keeping the coaching 'result-focused.' Keep the goal in mind. Always remember, it is the quality of your questions that determine the quality of the coaching. Challenge them to think.
- **Positioning**
  Making sure you sit in a position with your writing hand between you and the executive. This makes it easy and natural to make notes and they can see what you're writing. Ideally, sit at the corner of a table.
- **The 8/38 second rule**
  Always wait at least eight seconds for an answer when you're coaching and, if coaching a very analytical person, sometimes even longer – perhaps up to 38 seconds. People need time to formulate ideas and responses.

- **More of/less of**
  This makes people think deeply about what they want more or less of in their lives. Stating it out loud verbalizes an intention that may support them to make changes towards those ends.
- **No tips**
  Don't make suggestions or give advice about what we think they should do. It's a natural reflex to want give a tip every time we hear a problem but we need to control that reflex. Don't be 'Mr. Fix-it'.
- **'S.M.A.R.T' goals**
  This is an acronym to help you set clear goals: Specific, Measureable, Agreed upon action, Realistic and Timeable goals.
- **Follow up plan**
  Make a plan to connect with each other at some point in the future and provide an update on how things are going. It makes people accountable.

Coaching tips #2

- Atmosphere
- 20%, 30%, 50% Communication Rule
- Hilti/Black 'n Decker technique
- Open-ended questions
- 3rd person example with storytelling method
- Next week's goals
- Strengthen your strengths

- **Atmosphere**
  The right coaching 'atmosphere' is essential, find a quiet and comfortable place where you won't be distracted.
- **20%, 30%, 50% Communication rule**
  This represents how we communicate: 20% of our communication is through words, 30% of what we communicate is through our tone and a full 50% is conveyed through our body language.

Focus on using more tone and body language. This will be especially important for you engineers, don't just be a 'talking head.' It's not just about IQ.

- **Hilti/Black 'n Decker Technique**
  Use the 'Hilti Drill' like a master craftsman to keep probing, keep asking why? Press the person you're coaching to go deeper and be honest with themselves.

- **Open-ended questions**
  Ask open-ended questions and use paraphrasing to be an active listener. Ask questions like, 'Why is that important for you?', 'How did that make you feel?' and 'What will it look like in two to three years?' Draw information out of them.

- **3rd person example with storytelling method**
  There is power in using a third person storytelling technique. For example, if your client is struggling with poor communication on his or her team, you may tell them a story about a friend of yours who had the same struggle, but they found great tools and ideas in a book by Patrick Lencioni called 'The Five Dysfunctions of a Team.'

- **Next week's goals**
  Get the person you're coaching to tell you what they are going to do next week to get started. Make them commit to an action.

- **Strengthen your strengths**
  Strengthening strengths to become world class is something I really believe in. The key is to affirm and help the person you're coaching to see their strengths and create a developmental plan to strengthen those strengths.

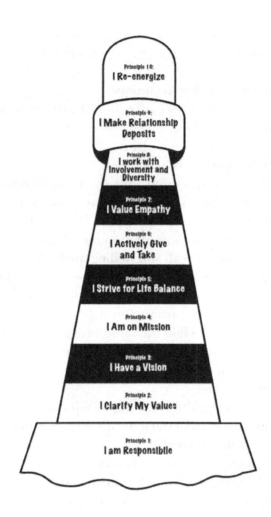

Principle 10:
I Re-energize

Principle 9:
I Make Relationship Deposits

Principle 8:
I work with Involvement and Diversity

Principle 7:
I Value Empathy

Principle 6:
I Actively Give and Take

Principle 5:
I Strive for Life Balance

Principle 4:
I Am on Mission

Principle 3:
I Have a Vision

Principle 2:
I Clarify My Values

Principle 1:
I am Responsibile

The Ten Principles of Leadership and Life

This is based on a whole person model, meaning both the private and professional sides of life. It is based on an inside out process that begins with you, through self-development and personal growth.

Principle 1: The Principle of Responsibility
This means taking life into your own hands, feeling like you are the programmer, understanding you are not the victim and that you always have a choice. It's a mindset of believing, 'Yes I can' and 'I pull my own strings.' It's the proactive mentality that is a prerequisite for all other principles.

Principle 2: The Principle of Values
To live this principle means taking time to think about what matters most and what is truly important. This will form the foundation for your vision and help you to make decisions. As an individual becomes more mature, clarity comes more easily. Some people wait for a crisis, failed relationship or health issue before they realize what is at their core and what is truly important. Clear values are needed both privately and professionally, as well as in the organization and the team.

Principle 3: The Principle of Vision

You need to start with a picture of success in your mind. You need to create a blueprint first and then start to build. Seeing your ideal future and visualizing it, even dreaming about it, is the essence of this principle. The power of visualization is what seperates the top athletes from their mediocre competitors. Entrepreneurs live this principle very well. As they see the future and know what they want to create. This focus keeps them aligned and moving in the right direction. A clear vision and values gives you a built-in GPS or an internal compass pointing steadily towards success.

Principle 4: The Principle of Being on Mission

The essence of this principle is having the discipline to execute based on your vision and values. This means do the right things first and saying 'No' to what matters least. This can also be called the Principle of Effectiveness, where you walk the talk and keep your promises. People who are 'on mission' set clear and challenging weekly goals and have a high Execution Quotient, which means they achieve most of their weekly goals. They live their values and consistently move toward their vision. Effective people find their professional priorities based on their M.C.C.L.S. model and their vision and values. They have the habit of getting the right things done first. People who live this principle often create a personal mission statement, which helps to keep them accountable and aligned to their purpose.

Principle 5: The Principle of Life Balance

This principle can also be called the Happiness Principle and it is the result of living Principles 1-4. People who are living their values and moving constantly toward their vision are naturally balanced and happy. This happiness shows when they smile because it is a real smile where 22 muscles contract and 14 muscles relax simultaneously and that smile is evident to everyone around them. Their positive energy will spread through, and almost take over a room. Their joy, gratitude and happiness is palpable. What they are doing is aligned, makes sense and connects to their purpose.

These first five principles are the inside work, or the personal development that is required before moving onto the outside work of leading, influencing, connecting and communciting with others. Living the first 5 principles will result in positive character development. You will begin to lead by example and become a role model for those around you. In summary, you make a promise based on your vision and values and then deliver on that promise. This demonstrates integrity and that is the number one thing that followers want from a leader.

That brings us to the outside principles, which are less about the individual and more about communicating with others. Succesful leaders realize that the only way to achieve success is with and through other people.

Principle 6: The Principle of Give and Take

This is the principle of fairness and respect and is the key to long-term relationships. You need a win-win mentality where you try to find long-term solutions that work for both sides. This principle is lived in every negotiation situation, both privately and professionally. It takes emotional intelligence, understanding and great patience to live this principle. It applies at home as much as it does at work. Privately, if mothers and fathers are too strong and dominant and constantly create a win-lose with their children, they will end up with weak children and that is the last thing you want. Profesionally, this principle is the key for good sales people, long-term business relationships and also for leaders if they want to retain their people.

Principle 7: The Principle of Empathy

This is all about understanding others and the ability to make other people feel understood. Being understood is one of the greatest needs for a human being. Your emotional intelligence plays a huge part of living this principle as it is your ability to use body language, tone, mimic, gesture and the use an appropriate volume when communicating with others. This principle is also called the Coaching Principle as great coaches live this principle.

Principle 8: The Principle of Involvement and Diversity

The essence of this principle is to create and surround yourself with a diverse team of people that provide you with different ideas, thoughts and suggestions. Their varied perceptions, paradigms and backgrounds will come together to create synergy and produce the best possible solutions. By involving others you empower them to think, contribute ideas and therefore increase their commitment to a solution. Remember, if there is no involvement there is no commitment and all the diversity in the world will be of no value. This means you must pull back and work as a facilitator and get the diverse ideas onto the table. The essence of leadership is to give your team a platform to identify problems and create solutions. This can also be called the Leadership Principle.

Principle 9: The Principle of Relationship Deposits

To live this principle you need to be aware of other people's needs for recognition, support, positive feedback and even compliments in order for them to feel valued. Sometimes, these deposits are the small things, such as a handshake, a hand written card, a touch on a shoulder or a small sign of appreciation, which conveys your respect for the other person. These deposits will strengthen that person's feeling of self-esteem and self-belief. For children, it is a sign of unconditional love and makes them confident that you believe in them. People who live this principle have the habit of catching people doing things right. There is a saying, 'What gets rewarded and acknowledged over time will get repeated.' Emotional intelligence and awareness of other people's needs is the key to living this principle.

Principle 10: The Principle of Re-energizing

This principle can also be called the Principle of Self-renewal. This cannot be delegated. You have to do it yourself. It is often the biggest weakness for most middle managers as they forget about themselves and, ultimately do not have enough energy to lead. This makes them overpaid for what they are actually doing at some point in their career. Such re-energizing needs to happen on five levels:

1. Physical – Your body
2. Emotional – Your heart
3. Social – Your social circles
4. Mental – Your mind
5. Spiritual – Your purpose

The key to this principle is listening to your body and finding time for yourself. Of course, healthy nutrition, drinking lots of water and living the 100 Day Challenge consistently are also major aspects of this principle. Having a clear purpose and knowing why you exist re-energizes your spirit and relights the flame that glows within you. Reading, taking courses and learning are part of mental renewal and spending time with friends is part of social renewal that will help you feel connected to others. We are pack animals after all! Emotional renewal happens when we invest one-to-one time with the person or people we love.

THE 100 DAY CHALLENGE

"Vitality is a choice"

These are the recommendations for the next 100 days, or for a lifetime, if you make the choice to increase your vitality. People who take full responsibility for their life and create a vision, quite often take full responsibility for their health and vitality as well. It is aligned with their vision and values.

1. **F.I.T.T. Principle**
   Do some type of aerobic exercise 3-4 times a week keeping your heart rate at 120-140 beats per minute for twenty minutes.

2. **The 4 minute workout – strengthening your core**
   Do four minutes per day of stomach crunches/sit-ups combined with back extensions and the plank. This needs to become a daily routine.

3. **W³ – Water, Walking, Wine**
   Drink 2-3 liters of water per day. Walk after meals to increase metabolism and fat burning 2-3 times a week. Drink 1-2 glasses of good red wine per day.

4. **Nutrition and 'The Zone' by Dr. Barry Sears**
   Increase fruit and vegetables, find the right balance of carbohydrates, proteins and fats: 40-30-30 ratio. Read 'The Zone' by Dr. Barry Sears.

5. **Vitamins and supplements**
   Find a good source of Omega-3 fish oil. Take 1-2g/day. 1g of vitamin C should also be part of your daily routine.

6. **Immune system**
   Research shows that 140-240 minutes per week of aerobic activity has an impact on the immune system. Try to increase your weekly movement to this amount.

7. **Strength training**
   Muscle burns fat, the best bang for your buck exercises are push-ups and pull-ups. Do daily push-ups. Use the formula: 80 minus your age to determine how many push-ups you should be able to do.

8. **Mental fitness, mental training**
   Find time for relaxation exercises and practice visualizing your picture of success twice weekly.

9. **Time for self**
   Do things you love to do and, if you are an introvert, find time to be alone.

THE LIFE BALANCE ANALYSIS

T he key to using a self-assessment tool is to be brutally honest and analyze how you are really spending your time.

Life Balance Analysis

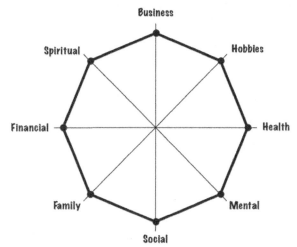

- Where am I today?
- What is important? What do I value in each area?
- Where do I want to be?
- My motive? Why do I want to change (benefits)?
- My actions within the next 100 days?

    What do I have to start doing?
    What do I have to stop doing?
    What do I have to do more of?
    What do I have to do less of?

A good first step is to define what each word means to you, write down what is important to you and what you really value under each word. Yes, that means writing down what matters most in every area. Then, rate yourself on a scale from one to ten on how you are currently living each of these values. If you are honest, you will see the gaps very clearly and, hopefully, feel some anxiety or discomfort. At this point, you should decide which 2-3 areas you want to improve upon and be very clear what benefits you want to experience in each area.

After seeing the "What's in it for me" benefits you will be ready to create a strategy or action plan to improve your targeted areas. The key questions you need to ask yourself are:

What should my first step be?
What do I need to start doing?
What do I need to stop doing?
What do I need to do more of?
What do I need to do less of?
What's the one thing I need to do more consistently and turn into a daily habit?

The answers to the questions above should lead to a 100 day action plan and, if maintained, sustainable results. Ideally, commit to these actions with a coach or trusted partner who is dedicated to holding you accountable.

MY TRUE CALLING

T his model will help you to discover what it is you are really meant
to be doing with your life.

My True Calling

Passion:
what I love to do

My Economic Engine
Things I can do to create value

My Strengths and core competencies
Where can I be best in the world? (10,000 hours)

The first circle focuses your attention on you **passions**, what you love to do and what you're passionate about. Seeing these will spark your fire and pull you toward your true calling.

The bottom circle encourages you to reflect honestly, see and recognize your **strengths** and **core competencies** and decide where you can become world-class or in the top 1% for that skill set. These strengths will be part of your true calling.

The last circle helps you realise what you can do to produce income or **drive your economic engine**, to add or create value. The more value you create, the more you will get paid over time.

Some people take a lifetime to find their true calling and others find it right at the start. The challenge is to keep searching, not to give up and to seize your opportunity when it comes. When you find your real True Calling, you will know it and it will feel right.

THE SOLUTION TO INDIANA JONES

To ensure that all participants escape safely with the treasure, Indiana and the beautiful woman cross first (10 minutes), Indiana returns across the bridge (5 minutes, for a total of 15 minutes now). He gives the flashlight to the banker and the businessman, they return together (25 minutes, with 40 now used up). The young woman goes back across the bridge and returns with Indiana (10 minutes each way, for a total of 60 minutes all together). Everyone is safe and escapes from the 'bad guy'!

Pyramid of Effectivity

The pyramid of effectiveness is so powerful! For a full explanation of the different levels, go back to pages 128 to 130 in the book, as Michael reflects on all he learned. The pyramid will show there is lots of work ahead, it will involve taking risks, but it is doable ...however only you can do it! Becoming effective leads to happieness, and in the words of Emerson...what else is there?

If you do not take risks,
You cannot grow.
If you can not grow,
You cannot be your best.
If you cannot be your best,
You cannot be happy.
If you cannot be happy,
What else is there?

ABOUT THE AUTHOR

As a Canadian – now living in Switzerland – I have my roots in the world of hockey. I worked for many years as a player, coach and manager for top teams in Germany and Switzerland. I also had the opportunity to work with Team Canada at six Spengler Cup tournaments.

Since 1999 I have worked full-time as in-house trainer, coach and keynote-speaker. My education (University of Manitoba, Bachelor of Education and Bachelor of Physical Education) provided an ideal foundation for my work today. I extended this with further education as a trainer and speaker in Australia and Canada.

Early on, I identified the link between high performance in sport and high performance in business as there are many parallels between these two worlds. Drawing on my past experiences in professional sport, I have many personal examples and exciting real-life stories to share. My passion is leadership development. This includes coaching, team vision, team work, motivation, high-performance, communication and psychology of winning.

I believe that the development of leaders and leadership is the competitive advantage.

The core of my philosophy is that leadership development is an inside-out process. It begins by defining clear values and creating a mission on a personal level. This leads to effective leadership on a professional level

Made in United States
Orlando, FL
10 January 2024

42357489R00176